Notes of a Newsman

Witness to a Changing Scotland

JOHN MacKAY

Luath Press Limited

EDINBURGH

www.luath.co.uk

First published 2015

ISBN: 978-1-910745-04-5

The paper used in this book is recyclable.
It Is made from low chlorine pulps
produced in a low energy, low emission
manner from renewable forests.

Printed and bound by
Martins the Printers, Berwick upon Tweed

Typeset in Meta and Sabon by
3btype.com

The author's right to be identified as author
of this work under the Copyright, Designs
and Patents Act 1988 has been asserted

For Jo, Kenny & Ross
who've heard it all before.

Contents

Acknowledgements

Thanks to Phil Taylor, Eddie Mair, Alison Walker, Dougie McGuire, Michael Crow, Sharon Frew, Howard Simpson, David Cowan, Mike Farrell, Pete Smith & Karen Greenshields for their written recollections.

Bernard Ponsonby whose on-air analysis is such a key element of the latter stages of the book.

James MacKay, Stephen Townsend, Stephen Daisley, Vicky Lee-Middleton, Laura Trimble and Stacey Carnie for their feedback.

www.euanandersonphotography.com for the cover photo.

Rachel Pike who delved into the recesses of the STV library often and without complaint.

Alistair Cairney for his help in preparing many of the images in the book.

Bethan Broster & Lisa Inglis who provided transcripts for some of the interviews.

STV for the use of their archive.

Excerpts from BBC Scotland News, courtesy of the BBC.

Too many colleagues past and present to thank individually.

Preface

On 19 September 2014, the result of the Scottish Independence Referendum was announced. Scotland voted No, but right up until the polls closed the night before it seemed too close to call.

That day also marked 20 years since I had joined STV. Few would have imagined then that Scotland would come quite so close to Independence so soon. The prospect of a Scottish Parliament was on the horizon, but that was supposed to extinguish any desire for Independence.

In that reflective mood, I looked back on how much had changed in Scotland, and how much has remained the same, since I started in journalism. As a reporter and as a news presenter, I had the privilege of witnessing many of these changes at close hand.

This is the result of these reflections, using contemporary reports, interviews, recollections and personal diaries.

It lays no claim to being the inside story. Quite the opposite. It is the story of a changing Scotland as it was heard and seen by the people of Scotland.

Introduction

In the summer of 1986 I was preparing to go to London.

I didn't want to leave Scotland, but my ambition of working on the *Evening Times* in Glasgow would have to wait because they didn't take on trainees. Radio Clyde rejected me because they said I didn't have a voice for broadcasting.

My years as a paperboy, my £10 Letter of the Week to *Shoot* magazine, my degree, my editorship of the *Glasgow University Guardian* and wearing my trench coat to cold call at every paper I knew had all delivered nothing.

So I was off to London and a postgraduate journalism course at City University. There is every chance that's where I would have remained. All roads led to London. I heard that then and I've heard it ever since.

Maybe it was the trench coat, I don't know, but *The Sunday Post* had seen something in me when I called and belatedly asked me back for an interview.

DC Thomson were good enough to give me a job as a trainee reporter and that was it. I was embarking on a career as a newsman in Scotland at the beginning of one of the most significant periods in the country's peacetime history.

1986

Thursday 31 July 1986

DIARY: I've got a job as a journalist! I went into *The Sunday Post* office in Port Dundas Road and the Glasgow editor Robert Miller said, 'Well it looks like we've come to the end of the road and we're prepared to offer you a job as a trainee reporter at £90 a week.' I have got my foot in the door and hopefully I'm embarking on an eventful and successful career.

The Sunday Post *was a hugely popular newspaper with a circulation of around a million during the 1980s. It was a fascinating throwback to a different Scotland. Like a scene out of an old black and white movie, it was a place suited to a trench coat. There were wooden-framed telephone cubicles at the far end of the office for talking privately to contacts. One of the office girls would summon you if a call came in. It was a throwback in other ways. It was non-union, non-sensational and by-lines were rare, but DC Thomson had a deserved reputation for giving a start to young journalists and many familiar names in Scottish journalism got their first break there.*

Most of my early scores in the paper were in the heartwarming stories in the middle pages. One of particular note was 'George is Scotland's Champion Whistler'.

Hercules the Bear

One of my early jobs was to meet Hercules the Bear. Everyone knew Hercules. He was the 'Big Softy' who starred in the popular Kleenex adverts. He lived with his owners Andy and Maggie Robin in a big house on the road to Perth.

I can't recall what the story was, but Hercules was a star so that was reason enough. When I arrived there was no sign of him, but I seem to remember an ominously open cage. As I sat in the Robins' lovely lounge, he suddenly sauntered in paying me no mind. I paid him plenty. I didn't take my eyes off him as he padded around amiably. But Andy wanted me to see Hercules perform. This grizzly could act. He could wrestle. So Andy started to playfully slap him. The bear pawed back, rearing up as he did so. Oh, but he was big. I mean really big. My student journalism had been limited mostly to the blathering of student politicians. This was the danger of front line reporting. From a lounge. In Perthshire. Wearing a trench coat. The truth is Hercules was so placid I think he'd have put a paw around my shoulder to show me out. He never got the chance. I was gone.

Sunday 31 August 1986

The Sunday Post

Some husbands may be in for a shock when the new Family Law (Scotland) Act 1985 comes into force tomorrow. For the first time, if a husband keeps his wife short on housekeeping, she can go to court and be awarded a fair amount. Previously she'd have to leave him before she could get a court order. Children living at home can also take their parents to court for their keep. 'Revolutionary' is how some solicitors see the new laws.

Revolutionary indeed.

DIARY: Good feeling that the *Post*, the paper I've read for so long, had some of my work in it.

Sunday 14 September 1986

The Sunday Post

A GHOST AT THE WEDDING IN LOCHBOISDALE

THREE CHEERS FOR THE FRIENDLY FIREMEN FROM STRANRAER

Sunday 5 October 1986

The Sunday Post

KIEV HERE WE COME

Celtic fans are already making plans to travel to Kiev to watch their team play – despite the Chernobyl threat. The city is only 65 miles away from the nuclear plant where there was a massive explosion earlier this year. Danny McCarron of the *Celtic View*, the club newspaper, insisted the club would not advise supporters to travel. 'Apart from the nuclear scare and the political situation, the difficulty in obtaining visas will discourage most people,' he said. A spokesman for the Scotland–USSR Society said, 'Official reports indicate the area is now safe.'

Celtic lost 3–1 to Dynamo Kiev.

DIARY: Three articles in today's paper. Particularly pleased that two were news stories.

Friday 10 October 1986

DIARY: Sent out to do a story on last night's big fire at the McLellan Galleries. The wedding shop next to it was thought to have a number of dresses for brides on Saturday ruined. I had to check this. No there aren't. End of story.

As I was writing this it was announced that the McLellan Galleries were to be re-opened after many years closed. The report included archive footage of the Galleries from the time of the fire. There in a shop window were the unharmed wedding dresses in all their pristine glory.

Sunday 2 November 1986

The Sunday Post

FIREWORKS TERROR FOR THOMAS

Playtime turned to terror for 11-year-old Thomas Reilly when an older youth stuffed a lighted banger into his pocket.

Saturday 8 November 1986

DIARY: Busy for first 2–3 hours – minor train crash, pitch invasion Darlington v Middlesbrough. After that nothing.

A regular Saturday night routine was driving round the city police stations with early editions of the paper. You were more likely to get a tip from speaking to the desk sergeant face to face than you would from a telephone call.

Sunday 21 December 1986

The Sunday Post

AMID THE GLOOM

In the shadow of the closed steel works, Gartcosh village was a place of laughter yesterday. Despite the loss of 550 jobs earlier this year, the children were treated to their annual Christmas Party as usual… only a small number of the redundant workforce have found new employment. The rest are on training schemes or have nothing.

The closure of heavy, nationalised industries and the fallout from that was a feature of the Thatcher era.

Sunday 28 December 1986

The Sunday Post

MYSTERY OF MISSING LAWYER

The disappearance of a Scottish lawyer, only hours after he left to visit clients, has left police in England and Scotland baffled.

This was my first front page, co-written as I recall. Tragically, the lawyer had committed suicide.

1987

Saturday 10 January 1987

The Sunday Post

NEW ROW OVER COLD PAYMENTS

Braemar, Scotland's coldest village, shivered in temperatures of 16 degrees below freezing on Friday, with underfoot temperatures even lower at 19.3 degrees below. But the freezing conditions haven't been enough for OAPs in the village to qualify for extra heating allowances under the Government's new Severe Weather Payments Scheme.

DIARY: Spoke to SNP Chairman Gordon Wilson. Pleasant and well prepared. His comment was more of a dictation eg 'stop, new sentence.'

Barlinnie Riot

A riot erupted at Barlinnie Jail on Monday 5 January 1987. One hall was trashed and some prison officers were taken hostage. Prisoners took to the roof of the jail. Banners were hung alleging brutality and slates were thrown. The siege ended peacefully on Saturday 10 January.

Thursday 8 January 1987

DIARY: Up to Barlinnie Prison. A real media circus had set up. I managed to get into the street closest to the prison and ask some of the residents if the situation worried them. General impression is no. It was cold, grey and foreboding out there.

Saturday 10 January 1987

DIARY: Stood around in freezing conditions waiting for a statement following the end of the Barlinnie siege this morning. When the Scottish Office spokeswoman finally came out I put my tape recorder out and taped the statement... only problem was the pause button was on so I never got anything! Fortunately the statement was also printed. In the end we waited around for hours for very little.

The tape recorder – strictly speaking a cassette recorder – had been a gift for an aspiring journalist. Such devices were only beginning to appear at news conferences. The spokeswoman had looked at me askance as I thrust it in front of her. Maybe it was because the pause button was still on. Now, even these recording devices are old news. Most reporters use their phones.

Thursday 22 January 1987

DIARY: Afternoon working on a domestic and another middle about a Rangers fan who pays a minister some cash each week so that he can shout abuse at games. Would like to do more news.

The headline from this was classic *Sunday Post* – 'It's Not Easy Sitting Beside A Minister At Ibrox'.

Saturday 24 January 1987

DIARY: Spoke to MP Robin Cook at length about the threatened closure of the Golden Wonder crisp factory with the loss of 40 jobs. Also rewrote story of the Queen's fury over the leaking of the Duke of Edinburgh's letter to the Marines over Prince Edward's resignation. So, five articles in this week's issue.

Friday 30 January 1987

DIARY: Got a total of £27.40 in expenses, so that'll keep me going until my salary is in the bank – what there is of it. The editor signing my expense

sheet says, 'you sport boys eat well.' I'm news.

Saturday 31 January 1987

DIARY: Was down in the case room for a while watching how they put a page together. It certainly is an art, but a dying one. It seemed very fiddly to me and the new processes should speed it up.

The paper was changing, as most did in that period, from the old method of hot metal type to new, cheaper computerised technology.

Saturday 14 February 1987

DIARY: Went to a wedding in Milngavie. The story never existed (all to do with nine brothers wearing the same suits).

This was a typical experience. Every reporter has gone out with a heavy heart knowing that what has been promised will bear little resemblance to what will actually meet them when they get there, but knowing, too, that they need to bring something back for the newsdesk.

Sunday 22 February 1987

The Sunday Post

ROLLS ROYCE PROTEST
Almost 2,000 workers at the Rolls Royce overhaul plant in East Kilbride will stage a two-hour walk out tomorrow in protest of privatisation plans.

Industrial unrest over privatisation was standard fare during the Thatcher years.

Friday 27 February 1987

DIARY: Out at a special AIDS press conference at Glasgow University. Professor Jarrett at the forefront of the race to find a vaccine said, 'The permissive society is dead.'

The AIDS scare was reaching its peak in 1987. A Government-funded campaign told us, 'there is now a danger that has become a threat to us all. It is a deadly disease and there is no known cure.' This was emphasised by a gravestone with AIDS chiselled on it and the slogan 'Don't die of ignorance.' It's questionable that it was ever really a threat to us all, but the advances in treatments for HIV mean that people can now live with the virus for much longer than thought possible in 1987. And it's probably fair to say the permissive society is still very much alive.

Thursday 19 March 1987

DIARY: Frustrating day. In work I was landed with a couple of shitty jobs, including collecting quiz questions. That after we'd had an informal meeting about making the news harder.

I've seen this time and again from young people starting in newsrooms. There is a natural desire to get on, but it is easy to forget that you have to serve your time. That includes doing basic jobs.

General Election 1987

In June 1987 Margaret Thatcher won an historic third term with a significant parliamentary majority across the UK. That picture was not reflected in Scotland. Labour won 50 seats, the Conservatives dropped from 21 seats to ten, the SDP Liberal Alliance got nine seats and the SNP won three, an increase of one.

As a junior reporter on a Sunday newspaper, I had little involvement in covering the 1987 General Election. The following report, to which I contributed

these vox pops, looked at first-time voters ahead of the election.

Sunday 22 March 1987

The Sunday Post

YOUNG SCOTS SAY 'NO' TO MRS THATCHER

Every party recognises that first-time voters are going to be a crucial factor in the next election. Since the last General Election in June 1983, 2.1 million voters have had their names added to the electoral register. They now account for almost five per cent of the total electorate of 43.4 million.

GILLIAN FISHER: There is no way I would vote for Margaret Thatcher and I have no confidence in Neil Kinnock. The Alliance will get my vote.

JAMES SMITH: The Labour Party is biased against Catholics, so I won't be voting for them. The Alliance just don't appeal to me and there's no way I would vote Tory. It seems the SNP is all that's left.

ANDREW WITHERSPOON: I don't have to think twice. My parents have always voted Conservative. Coming from a private school, which Labour want to abolish, I think I'll stick with that philosophy.

Friday 27 March 1987

DIARY: **I'm doing a story over a rumpus about taxi licences in East Kilbride (EK) and one of the main characters is avoiding me. I'll come up against that often I'm sure.**

Saturday 16 May 1987

DIARY: **Down in Greenock. Princess Anne visiting a charity fete as President** of Save the Children. From 11.00am to 4.00pm and it was dull. I reckon we could have left after the Princess arrived at 12.15pm. Not much of a story. Felt sorry for her if she has to visit these affairs so often, meeting dull dignitaries and watching the same displays. Having said that, the fetes are great for locals – the whole town seemed to be out.

Back just in time for extra time in the Cup Final. St Mirren beat Dundee United 1–0 which is a surprise, but good for Scottish football.

Sunday 17 May 1987

DIARY: My best day in the paper yet. P2 lead, P2 photo caption, Raw Deal lead, two middles and lead book review.

During that summer, I saw an advert for news trainees at BBC Scotland. I initially ignored it because I didn't think broadcasting was for me. A combination of curiosity and youthful optimism made me submit an application later on, but with no real expectation of being selected from the thousands of others who applied.

Friday 18 September 1987

DIARY: Big day as regards the Radio Scotland job. Final interview and voice test. Given a selection of news items which had to be whittled down to two minutes. I selected international, national and Scottish stories and made two takes. Taken to conference room with another six Radio Scotland officials – News Ed, Current Affairs Ed etc. Grilled me solidly for about 45 minutes. Mostly about news with a Scottish flavour – what Scottish stories should be given more exposure, most important Scottish stories of the week etc.

Thursday 24 September 1987

DIARY: I am going to work for the BBC! Got the phone call this evening. A two year contract at £8,280 (+£634 shift allowance). A great opportunity.

Ironic that earlier Flash (Bill Anderson – *The Sunday Post* editor) was down from Dundee. He pulled me into the TV room on my own… turned out to be a pep talk. I mentioned not being satisfied with my news contribution, but he said he was perfectly happy and I was scoring well throughout the paper.

Saturday 26 September 1987

DIARY: Very dull Saturday. Later a small news story on the effects of demolition of the Apollo Theatre.

Glasgow's famous Apollo Theatre was demolished following its closure two years previously. The Apollo had hosted most of the major rock acts of the '70s and '80s and still holds a special place in the hearts of the city's music fans.

I'll always be grateful to The Sunday Post. I got my start on the paper and my colleagues took me under their wing. Many of them went on to success elsewhere. Others established themselves as significant figures in the DC Thomson operation.

I started at BBC Radio Scotland in November 1987. My initial training was on the news desk preparing the news bulletins. It was an entirely different culture with hourly deadlines. Central to the news output was a bank of telex machines. Every hour at 20 to the hour, they would start chuntering out three minutes' worth of news material from London, covering UK and international stories. In addition a news voicer might be sent, which had to be recorded onto a cartridge. This was all complemented by Scottish stories and voicers from our own reporters and copy from local correspondents. The rip 'n' read was so called because that is exactly what you did with it – the stories were printed on a long sheet of telex paper and, using the edge of a ruler, you tore out the ones you wanted, stapled them onto a sheet of A5 paper and arranged them into the running order. You then descended two floors to where the newsreaders had their small continuity studios. That was how it was supposed to work, but news never does. The rip 'n' read was frequently late, or there was a problem with the audio or there was a breaking story. Too often I would burst through as the pips were marking the final seconds towards the hour. I loved it. This was news as it was happening, or as close as it could be for the time.

Tuesday 17 November 1987

BBC Radio News

A demonstration organised by the National Union of Students marched through Glasgow city centre this afternoon to protest against Government plans for education. Students from the 32 affiliated colleges in the west of Scotland took part in the protest. John MacKay reports…

This was my first BBC report.

Monday 7 December 1987

BBC Radio News

Police in Glasgow are investigating the possibility that a batch of bad drugs have been responsible for three deaths over the weekend. The bodies of three men were found each with a hypodermic syringe beside them. John MacKay reports…

Drug deaths have remained a consistent presence in news bulletins.

Tuesday 15 December 1987

BBC Radio News

The bridge that leads to nowhere at last seems to be going somewhere. Developers have submitted a plan to Glasgow District Council which will transform the concrete eyesore into part of an £18 million office development, linking with a new complex to be built at the bottom of Bath Street. Here's John MacKay with the details…

The bridge had been constructed in 1972 as part of the city's inner ring road. It was supposed to be part of a pedestrian walkway above the motorway, but that didn't happen and it was considered too costly to demolish. The development is the distinctive brown office block sitting over the M8 motorway at Charing Cross.

Undated news report 1987

BBC Radio News

Over two thirds of Scottish people see no need for shops to open on a Sunday, according to organisers of a new movement – the Scottish *Keep Sunday Special Campaign*. They claim that Scottish society does not want or need Sunday trading. And they are backed by traders and trade unions. John MacKay reports…

There was no legal restriction on shops being open on a Sunday, but it was the custom. Town and city centres would be dead on a Sunday. That began to change rapidly in the 1990s.

1988

BBC Radio Scotland trainees were sent to 'out stations' around the country – Aberdeen, Highland, Orkney, Shetland, Border or Solway – to gain intensive practical experience. I was assigned to BBC Radio Orkney under the guidance of station manager John Fergusson.

Thursday 7 January 1988

DIARY: Sent out on a 'jolly' today to the island of Sanday to the north-east. The flight was on a Loganair Islander. Ten seats, including pilot and co-pilot. A ten minute flight from Kirkwall and when we came in to land I was amazed to find that we were coming down on a field with sheep scattering beneath us.

Monday 11 January 1988

DIARY: Committed the cardinal sin this morning. I had arranged to be in the studio with John again this morning – and I slept in. I'd set my alarm for 6.30am last night, but I hadn't switched it on. So when I finally awoke at 8.30am the programme had already gone out. Fortunately John took it in good part, but it can't happen again. At least I wasn't presenting so I've learned a lesson the best way.

Tuesday 12 January 1988

DIARY: On a boat for half an hour to sail to Shapinsay. Met by shepherd – Jim Foubister – who took me to his home where his wife Ina gave me dinner (*lunch actually, but I wasn't so sophisticated then*). Did an interview with him about wintering sheep and then he took me to see another bloke about the same. Finally he took me to the local laird's son who is breeding ducks for wild shoots. Crammed all

that into a two hour stay before the ship returned. If it hadn't been for Jim, I'd never have made it. I can't get over how welcoming and helpful the islanders are.

Thursday 21 January 1988

DIARY: I had the continuity announcement at lunchtime sprung onto me. It meant introducing a tape of personal choice and doing an outro for it. I was quite nervous as I flicked open my microphone for my first ever 'live' broadcast. I stumbled a couple of times and crashed into Robbie Shepherd's programme a bit early. It was the old dry throat, thumping heart syndrome. But John reckoned I'd done okay and it didn't sound as bad as I thought it had. I'm glad to get it out of the way because I'm presenting my first breakfast programme tomorrow.

Friday 22 January 1988

DIARY: Presented my first live show this morning and it went well. It helped to have got yesterday's out of the way. As soon as I opened the mic I was away and relaxed very quickly.

Tuesday 26 January 1988

DIARY: Caught the 5.05pm flight to Shetland. Met Andrew Anderson (BBC Radio Shetland) and Duncan Kirkhope (a BBC Radio Scotland colleague also on attachment). He and I went to see the 'Up Helly Aa' procession – which was spectacular – with up to a thousand men marching with flaming torches. The burning of the traditional galley was quite a sight.

Tuesday 2 February 1988

DIARY: Big mistake this morning. We have market reports from two different

Marts – one is the Kirkwall Auction Mart, the other is the West Mainland Mart and I spoke about them as if they're one and the same.

The islanders were very welcoming, but it must have pained them at times to hear someone like me make such basic errors. Pronouncing the island of Foula (Foola) wrongly was another one. It might seem trivial, but it matters. If you can't get the basics right, how can people be sure your other facts aren't as sloppy?

DIARY CONT: At a council meeting. I found it dull, uninspiring and full of old farmers and prim maids with starched drawers. Dry stuff.

Ah, the clichéd arrogance of youth. This was local democracy in action.

The first Comic Relief Red Nose Day was held in February 1988. I had interviewed some children from Stromness who were going to school in their pyjamas to raise money. The interview ran the following day.

Thursday 4 February 1988

DIARY: Just before the final item finished I ran downstairs to check with Mairi (Mairi Fotheringham – station assistant) whether the weather summary had arrived on the telex machine. I ran back upstairs and ended up breathless.

What this entry doesn't detail, probably because of overwhelming embarrassment, is that the final item was the piece about the Stromness children. The very last clip was a young girl describing the night clothes she was wearing. I arrived back at the sound desk to fade up the mic just as she finished speaking. Having just run upstairs I was panting like a pervert and I knew it. In these situations there is no

short remedy, you just have to wait until you get your breath back. It took a few of the longest seconds of my life.

Wednesday 10 February 1988

DIARY: Interviewed the Celtic manager Billy McNeill today. Very impressed by him – genuine, warm and articulate. I'd half expected the 'big shot from the big city' syndrome, but no. I liked him a lot.

Saturday 27 February 1988

DIARY: I had an interview to do on North Ronaldsay and we travelled in the wee Loganair Islander. Unfortunately there was a blizzard on the way and it was a turbulent flight. I only had five minutes to get my interview, but I'd arranged to meet the guy at the airfield. On the way back it was just as bad, and on the approach to the runway the pilot had real problems holding the plane level.

There was a big storm coming in and the pilot told me that if I wasn't back in five minutes he would have to leave. I ran out to a small outbuilding, met my interviewee, recorded the interview and ran back to the plane, unknowingly stepping in cow dung as I did so. As we flew quickly back from North Ronaldsay, the plane heated up much as a car would and as the heat spread, so did the pungent stench of shit emanating from my seat. There was evident suspicion among my fellow passengers that the turbulent flight had been too much for me.

Friday 4 March 1988

DIARY: Got a real scare on the flight home. We'd just taken off from Inverness (the Orkney flight to Glasgow went via Inverness) and reached our cruising altitude when the plane suddenly turned sharply and seemed to dive through the clouds. The pilot said we had to return because of a technical fault, but we had fire tenders on the runway and it was all very rushed. I now know the meaning of the term 'shaken'.

As we descended rapidly below the clouds, all I could see was flashing blue emergency lights along the runway. The cabin was suddenly full of anxious chatter when previously it had been almost silent. Across from me were an elderly woman and a younger man. They didn't know each other, but she grasped his hand. The plane landed safely (the cause of the alarm had been a flashing warning light in the cockpit). In the arrivals lounge there were two coin-operated phones on the wall. I ran to one to alert my newsdesk. I could hear the other phone was being used by another reporter (a freelance). Meanwhile, the rest of the passengers lined up behind us, waiting to phone their loved ones to tell them the drama behind their delay.

I left Orkney at the end of March 1988 with some regret and returned to the BBC Radio Scotland Newsroom in Glasgow.

Tuesday 19 April 1988

DIARY: Had to do a piece on a report which claims that Scotland isn't doing enough for refugees. But the organisers couldn't even line up a refugee family. Incompetence.

This is still a regular complaint by reporters. There is no point in sending out a news release to broadcasters if the main figures are away on holiday, unavailable for interview, don't want to speak etc. If you want good coverage for your story, provide an example who is willing to talk about their experience and a specialist who can give it authority. That's what the best PR people do. Time is often against reporters and the more you can set up, the better the coverage of your story will be. A reputation for providing tea and bacon rolls is a big plus, too.

Wednesday 20 April 1988

BBC Radio News

Scottish Opera have announced details for their new season and there is one rather surprising introduction. Rikki Fulton – better known for more light-hearted roles – is playing the Lord Chancellor in Gilbert and Sullivan's 'Iolanthe'.

DIARY: First time I've felt the pressure of a deadline. Rikki Fulton – the popular comic actor – was there and I had to get an interview with him and the Opera's Managing Director. I couldn't interview them until midday, although the conference started at 11.00am. Boy did the organisers gab. I had two snatches of interview on just after 12.45pm, so I was pleased.

In the pre-digital era, I would return from my story with the material recorded onto quarter inch tape. It was edited by marking the tape with a white chinagraph pencil and literally cutting it using a razor blade on an editing block. The edits were joined with sticky tape. Finally, a length of yellow, quarter inch lead-in tape was required to mark the start of the piece, and red tape to mark the end.

The Glasgow Garden Festival

The Garden Festival was a huge success for Glasgow. Created on the site where STV and the BBC are now, it converted a

*rundown dockland area into a garden
wonderland with theme parks. Millions
visited between April and September and
it is remembered fondly. Many wondered
why it could not be maintained
permanently, especially when the housing
which was supposed to be developed on
the site never happened.*

Thursday 28 April 1988

DIARY: The first day of the much-
heralded Glasgow Garden Festival. It's a
credit to the city and while some parts
seem to be bustling, the gardens are
quiet and serene.

Monday 6 June 1988

DIARY: Down to Dalmuir to do a piece
on asbestos burial and for the first time
I used the cellnet phone to file copy.

My News Editor Robin Wyllie had handed
me a heavy black box with a telephone
receiver on top to try out. The contraption
was so big it came in its own briefcase and
clamped to the roof of the car. It was many
years before the use of mobile phones
became widespread.

Piper Alpha

*On the night of 6 July 1988 the North Sea
oil rig Piper Alpha exploded, killing 167
men. It was caused by a gas leak during
maintenance work and remains Britain's
worst ever oil disaster. The blaze took
three weeks to extinguish.*

Thursday 7 July 1988

DIARY: Today's news dominated by a
tragedy in the North Sea. An oil rig
– Piper Alpha – blew up and there are
believed to be some 160 people lost.
Apparently flames were reaching up to
400 feet and some TV pictures of it
were dramatic. There were also pictures

of relatives severely distressed, screaming
in the street. I think that is intrusive.
Amazing how these stories develop.
Peter Aitchison (*BBC colleague*) joined
us in the bar last night from the
newsroom after his shift. 'There's a fire
on a North Sea rig, but it doesn't seem
to be much,' he said. Then I woke up to
hear that. A real shock.

*The subsequent inquiry was covered
extensively in our news bulletins for
months afterwards, much of it very
technical. The word 'flange' (a metal disc
to seal the end of a pipe) became one of
the most commonly used words in news
reports.*

I was temporarily off news at this time.
BBC Radio Scotland decided it needed to
reach out to a more youthful audience.
Very reluctantly, I was part of the team
which developed and produced the 'No
The Archie Macpherson Show'. The
Executive Producer introduced a new
comic writer who wrote sketches and a
weekly soap. I thought him a pleasant guy,
but I didn't connect with his humour. At
production meetings I would argue that
this or that sketch just wasn't funny.
Armando Iannucci went on to have a
hugely successful career as a comedy
writer in the UK and Hollywood. I never
produced another non-news programme
again.

Saturday 10 September 1988

DIARY: My first football report today.
No Premier League games on because
of the forthcoming World Cup qualifier
against Norway midweek. So the focus
was on the First Division. I was at
Broomfield for Airdrie versus
Kilmarnock. Must have been one of the
first there. Settled in time for my tee-up

piece just after 2.00pm – and from then until half time I was doing a series of short pieces. Only one in the second half and a final summing up at full time. Also got Airdrie manager Gordon McQueen to do a telephone interview.

Airdrie won 5–1. Their first goal was scored by full back Tom Black who had a thick black moustache. I dialled the studio to update them and as presenter Tom Ferrie threw to me, my note with Tom Black's name on it blew over. There was a momentary panic as I announced the goal scorer was '... the man with the moustache...'

Everything was still done using a dial-up telephone. Far from the open mics now, you had to dial in if anything happened and hope the studio number wasn't engaged.

Friday 4 November 1988

DIARY: My last *Good Morning Scotland* as a producer – for quite a while at least. I've enjoyed the producing, but I'm not sure I'll miss it.

Producing GMS involved a long working day, a short sleep and then back in to put the programme out between 6.30am and 9.00am. It was two and a half hours of live radio, reacting to stories that could be international or local. Taped reports would be commissioned, live interviewees set up, presenters briefed. It was challenging, but enjoyable.

Such was the status of the BBC, there was some incredulity in my family that I was working there. When a friend told my mother that she'd heard my name as producer in the credits for *Good Morning Scotland* my mother had said, 'I don't think that would be our John.'

Undated report November 1988

BBC News

All police interviews with suspects in Strathclyde will soon be tape recorded. The Strathclyde Police Force are introducing a £1.3 million programme which will start with Maryhill Division next month. Other divisions will be included in the New Year.

This is now standard procedure for serious crimes.

Friday 11 November 1988

DIARY: Jim Sillars won the Govan by-election – turning a 19,000 Labour majority into a 3,000 SNP one. It's caused massive reverberations and what is clear is that the Tories are doing nothing for Scotland and Labour's 50 Scottish MPs are ineffectual.

Wednesday 23 November 1988

DIARY: Rangers have been bought by Scots businessman David Murray.

Rangers had begun their transformation two years previously under the chairmanship of David Holmes. His hiring of Graeme Souness as the new player manager and then an influx of top English players had transformed Rangers and Scottish football. Murray took Rangers to another level and invested huge sums trying to achieve success in Europe. It all came to a crashing end more than 20 years later.

David Murray would readily take direct calls from reporters which was great from our point of view, but also gave him a degree of manipulation. He liked to mess with reporters too. During a series of media interviews I went in after the BBC's highly regarded Alan Mackay. As my cameraman was setting up, Murray spoke of how good Alan was and what an interview he'd just done. I was followed in by a former colleague, Alison Douglas. She told me afterwards that he'd said the same about me. All of it just to put the reporter facing him a little on edge.

Monday 5 December 1988

DIARY: A press conference at police HQ. There's some nutter loose in the city.

Ah, Glasgow.

LOCKERBIE BOMBING

On Wednesday 21 December 1988 a Pan Am jet, flying from London to JFK Airport in New York exploded over the Scottish town of Lockerbie. After a long, complex investigation, two Libyans were put on trial in 2000. One of them, Abdelbaset al-Megrahi, was convicted and sentenced to life imprisonment. Controversy over who was responsible for the bombing continues to this day. The Scottish investigators remain resolute that the right man was convicted.

The BBC Radio Scotland newsroom had deserted quickly that evening, many to a Christmas Party being held elsewhere in Broadcasting House. I had brought a book in anticipation of a quiet shift.

Wednesday 21 December 1988

DIARY: Answered two very important calls just after 7.20pm. One said there was an explosion in the town of Lockerbie. A minute later the AA called – a patrolman had seen a plane come down on a housing estate. Quickly established that it was a Pan Am 747 flying from London to New York and all 259 on board were dead, plus 11 on the ground. As the night wore on the

full scale of the disaster became clear and we broadcast through the night.

One of the first questions was, where was Lockerbie? It was one of those names we were vaguely familiar with because we'd passed it driving south, but I don't think anyone could have said precisely where it was. It quickly became apparent that it was not a military, but a passenger jet. We immediately thought it must be the London to Glasgow shuttle. Calls to air traffic control and airlines soon established that the plane missing was a Pan Am 747 flying from London to New York.

Duty News Editor Phil Taylor bashed out a script and told me to go to a studio and record it for transmission on Radio 4 at 8.00pm. In the days before 24-hour rolling news, the first that much of the UK would have heard about the tragedy was my young Scottish voice reading that script.

BBC Radio 4 News

Police in Dumfries say that 'many bodies' have been recovered from the wreckage in Lockerbie town centre where a Pan American Airlines Boeing 747 crashed in flames earlier this evening. The injured are being treated in hospitals throughout Dumfriesshire and Carlisle. Doctors and medical staff are being called in from a wide area. Police say that any members of the public offering blood should contact Dumfries Infirmary. The plane, flying from London to John F Kennedy airport had 259 passengers on board. It's reported to have struck a petrol station, exploding and setting alight nearby houses. An eyewitness spoke of a 300 foot fireball shooting into the sky.

Police believe there are a 'huge number' of casualties. They have appealed to motorists travelling north or south to avoid the main A74 Glasgow to Carlisle road for the next few hours.

Kenny Macintyre – a reporter who worked off his wits – went straight to the phone book, looked up the number for the post office in Lockerbie and called. That quick reaction got one of the first eyewitness accounts of what people in the town were experiencing.

Phil Taylor (BBC Radio News Editor)
Like all the truly memorable/ remarkable/terrible stories of a life in journalism, the Lockerbie bombing from a personal standpoint was one of those lurches from the mundane to the extraordinary and chaotic.

I was on a back-shift, working as a duty news editor, although the title used by the BBC at the time must have had its roots in the Imperial Civil Service: I was titled a Chief News Assistant!

In those days, calling around the principal emergency services by 'phone was an almost hourly routine. These days I gather the police tell journalists anything they have to say will be 'on our website.' Another example, dare I say, of the degradation of what should be an open and honest relationship between authority and journalists trying to monitor those who exert power. Our sub-editor hung up the phone, paused, and then turned round to the newsdesk and said, 'It appears a plane has come down in Lockerbie.'

Within minutes of that conversation, we were getting calls from BBC Scotland journalists down in the South West. Kenny Macintyre, being the genius journalist that he was, was also bashing the phones, trying all the contacts he could think of, including – no doubt – members of Mrs Thatcher's cabinet. The next stab at what was really going on was a rumour that an RAF jet fighter on a low-level training flight had crashed in to a petrol station. All these years later, writing this prompts me to go to Google Earth and to gaze down at the A74 as it passes the ill-fated Sherwood Crescent where a wing section from Pan Am Flight 103 created a crater 150 feet long, killing 11 people. Where did the petrol station rumour come from, I wonder? The nearest services are at Annandale 8.2 miles to the North. I guess the grim answer is: how else do you explain sheets of flame rising hundreds of feet from the side of a motorway on a chill December evening?

Over the next hours, our newsroom did what newsrooms have always done at such times of drama; we drafted in every member of staff we could reach. We despatched reporters – including a young Eddie Mair – producers, TV crews. Staff from BBC Scotland's Dumfries office became the point men and women, getting to the scene first, or as near the multiple sites of destruction as the emergency services could allow. The calls began flooding in from all around the world. Could we put one of our staff on the line to tell the story? Very quickly it started to emerge that 35 of the passengers were young students from Syracuse University in New York. They were returning home for Christmas. We began calling the university for reaction – and New York radio stations were calling us.

Eddie Mair (BBC Radio Reporter)

I was coming to the end of a three month secondment acting as a reporter. I barely knew which end of a microphone to talk into, but during a late shift one evening – while an office Christmas party was in full swing, we got reports of some kind of incident near the A74. A small plane had hit a petrol station?

I was despatched to get a colleague, David, out of the Christmas party and drive us both down to the scene. With my usual nose for news, I recall telling my editor it was probably nothing and why were we driving all that way?

En route, we turned on the radio news to hear for the first time reports of a passenger plane being lost. It was shocking to us both. We arrived somewhere close to Lockerbie to find the A74 closed and jammed with traffic, blocking our way. We were stuck some distance from where we needed to be. In a fit of inspiration/ stupidity, I drove the car onto the central reservation and followed emergency service vehicles down the bumpy grass. That at least is my memory though I wonder whether it's false. The road has been upgraded and now there is no grassy division

between carriageways. Did I really do that?

A deeply inexperienced 'reporter', I recall walking around the deserted streets of Lockerbie where front doors stood open, and Christmas lights twinkled. I recall seeing a woman's body in a garden, but that sight made no sense to me.

Where were all the people? I found them in a pub on one of the main streets, crowded into the bar, watching the *Nine O'Clock News*: a slightly surreal moment interviewing traumatised witnesses about what had happened while they watched news from London which seemed to know more than they did.

BBC Radio News

The airline says it appears certain that all those on board – believed to be more than 250 – have been killed. And in the last hour, there are reports of motorists who were travelling on the A74 just after seven o'clock this evening having been killed. A few minutes ago a local hotelier told us he'd seen several cars on fire. (*In fact, no motorists were killed. All 11 fatalities on the ground were in the town's Sherwood Crescent.*) In Lockerbie itself, the situation is still unclear although it's known that two residential areas have been flattened. Some houses were set on fire when the plane crashed into a petrol station and exploded. Eye witnesses spoke of a fire ball... at least two explosions before the plane hit the town and a sense of the area being struck by an earthquake. Helicopters have been

31

ferrying the dead and injured to local hospitals. It's known that three babies and a number of American military personnel and students were on board the plane. Police have sealed off part of Lockerbie and warned motorists that they must stay away from the A74 to allow the rescue operations to proceed.

The phone calls started coming in, firstly from stations elsewhere in the UK and then from abroad. I reported to several American, Canadian and Australian stations.

Some extracts from my reports reveal how the story changed as the evening moved on.

(KSRO, Santa Rosa California, USA) 'Live Line' with Larry Chiaroni

'The two nearest hospitals that have been dealing with casualties have been told to stand down. Everyone on board is understood to have been killed. There are no casualties coming in. At the moment, though, we do not know how many people on the ground have been killed, if indeed there have been any.'

'The plane was on fire when it hit the ground… it may have hit another plane or there were a number of American servicemen on board, so there are rumours that it may have been a bomb, but I stress that is purely speculation at the moment and we have no way of knowing as of yet.'

'There are large craters in the town centre. These craters are up to 30 feet deep. A number of houses have been destroyed, there are burned out cars on the roads. The police have imposed a two mile exclusion zone around about the area where the plane came down.'

'The plane left London Heathrow at six o'clock in the evening and it disappeared from radar screens at 19 minutes past seven.'

(XTRA, San Diego, California, USA) News Talk Hotline – Mark Williams

MARK WILLIAMS: John, we are getting reports here that it is apparently certain that this jet liner was blown out of the sky. What's being said there?

JM: That is certainly the speculation at the moment. There was no Mayday call and the plane just disappeared from radar screens without any panic coming from the pilots. It seems that whatever happened, happened very quickly and that would suggest it was a bomb. We're also led to believe that a warning went out to staff at a number of American embassies a few days ago informing that a threat to place a bomb on board a Pan Am flight from Frankfurt to the United States had been made, although the warning did not specify what flight would be affected.

MW: Are we getting any information on who was on board the aircraft?

JM: It's believed there were a number of students on board. Perhaps more significantly, is the fact that there were servicemen on board who were returning from Frankfurt in Germany.

MW: Is there any speculation as to – if

a bomb was planted on this aircraft – where it was planted, in Frankfurt or in London?

JM: The flight was Pan Am 103 and that originally left Frankfurt via London. It's believed that the plane that left Frankfurt is not the same plane that left London. Although it was the same flight number it may have been a different plane (*it wasn't*). But that is purely speculation. We can't be certain on that.

MW: Do we have a count of how many people are dead?

JM: We understand that there were 260 people on board the Pan Am Boeing 747. They are all dead. At the moment we do not know how many people have been killed on the ground, but certainly we're talking in terms of at least 300 people in total, probably more (*the death toll was 270*).

MW: Have they recovered the black box?

JM: There were two black boxes. They have been recovered and are being investigated.

Phil Taylor (BBC *Radio News Editor*)

Most of us, I think, worked through the night. One of the things that does stand in my mind is the absence in those days – of course – of any 24-hour, rolling news capability in the UK. However, CNN had launched in the US eight years earlier and by 1988, was available in some BBC news rooms including ours. Ironically, the first images of fire and smoke in the night sky of Lockerbie that I watched was on that CNN feed.

By the morning, we were beginning to see more of those dreadful scenes on our domestic TV services. The most terrible of all, surely, was the surreal image of the nose cone of the clipper *Maid of the Seas*, lying on her side in a field at Tundergarth Church, just outside Lockerbie. What does hindsight tell me? Not much; just how terrible it is to think of all those lives lost and other lives changed forever in the inkling of an eye at a few minutes after 7.00pm on the night of Wednesday 21 December 1988.

1989

Wednesday 4 January 1989

BBC Radio News

Leaked details of the proposed restructuring of the National Health Service (NHS) include plans to allow hospitals to opt-out of the system. The proposals were contained in a draft White Paper which has been considered by the Prime Minister.

Proposed changes to the NHS have always been and remain a fixture of any self-respecting news bulletin.

Thursday 5 January 1989

DIARY: A TV crew was in the newsroom covering our day as part of a programme to let the public see what we do. They covered the morning meeting and were then assigned to follow me as the reporter. I was covering a fairly dull story on a Loch Lomond development. They filmed me setting the story up, doing my interviews and editing the story together. It was very interesting and I was pleased to be part of it. Got a bit of slagging in the office about being a 'star'.

I got an even bigger slagging because I got lost on the way to the interview and managed to lose the film crew. Inevitably, that made its way into the diary of the Glasgow Herald.

Monday 9 January 1989

BBC Radio News

Scottish Ballet have attracted one of the world's foremost artistic directors to choreograph a new production in the spring. Oleg Vinogradov of the Kirov Ballet will work on an original version of *Petrushka*.

DIARY: Obviously he's quite a big fish in that world. No English, so done through interpreter. Good interview, but had a bit of difficulty putting it together with his Russian dipping under the translator's voice.

'... quite a big fish in that world' did not do Oleg Vinogradov quite the justice he deserved as a choreographer of international renown.

BELLGROVE TRAIN CRASH

Monday 6 March 1989

Two people died and more than 50 were injured when two passenger trains collided near Bellgrove Station in Glasgow. An inquiry later found the cause of the accident was one of the drivers going through a danger signal.

I was sent out as a secondary reporter to get a sense of the scene. It wasn't one of devastation – as both trains were still on the track. They had collided head on and the front of one had risen up on top of the other one. I picked up as much as I could and headed back to the BBC. I did a rushed live two-way into the PM programme on Radio 4 with Valerie Singleton, whom I used to watch on Blue Peter. It was a surreal moment.

Undated report March 1989

BBC Radio News

A Scottish Member of the European Parliament has claimed that many Scottish football clubs face financial ruin with the introduction of the European Market in 1992. Strathclyde West MEP Hugh McMahon says the proposals for the free movement of workers could mean financial doom for clubs which rely on transfer fees to survive.

This was pre-Bosman ruling. A player could not move to another club unless his current club agreed and they would have to be paid a transfer fee. These transfer fees helped sustain many clubs in an era before big television money.

Undated report 1989

BBC Radio News

Strathclyde Police have introduced a new video car to the roads of the region in an effort to combat bad driving. The unmarked car has been fitted with video equipment which can film a driver's errors and even be used in evidence in a court action.

This is now standard practice.

Sunday 28 May 1989

BBC Radio News

The President of the Scottish Football league says the future of the Scotland England international should be reconsidered following the violence before and after yesterday's game in Glasgow. His remarks came after more than 250 fans were arrested during a day of street fighting in the city.

Scotland lost 2–0. This was the last of the annual Auld Enemy clashes.

Undated report June 1989

BBC Radio News

The annual rate of inflation has reached its highest level in seven years. Last month's figure of 8.3 per cent was lower than analysts had predicted, but it was still the 16th in a row which has seen a rise. The main causes of the increase were the rise in mortgage rates and the price rises for petrol and food.

RANGERS SIGN THEIR FIRST CATHOLIC PLAYER

1989 was the year when the Berlin Wall came down and Eastern bloc countries revolted against Communist rule. Rangers signing a Catholic footballer hardly stands as a comparison, but for many in Scotland it was just as seismic.

Monday 10 July 1989

ALISON WALKER, BBC Radio Sports Reporter

I was relatively new to the world of football journalism – a rookie reporter in sport. I'd done my share of interviews with managers and new players and been to a few press conferences. The newsroom generally wasn't interested in these – but on that day in July 1989 when Rangers called a press conference to announce the signing of a new player, I was told I wouldn't be going on my own to Ibrox.

The seasoned newshound Kenny Macintyre would be going with me. There had been talk of Rangers signing their first Catholic player and this was potentially a major story.

I remember reading the *Scottish Sun* that morning. They'd run an exclusive, saying it would be Mo Johnston, yet most of us didn't believe it. We thoughts they'd taken a flyer because, after all, it wasn't in the 'Daily Souness' or the 'Daily Ranger' as we used to call *The Daily Record*.

We headed for the Blue Room at Ibrox. I remember it felt quite tense. There were loads of newspaper journalists in that room, every seat occupied and some standing. They kept us waiting – I wonder now if that was on purpose too.

The door at the end of the Blue Room, behind the press conference table opened, and as the assembled group walked in, there was a collective gasp of air from the audience. It was quite surreal. There was Maurice Johnston grinning widely, almost as widely as Graeme Souness and David Murray. Also in the line-up was key agent, Bill McMurdo.

One or two journalists rushed out, falling over themselves and each other. There weren't mobile phones in those days so this really was news to spread as quickly as possible. The announcement was made. The top table spoke and then there was a barrage of questions.

I am not sure I really understood the significance or magnitude of this signing until the moment when Mo walked into the room. I remember thinking, 'what is life going to be like for him now. Is he brave or stupid?'

As it turned out, he ended up being a huge footballing success at Rangers, but it can't have been easy for him. Thank goodness times have changed.

I won't forget that day in July 1989. It was, for sure, one of those 'were you there?' moments.

I came in for a late shift, having followed Rangers' signing of Maurice Johnston throughout that morning. A young female English colleague was preparing the 2.00pm bulletin and sought my opinion on whether Rangers' new signing was still worthy of being lead. It illustrated how localised this story was. Someone from elsewhere in the UK couldn't quite grasp, understandably, that such a practice would have still been going on.

STV News

MAURICE JOHNSTON: 'I've come to a really big club, possibly one of the biggest in Europe.'

GRAEME SOUNESS, Rangers Manager: 'Obviously there were a lot of considerations we had to take into account – the main one being that he's an out and out quality player.

REPORTER: Are you troubled at all by the pressures that will be on him as the first Catholic to play here?

GS: There'll be pressures on all my players next year because we have a big squad, there's no one going to be an automatic choice and that includes Maurice. There's pressures playing at Rangers. You have accept these things when you come here.'

A couple of scarves were set on fire outside Ibrox and a significant number of the gathered fans were unhappy.

(*Fans' vox pops*)

'They should keep to their own.'

'It's just unbelievable. I can't get over it. I'll maybe wake up in the morning and it'll not be true.'

'Everything is away now, isn't it? Religion and everything.'

Johnston was at Rangers for more than two seasons and was generally considered to be a success. Celtic fans have never forgiven him. Rangers signing a Catholic is no longer news.

Some ten years later, the *Daily Record* did a feature on Rangers' Italian captain Lorenzo Amoruso, including a photo of his mother at home in Florence. Side by side on her mantelpiece were photos of the Rangers captain – her son – and the Pope. It was as vivid a statement as any that times had moved on.

Monday 25 September 1989

BBC Radio News

Nearly a quarter of a million council house tenants applied to buy their homes between the introduction of the legislation allowing them to do so in 1980 and the end of 1988. According to figures published by the Scottish Development Department, over 138,000 dwellings were sold to sitting tenants in the same period.

The sale of council houses to their tenants was one of the principal policies which brought Margaret Thatcher to power in 1979.

Thursday 19 October 1989

BBC Radio News

Three of Scotland's senior judges have ruled that the victim of a sex attack should not be asked her views on the sentencing of her attacker. They said that given the circumstances of the case and knowing the background of the accused, no judge could impose anything but a prison sentence for a substantial number of years. The case came before the Appeal Court in Edinburgh after Lord McCluskey deferred sentence on the attacker.

Tuesday 17 October 1989

DIARY: Drove through to Perth for the official opening of St Johnstone's McDiarmid Park against Manchester United. I was doing a piece for *Good Morning Scotland*. Interviewed Alex Totten, Alex Ferguson, the team chairman and even the tea lady. Very pleased with it. Driving back I listened to the two tapes of material. One of them was blank! I was really pissed off. Very frustrating because it was a fault in the recorder – honestly!

As well as Alex Ferguson, I had got United captain Bryan Robson and star forward Mark Hughes. They were all relaxed and had given good interviews. I had my report already prepared in my head. I knew the clips I wanted and how it would all fit together. The GMS producer Peter Aitchison had set aside a good few minutes of his programme for the piece I had promised him. All reporters have been there in one form or another – that futile pressing of buttons on the tape recorder, play, stop, rewind, play, stop, rewind further. Nothing. Of course, it's always because of faulty equipment!

Sunday 29 October 1989

DIARY: On an early shift and I was still drunk when I arrived (following a stag night). So as the morning wore on I could feel myself sobering up. At about 10.00am I was sitting in the chair with the sun streaming onto my face and not a sound. I drifted into a blissful doze.

That blissful doze caused me to miss the 11.00am bulletin, forcing the news reader to use the 10.00am again. It was only his anxious call as we approached the midday bulletin that woke me up. Never again.

Thursday 2 November 1989

Sometimes the detail thrown up by the insignificant stories from local agency copy is wonderful. The following still makes me smile.

BBC *Radio News*

A supervisor in a fish factory who was sacked for hitting a teenage girl in the face with a fish has won his claim for unfair dismissal. The incident arose from a row over the size of fish he was giving filleters at a seafood factory in Peterhead. This report from John MacKay...

An industrial tribunal in Aberdeen heard that the size of the fish had a direct bearing on the earnings of the filleters. When they complained to their supervisor, WP (*I think it's only fair to use initials here*), that the fish were too big, he became involved in an argument with AM. Mr P pulled a fish from one of the boxes and hit her on the side of the face with it. Miss M told the tribunal that she was upset and the side of her face was covered with fish slime. Mr P accepted that he had been arguing with Miss M, but claimed that he had accidentally struck her with the fish. The Tribunal said they had taken into account Miss M hadn't complained herself, and that she was known to be cheeky. The tribunal awarded Mr P £1,290 in compensation, but said he was 20 per cent to blame.

Thursday 2 November 1989

DIARY: Eddie's (*Eddie Mair*) leaving for television where he'll be part of the *Reporting Scotland* team. I've thought of television myself and I think ultimately I'll find myself doing that. But what I enjoy about radio is the independence. If I want to do a story

myself I grab a Uher (*tape recorder*) and that's it. TV is much more complicated and a lot slower. But that is where the future of broadcasting lies and I suppose I'll have to try and get in some time.

Tuesday 21 November 1989

DIARY: Parliamentary and broadcasting history were made this afternoon when the House of Commons was televised live for the first time. Watched it and it wasn't particularly dramatic. Debates on the Queen's Speech. It'll get better when we get into *Prime Minister's Question Time.*

Coverage of Parliamentary proceedings only began on radio in 1978. Throughout the 1980s any TV coverage of events in Parliament was audio-only covered by a photograph of the Commons chamber and an inset photograph of the politician speaking.

Tuesday 28 November 1989

BBC *Radio News*

Scotland will be left in an economic backwater when the Channel Tunnel is opened, unless there is a major investment in the railway network. The warning came from the General Secretary of the Scottish Trades Union Congress, Campbell Christie, who was speaking prior to the special conference on railway investment which is being held in Glasgow today.

Monday 4 December 1989

DIARY: Eddie Mair made his debut as a presenter on *Reporting Scotland*. Didn't see it, but I'm sure he did well. Would maybe like to do something like that myself in the future.

Undated report December 1989

BBC Radio News

The High Court in Glasgow has been hearing how sectarian violence flared when two neighbouring households watched this year's Old Firm Scottish Cup Final on television. A woman draped in an Irish tricolour ran from her house shouting insults at the family across the road. They in turn brandished a Union Jack and street battles broke out ending in the death of a man. John MacKay reports...

1990

Wednesday 24 January 1990

DIARY: Just before 3.00pm we got a call saying a helicopter had crashed into a block of flats at Eastwood Toll. I was dispatched in miserable weather and traffic jams meant I had to abandon the car and walk the last mile, which was very unpleasant. I just missed a press statement by a police officer, but I got a couple of good eyewitnesses.

A policeman on board was killed.

Tuesday 13 February 1990

BBC Radio News

As police in Glasgow continue the hunt for the killer of ten-year-old Christine Lee, her family have appealed for anyone with information to come forward and help the inquiry. Her body was found late last night in the Castlemilk area of the city, five hours after she'd gone missing.

DIARY: I covered the story throughout the day. I attended a police press conference, interviewed the man leading the hunt and packaged for 1.00pm. Also voiced for lunchtime and London (*Radio 4*). Then I went out to Castlemilk and spoke to the dead girl's uncle. Normally I hate doorstepping, but this guy was willing enough and gave me a good interview. Also spoke to some young mothers in a nearby community centre. Packaged for *Good Evening Scotland* and for Radio 4, voiced for our 5.00pm and 6.00pm and also London's 6.00pm. I was extremely busy and didn't have a moment, but when you get into such a story you thrive under the pressure.

The devastation of the victim's family was rather overlooked by the enthusiastic young reporter caught up in the rush of a strong news story.

Friday 2 March 1990

BBC Radio News

At the funeral of the murdered ten-year-old Glasgow girl, Christine Lee, the priest appealed for her killer to come forward and seek help. And he led mourners in praying for the person responsible for her death.

Wednesday 19 September 1990

BBC Radio News

A pathologist has told the High Court in Glasgow that Christine Lee was killed by strangulation. But he was unable to pinpoint the exact time of her death.

Nineteen-year-old John Dowling was jailed for the rape and murder of Christine.

I was never a crime correspondent, so it was unusual for me to follow a case through to its conclusion. More typically you would dip in and out of court cases, depending on the availability of the crime correspondent or more senior reporters.

Saturday 17 February 1990

BBC Radio News

It's been confirmed that Rangers have been approached to take part in a new European Super League. Only three British teams have been invited to take part and Rangers will be joined by Liverpool and Arsenal if the ban on English teams taking part in European competitions is lifted. Celtic have not been included. This report from John MacKay…

JM: The new competition, which will replace the existing UEFA Cup, will feature the elite of European football, including AC Milan and Real Madrid. The league games will be played on Wednesday evenings and will begin in November next year. It's understood that fans will not be encouraged to travel to away games and, instead, visiting teams' supporters will see the game via satellite television. Rangers say they will continue to play in the Premier League. A provisional fixture list has been drawn up for the first Super League season in 1991–2, with plans for a grand final at Wembley in February 1992. The news will come as a shock to Celtic and Manchester United who are being left out because they are considered to lack the necessary business expertise and all-seater grounds.

This was the beginnings of what became the Champions League.

Monday 30 April 1990

BBC Radio News

Ten people have been killed after a plane crashed into a hillside in Harris in the Outer Hebrides. The plane, a Shackleton, was taking part in an RAF exercise when it came down in low cloud. The Shackleton, a maritime reconnaissance aircraft, was based at RAF Lossiemouth.

Saturday 26 May 1990

BBC Radio News

The Labour leader, Neil Kinnock, says that under a Labour Government a future Scottish Assembly would be free to raise taxes without cash limits set by Westminster. In an interview in the Observer, Mr Kinnock claims that is what the country wants and that's what it will get. John MacKay reports…

JM: In the interview, Mr Kinnock says there is a huge majority support for a form of Scottish Government with tax-raising powers. He pledges that a Labour Government would create such an assembly and it would be up to it what taxes could be levied. Mr Kinnock says the members of such an assembly would be conscious of not hoisting taxes too high. Not only would this inflict a burden on the Scottish people, he says, but it would deter inward investment.

Tuesday 26 June 1990
BBC Radio News

The mother of a four-year-old girl has failed in her attempt to order a man to undergo genetic fingerprinting to prove whether he is the father of her child. At the Court of Session, three appeal judges ruled that under existing law the court had no power to order the test.

Tuesday 17 July 1990
BBC Radio News

The offside rule in football is to be changed. The rule, which has probably caused more arguments in the game than any other, is to be adapted so that an attacker can now be in line with the defender instead of behind him. FIFA hope the change will lead to teams playing a more attacking game, and more goals. The change will come into force at the end of this month.

The offside law remains one of the most controversial in the game and has become even more complex with the concept of players being 'active' or 'inactive'. However, this change established the principle of the advantage being given to the attacking player.

1991

During the early part of 1991, I was working mostly as a Duty Editor producing the main bulletins on BBC Radio Scotland. This covered the period of the First Gulf War.

Wednesday 9 January 1991

DIARY: Work dominated by late news that American–Iraq talks to avert a Gulf War had failed. The UN deadline is Tuesday and no sign of Iraq pulling out of Kuwait. War seems likely. We won't really be affected, but people will die.

Wednesday 16 January 1991

DIARY: War has begun in the Gulf. Allied planes have attacked various targets throughout Iraq and Kuwait. I had covered the *Six O'Clock* and the *Ten O'Clock* tonight pointing at the last hours before war. One of my headlines was 'More than a million troops now poised for war in the Gulf.'

The attacks began at midnight.

DIARY: Much of (the coverage) was given over to the American TV network CNN. Two of their reporters were giving a live commentary from an hotel in Baghdad, describing the explosions and the tracers in the sky. Sad though it is, I think the allied response was justified. I expect it will be quick and there's no question we'll win. But what follows could be nasty – terrorism.

Thursday 17 January 1991

DIARY: I produced the *Six O'Clock* and the *Ten O'Clock News*, dominated of course by the outbreak of the war in the Gulf. There was some great material. A British Tornado jet has crashed and the race is on to rescue the two-man crew who were ejected. At midnight, word came through that Iraq had fired missiles at Israel. In the event the Scud missiles caused little damage and minor injuries, but it's a whole new aspect to the war. I sat on until Robin (*news editor*) came in a 5.00am, just cutting and cueing tapes to leave as much for the early bulletins as possible.

Tuesday 22 January 1991

DIARY: Had to completely redo the *Ten O'Clock* because Iraq had again launched Scud missiles at Israel. Three dead. How long can Israel stay out now?

Thursday 7 February 1991

DIARY: It was looking like a quiet morning when news broke of a mortar bomb attack on Downing Street at about 10.10am. We didn't start getting material on it until nearer half past, but we got a news flash on and had an extended bulletin at 11.00am news. I was cutting tapes coming in. It was an education to watch Robin in action. I just wonder how I'd have handled it on my own.

Saturday 9 February 1991

DIARY: I was covering the second division game between Queen's Park and Dumbarton at Hampden – my first visit to the press box of the national stadium. The Radio Scotland point is a room on its own on top of the stand at the end of the press box. And bloody cold it was too. Was provided with a cup of tea, cake and a biscuit at half time which was very civilised. Game ended 1–1.

Wednesday 27 February 1991

DIARY: The Allied advances in the Gulf continue to be remarkable – and the retreating Iraqi forces have been surrounded in Kuwait. One tragic incident, however – nine British soldiers, three of them Scottish, died when American planes accidentally bombed their trucks. We've lost more men through accidents and 'friendly fire' than we have from the Iraqis.

Tuesday 5 March 1991

DIARY: Major story in Scotland just now is about allegations of child abuse in Orkney – children taken from home by social workers etc. It's a legal minefield.

Thursday 4 April 1991

DIARY: News dominated by the Orkney case being thrown out by a sheriff far earlier than expected. The children arrived home in the islands this evening, so I managed an extended voice and clips from Orkney. It came late and was very long. I was editing it with two minutes before going on-air. Tight, but worth it.

Monday 15 April 1991

DIARY: Kept late this evening because of a tip-off Graeme Souness was leaving as Rangers manager to take over at Liverpool. We couldn't get anyone to say anything more.

Friday 19 April 1991

DIARY: Hectic 1.00pm. Rangers due to announce new manager – Walter Smith – at 1.00pm. I had three people there with the Radio Car and had three contingency plans. What I hadn't counted on was a fire alarm delaying the announcement and while I had enough material to fill, just, I was anxious to get it. Well, Derek Rae came on at 1.24 (we're off air at 1.28) and

the line wouldn't work properly. I was snapping instructions all over and the adrenalin was pumping. We got him on the telephone with two minutes to spare. All hectic, but we got it.

Tuesday 23 April 1991

DIARY: Government has announced a new Council Tax to replace the Poll Tax – a u-turn if ever there was one.

The Poll Tax for funding local government was introduced in Scotland in 1989, a year before the rest of the UK. It was hugely unpopular and opponents argued that it meant the less well off were having to pay more while the better off paid less. There were widespread protests and a mass non-payment campaign. It was key to the downfall of Margaret Thatcher as Prime Minister.

Saturday 27 April 1991

DIARY: Onto Ibrox for a press conference announcing the new assistant, Archie Knox. Bit of hassle when they said it should only be for the Sundays. However, I got my interviews in the end with chairman David Murray, manager Walter Smith and Archie Knox himself. I did have a minor gaffe – asked in usual fashion if Smith would identify himself on the tape to establish level and he must have assumed I wasn't sure who he was. The conversation went, 'Would you mind identifying yourself for the tape?' 'You must be fucking joking!' It was done with humour.

Monday 22 July 1991

DIARY: Stroll in at the back of 5.00am and see a TV sub. 'How are you doing?' 'Been here all night.' Immediately alarm bells ring. 'Don't you know? A train

43

crash, four dead.' Alarm bells ring, lights flash and off running. Fortunately, the late sub and reporter had it all under control.

Four people died in the Newton Rail Crash, including both drivers.

Saturday 10 August 1991

DIARY: A new football season and it makes Saturdays feel more like they should. Covering the Morton 2–1 Partick Thistle game from Division One.

A new season always felt vibrant with new grass, new strips and new hope.

I thoroughly enjoyed radio, but there was no question it was the poor relation to television. I wanted to expand my experience and applied successfully for an attachment to the TV newsroom.

Monday 30 September 1991

DIARY: The start of my television attachment today and a whole new world. Watching *Reporting Scotland* going out from the gallery was fascinating. I don't like the thought that all the elements – studio, VT, graphics – come from different parts of the building.

Wednesday 2 October 1991

DIARY: Got my first piece on *Reporting Scotland Tonight*. It was just my voice under shots of Stornoway coastguard station with two interview clips included. All to do with a search for 16 Spanish fishermen. I didn't find it that difficult to do, although I did have to rewrite my first draft and alter it slightly to match the pictures when we got them later, because it told the straightforward story radio style. I'm enjoying it more than I expected.

Thursday 3 October 1991

DIARY: Prepared my own bulletins this morning. It seems straightforward enough once you get into the way of it, but there really is not the same reaction time. Added to that, there's only 1.15 to fill and with weather it isn't much.

Thursday 24 October 1991

DIARY: Made my first camera appearance on *Reporting Scotland Tonight*. It was a fairly quiet day all in, but I voiced a story on a Fatal Accident Inquiry into a toddler who drowned when her mother tried to cross a swollen river in her car. By the afternoon we had some more on it, including pictures from the original tragedy. There weren't a lot of them so I decided to do a piece to camera. It was three sentences and I did them from memory. I did it in one take. However, the sound man wanted another one to be sure and it took me about five more after that.

Saturday 26 October 1991

DIARY: Airdrie were playing Dundee United. Not a great game, United won 3–1, so there was plenty to say. Jim McLean, United's manager, wouldn't allow any interviews because of the SFA's policy of clobbering anybody who says anything controversial. He wants 'freedom of speech'.

I don't think I ever did interview Jim McLean, who delivered Dundee United to the brink of European glory. He was forever in dispute with the football authorities.

1992

Wednesday 8 January 1992

DIARY: Today's main story being the closure of Ravenscraig two years earlier than expected, and all that entails in terms of job losses and the effect on the Lanarkshire economy.

Many of the news bulletins I produced in the late 1980s included stories about the demise of these big nationalised industries. Ravenscraig was the last of them. The explosive demolition of the Ravenscraig towers was an iconic image of the time.

Monday 13 January 1992

DIARY: I have to remember that my news values are sometimes affected by what pictures are available. I still work along the lines of the story on its own merits and while that is ideally the best method, it can lead to dull TV with straight reads.

Tuesday 21 January 1992

DIARY: Dull shift in the TV Newsroom – at one point Eddie and I were playing Hangman!

Monday 27 January 1992

DIARY: Presented my first-ever programme on national radio today. I co-presented *Newsdrive* with Clare English. My familiarity with live broadcasting through my sports stuff helped. The programme went very smoothly.

Wednesday 26 February 1992

DIARY: Presented *Midweek Sportsound* tonight as a taster before fully presenting Saturday's programme. We were featuring a number of Scottish Cup ties, but principally the St Johnstone – Inverness Caley tie. Bob Crampsey joined me in the studio and he is very good – he's so knowledgeable about sport and you can throw a question to him and know he can fill the time. Also interviewed John Beattie about rugby and he, too, is a good speaker. I thought I did reasonably well, without clearly being a born presenter.

I noted that 'I doubt I could ever do presentation as my prime work, but it is a good sideline to have.'

Saturday 29 February 1992

BBC Radio Sport

ANNOUNCER: 'Now at just after two o'clock, John MacKay is your host for four hours of top class sporting action. In *Sportsound*.'

Saturday 29 February 1992

DIARY: Today was the big one – presenting *Sportsound*. I was undoubtedly helped by the fact that I'd been in the studio last week and presented the programme on Wednesday. Went in early and trawled through the wires for pieces which might be useful to me. Soaked in as much information as I could before lunch. Again I was fortunate in not being too nervous beforehand. We went on-air at 2.00pm and I was anchoring for the next four hours – and doing so with hardly anything in the way of scripts. I have a running order and that is my guide. I wrote plenty of notes on it, cues to reporters etc, but the more I force myself to ad-lib the better I'll become. Bob Crampsey wasn't in the studio, instead he was at a ground – Hearts v Celtic – but he was still the man I was having the discussions with.

The first hour and a half and the last hour are the times when I had to be on my toes. Football, snooker, racing – we had it all. When I came out my head was absolutely thumping. Again I felt I had done okay, but I could do a lot better.

Friday 3 April 1992

DIARY: This afternoon I had a training session on the autocue. I'd expected a small scale attempt in the continuity cubicle, but News Editor Gordon Macmillan had organised a full scale rehearsal from Studio A with the works – lighting, director, VT etc. Even had to go via make-up. I'd been wanting to play it so low key that I left my suit jacket in the car. I did it immediately after the 3.55pm bulletin. We actually did it twice – the first one being a rehearsal. I didn't stumble and I followed the directions without a problem. My timings were fine too, so I was pleased. Dropped my jacket back in the car, washed off the make-up and returned low key to the newsroom. Walked in and they all applauded me! It had been put through the internal system and they'd all seen it. So much for low key.

The applause was not to mark my performance, but to let me know that everyone had seen it. Screen tests are never done on the quiet. Never.

The screen test was during the Election campaign and included this story.

BBC TV News
In an attack on the SNP, Labour's John Smith has described independent economic power for Scotland as 'an illusion'. But the nationalists insist Independence is coming.

JOHN SMITH, Labour Leader
I don't think it would be realistically financially viable because we would still be so much part of the United Kingdom economy that any sort of Independence would, I think, be illusory. I think it would make much more sense for us to establish a Scottish Parliament within the United Kingdom.

ALEX SALMOND, SNP Leader:
We're the Tory busters in Scottish politics because we are going to end Tory rule in Scotland, not just for one election, but we're going to end Tory rule in Scotland for good.'

GENERAL ELECTION 1992

Thursday 9 April 1992

DIARY: Election Day, which has been getting built up so much since everyone began predicting the election would have been last summer. Also there has been great interest in the Scottish Nationalists – who've been high profile. My own sense has been that while it may be causing great interest in the media and among the pundits, Independence is just not the burning talking point among the voters. Labour's star has been rising and it's being seen as a close run thing, possibly a hung parliament.

I worked in the VT area logging and delivering tapes. It was a frustrating experience because it felt detached from the action.

DIARY: The first of the crucial seats to be called, Basildon, went to the Tories and it was instantly clear that the Labour breakthrough wasn't going to happen. So it was, the Tory majority slashed, but still 20 or so and an improvement against all predictions in Scotland. SNP down one – Jim Sillars out.

Friday 10 April 1992

DIARY: The atmosphere was one of after the party – subdued and reflective – although amazement at the poor showing of the SNP. One or two people were actually very angry at the return of the Tories. The day's programme was dominated by reaction to the result. The Tories are cock-a-hoop, with Scottish Secretary Ian Lang making the most of it. Who can blame him?

I returned to radio as the Sports Correspondent at the end of my TV attachment.

Friday 22 May 1992

BBC Radio News

25 years ago today, 11 Scottish footballers walked on to a pitch in Lisbon to play for the premier trophy in European club football. They faced the might of the legendary Italian side, Inter Milan. Celtic won by two goals to one. That match, the most famous victory in Scottish football, is now part of the game's folk lore. John MacKay looks back...

I was quite daunted by interviewing these legends. They'd gathered in their green blazers for a celebratory event and had such an evidently strong bond. They were great, full of fun and happy to oblige my interview requests.

Friday 19 June 1992

DIARY: The Scotland squad returning from the European Championships in Sweden (Scotland lost two matches and won one) and I went down with the radio van to meet them. Hundreds of supporters were there and there was a real media scrum to get clips. Sent them back just in time for the *One O'Clock News*.

Friday 26 June 1992

BBC Radio News

Scottish football is set for the biggest shake-up in its history with the announcement that the country's main five clubs intend to resign from the Scottish League. The chairmen of the clubs sent letters to the league tonight giving notice of their intention to breakaway. They are to set up their own league, the Scottish Super League.

Thursday 16 July 1992

DIARY: On to the Scottish Football Association (SFA) news conference on the changes to the laws of the football game. The pass-back to the goalkeeper will now be punished with a free kick if the keeper picks it up. Fine in principle, but it'll just see the ball getting humped into the crowd. Personally, I think if they really want to improve football, they should radically alter the offside law.

This was part of the continued and generally successful attempt to make the game more attractive. Passing the ball back to the goalkeeper who could pick it up was a notorious time-wasting tactic and an easy way out for defenders under pressure. An ability to play the ball has now become part of a goalkeeper's essential skills. And my concern about the ball 'getting humped into the crowd'

47

*didn't really come to pass. Not too often
anyway.*

Tuesday 28 July 1992

DIARY: Plenty of Olympic material,
although it has to be said the Games
have still to come alive. The track and
field events should be spread out more
to maintain interest. Personally, I think
the number of sports should be reduced
(basketball and tennis, for example,
have no place at the Olympics). For me,
indeed for most, I think the Olympic
Games are about track and field. I can
see why swimming, gymnastics, cycling
etc are included, but much of the rest
should be ditched.

Friday 31 July 1992

DIARY: Used phrases like 'The Olympic
flame will burn more fiercely today with
the beginning of the athletics.' A bit
colourful perhaps, but interest in the
Games will really start now. I'd also
done a package on Yvonne Murray,
Tom McKean and Liz McColgan – the
Scots who'll be running this weekend.

Later I completed a package on why a
country like Denmark can produce
good international sides (they'd won the
1992 European Championships), but
Scotland with a similar population can't.

*Another of those issues that comes round
again and again, with consistent
regularity, especially with regard to
football. Listening to the shouts from the
sidelines at children's football on a
Saturday morning is a real insight into
why we consistently fail to match our
footballing aspirations.*

Tuesday 4 August 1992

DIARY: Went up to Scottish League

offices on West Regent Street – a shabby
affair compared to the SFA – cheap
wood panelling and plastic 'farting'
chairs. Waited just over an hour for a
meeting to discuss Super League to end.
Statement read and some questions
taken. Basically a stand-off with rebel
clubs which fails to address the
problems of the game. Too many egos
involved overriding football itself.

Thursday 6 August 1992

BBC Radio News

The Scottish Super League will be
going ahead as planned, says its
organisers, despite the refusal of the
Scottish Football League (SFL) to
accept the resignations of the rebel
clubs. And the Super League will be
expanded from the original eight
clubs to ten, with Motherwell being
introduced as a new member today.
As ours sports news correspondent
John MacKay reports, the clubs insist
they mean business…

DIARY: A news conference by the
organisers of the Scottish Super League
at the Royal Scot Hotel on the outskirts
of Edinburgh. Asked to take two
Romanian journalists who are on work
experience. They're going ahead with
the Super League regardless of SFL's
arguments. Interesting observation from
the two Romanians that, although
Wallace Mercer (*chairman of the Super
League*) is the mouthpiece of the Super
League, both recognised that Rangers'
David Murray was the main man,
despite not saying much.

Friday August 28 1992

DIARY: I've found while I've done this
sports correspondent job that most

people are helpful and friendly. But football, particularly the higher you go, and particularly the administrators, are for the most part difficult and pompous. Given what an arse they have made of the national game and given its current state (too many games and no European threat) they hardly have reason to be.

Wednesday 16 September 1992

DIARY: I went out to Celtic Park to interview the manager Liam Brady. I'd been given the wrong time for the news conference, but he was happy enough to be interviewed. Come across as a very amenable, laid back character and the interview worked well. Pity they weren't all like that.

DIARY: Major disruptions in the financial world with the pound's value plummeting. In a response that smacked of panic the Government raised interest rates twice in the day, first by 2 per cent, then a further 3 per cent this afternoon. Everyone worried about the impact on mortgage payments, although building societies said they'd bide their time. Later still, the pound was suspended from the ERM (*Exchange Rate Mechanism*) and interest rates were cut again. All this caused quite a commotion in the newsroom and it's good having that sort of buzz. It'll be interesting to see whether the Chancellor (*Norman Lamont*) keeps his post. I'm not sure that it meant very much to people. If mortgage rates go up then obviously it will, but for the moment it all seems to be about invisible dealings by the city cats.

Wednesday 14 October 1992

DIARY: Scotland v Portugal World Cup qualifying tie at Ibrox (Scotland lucky to get a 0–0 draw). I was doing the trackside interviews and I grabbed a couple of players when they came out to check the pitch (Craig Levein & Derek Whyte). I also interviewed Ian Durrant. My introduction to him said he was going to be a substitute and then I asked him, 'What will your role be tonight?'

Monday 26 October 1992

DIARY: I was doing the *One O'Clock News* and *Newsdrive*. Big issue now is Prime Minister John Major threatening Tory rebels with a General Election if they don't support him on Maastricht. Major has gone from Mr Nice Guy to Mr Incompetent in public perception.

Friday 30 October 1992

DIARY: A football fan's dream today – I stood on the centre spot at Hampden Park and Lisbon Lion Billy McNeil bought me a pint. The contractors start on the redevelopment of Hampden on Monday, so I was preparing a piece for that. I'd arranged to meet football oracle Bob Crampsey there, to hear some Hampden's history. We were allowed to go on the pitch. What struck me was how short the pitch appeared to be, although it is certainly wide. A thrill ran through me as I stood on the turf looking to the terraces, dreaming. Later called at Billy McNeill's pub to hear some of his memories and he bought me a pint while there. I've always liked McNeil whenever I've met him.

Thursday 5 November 1992

Rangers defeated Leeds United 2–1 in the Champions League with goals from Mark Hateley and Ally McCoist to win 4–2 on aggregate.

DIARY: As much as anything else I'm pleased about the fact that the English media have been put in their place – the way in which they dismissed Rangers over the past few days has been irritating. Out to Ibrox later with the radio van to interview Walter Smith, the Rangers manager. He seemed to think he should only have been doing the newspapers, but eventually agreed to do radio and TV together. The whole newspaper/broadcast split in football is incredible and must be the only area in the reporting world which continues in that vein.

Football news conferences were heavily slanted in favour of the written press. There was quite a division between the two, however well you may get on with individual reporters personally. We would all gather, the 'electronic' media would ask our questions and then have to leave. Newspaper sports reporters wouldn't ask questions while radio and TV were there. The idea was to keep stories for the following day's papers. It didn't apply to any other area – politics, crime, etc so why sport? Indeed, the Sunday newspapers often had an entire press conference to themselves. It seemed antiquated to me at the time and I couldn't see why football managers indulged it. They still do.

Thursday 10 December 1992

DIARY: A train to Edinburgh for the launch of a new venture to build a national stadium – this time in Lanarkshire. Bad day to launch it as all the European heads of state were arriving in Edinburgh ahead of the summit. They did their presentation – outnumbering the four media bods by three to one – and quite impressive it was too.

The proposal was for a futuristic stadium next to the M8 motorway. Looking towards the new century, it made sense to take the stadium out of an urban area with transport and parking limitations to a location where all that could be easily addressed. Even as I reported on it I knew it didn't have a chance. I'm sure the cost played a part, but lack of vision wouldn't have helped.

Saturday 12 December 1992

DIARY: Bad morning. Playing football before work. During the 3–1 defeat by Spatz in Coatbridge, I got an elbow in the mouth which split my lip badly and has chipped three of my front teeth. The lip, though badly gashed, will heal, but the teeth will need dental treatment. Added to that the team played poorly. I was doing the Airdrie–Motherwell game for TV and since I was playing in Coatbridge it seemed pointless to go home, so I cleaned up my wound as best I could. I should have gone to hospital, but decided to wait. No problems at the game – bottom of the table clash which Motherwell won 2–0.

I did my match reports and interviews and then returned to my car to come home. As I checked the rear view mirror, I saw a track of dried blood from the corner of my mouth to my chin. No-one had said a word all afternoon. Obviously not unusual in these parts of Lanarkshire.

1993

Friday 8 January 1993

DIARY: Celtic's announcement that they have effectively withdrawn from the Scottish Super League. We were told last night that the chairman would speak after 7.00am – he hung up on me. So I phoned straight back and after some discussion he agreed to do me later, but refused an early live. Yet another PR disaster for Celtic, who're stumbling from one fiasco to another.

When I say the main story was Celtic, that was in a sports context. The story of the week has been the grounding of an oil tanker off the south coast of Shetland and the consequent pollution. I'm enjoying sport, but I wonder whether I'm losing touch with news.

The Braer ran aground off Shetland spilling more than 80,000 tonnes of crude oil and causing widespread damage.

Saturday 9 January 1993

DIARY: As well as radio I was to cut a package for tonight's *Sportscene*. Had to provide three minutes. Cut the pictures first so I had my time spot on, then wrote my script to suit. (*St Johnstone 6–0 Forfar*)

Tuesday 26 January 1993

DIARY: Football legend Bobby Charlton was doing a promo for one of his soccer classes. For a man who was/is such a well known figure, and in footballing terms 'legend' isn't too strong a description, I was impressed by what a genuinely nice man he was.

Thursday 11 February 1993

DIARY: I did another screen test for television. I did one last year and they said they were happy with it, but they've not needed any newsreaders since. The news editor Gordon Macmillan said he wanted me to do another one today with the new set. I felt quite relaxed about it and perhaps last year's experience was a help.

Friday 12 February 1993

DIARY: I've to do my first television bulletin at the end of this month. They seem to have been happy with yesterday's screen test and I'll be doing the 21.28 on 26 February. It could be the beginning of a new avenue in my career or I could make an arse of myself.

Saturday 13 February 1993

BBC Radio & TV Sport

Duncan Ferguson was the man everyone thought would be the star of the show, but in fact it was Paddy Connolly who caught the eye. Two goals, in actual fact three goals, but one the ref didn't see, and a performance which mesmerised Thistle. Just before half time Connolly had the ball in the net, but it came off the back stanchion inside the goal and while Utd celebrated Thistle played on. Referee Les Mottram clearly didn't think the ball had gone in.

The ball rebounded from the stanchion inside the net and one of the Thistle players caught it in disgust. As the United players celebrated, the Thistle players walked back to position for the restart when it became apparent the ref was waving play on. There was incredulity on the pitch, around the ground and in the press box. It's the most bizarre refereeing decision I've ever seen in years of watching football.

Friday 26 February 1993

DIARY: I made my live television debut tonight, presenting BBC Scotland's 9.30pm news bulletin. It went smoothly enough, with no glaring errors and only one minor stumble. The lead story – strike at Yarrow's, then a court case about two youths killing a woman by rolling a car down steps, and the financial problems at Monktonhall Colliery. Straightforward, although perhaps more reading than usual. Problem before we went on-air when I couldn't hear talk back. Technician sorted it out, but it left time for only one rehearsal. Shortly after that was it, I was on-air. Happy and relieved when it was all over, although I felt quite comfortable doing it.

I'm not sure I looked comfortable, certainly not at the start. My face was flushed and there was a hint of perspiration on my forehead. The mouth was going like a washing machine to make sure I got the words out properly. Still, I began to present bulletins regularly so it couldn't have been too bad.

Monday 8 March 1993

BBC TV News

A nationwide campaign to abolish the criminal verdict of 'not proven' has been launched. The verdict is used when a jury is unsure about the guilt or innocence of the accused. 36,000 people have already signed a petition calling for a change in the law.

KATE DUFFY, mother of murder victim Amanda Duffy:

There are a lot of families out there who have gone through similar circumstances to ourselves and at the end of a trial, with a not proven verdict, you come out of that trial feeling that you have a life sentence.

Despite such campaigns and continued public disquiet, the 'not proven' verdict, famously described by Sir Walter Scott as 'that bastard verdict', remains.

Saturday 20 March 1993

DIARY: A new job reading the results on *Afternoon Sportscene*. I remember as a young child I used to lie in front of the TV writing down the results in the paper for Faither as they were read out. And here was I reading them out! The guy whom I used to hear still does it from London and I had him coming through my cans (*headphones*) and tried to keep pace with him. It was an education sitting beside Dougie Donnelly as he presented – no scripts and little guidance – and he held the programme together seamlessly.

The graphics were generated from London, so you had to keep up with their announcer. I had listened to the results for as long as I could remember, so I knew how to do the classic delivery – a high score up, a low score down.

Wednesday 7 April 1993

BBC Radio News

Rangers play one of the most important games in their history tonight when they meet Marseille in the European Champions League. Victory would almost certainly assure either side a place in the European

Cup (first Champions League) Final. The teams drew 2–2 at Ibrox in the first match in the section.

The match ended 1–1 and because of other results, Rangers failed to make the final.

Thursday 29 April 1993

BBC Radio News

It had to happen. Scotland were due a football humiliation after several years of respectable, if unspectacular results. Humiliated we were, thrashed 5–0 by Portugal in Lisbon. It means that Scotland will not be competing in the World Cup Finals in the United States next year, the first time we've failed to qualify since 1970. The National Coach Andy Roxburgh said he was shattered.

This was my final report as sports correspondent. I enjoyed sport, but I felt detached from news and I didn't want that. It took me some time to be able to watch a football match for its own sake without composing a quick update in my head every ten minutes.

Monday 3 May 1993

DIARY: I presented my first ever *Good Morning Scotland* today along with Alan Douglas. He's a nice fellow and it was a fairly easy introduction to our flagship programme. Bosnia, riots in Moscow, political dispute in the UK over Maastricht. A busy morning.

Tuesday 4 May 1993

DIARY: Officially back on the reporters' rota today. No longer a trainee, a sub, a CNA – I'm a BBC reporter.

Becoming a reporter had been my ambition since I joined the corporation. I had enjoyed all my roles, the newsdesk especially, but to be a reporter on the BBC – that was beyond anything I could have hoped when I started in journalism.

Friday 7 May 1993

DIARY: I was following the story of a baby found abandoned in Kilmarnock. She was only hours old and it made me sad to think of the child's start in life. And pity the mother, she must be frightened and confused. In the office at 5.22pm and I was the 5.30pm lead.

Wednesday 19 May 1993

DIARY: A call came through about a shooting incident in Cambuslang and I was sent out in the radio van. I didn't think I'd make it in time for the *Six O'Clock News* (left at 5.40pm), but I did – moving at a fair rate and even following a police van at one stage. The incident was on the town's Main Street and I parked on the main junction and put up the mast. Quickly spoke to a CID officer and a couple of witnesses – the first confirmed three injured, but said nothing more, the others spoke of a shopkeeper, woman and policeman being hit. Did an unscripted piece into the *Six O'Clock*. The police trapped the gunman in a house and there was a siege situation for a couple of hours before he was taken out.

Friday 21 May 1993

BBC Radio News

The shopkeeper who was shot in the head during an armed raid in Cambuslang on Wednesday has died. Earlier today a man appeared in court in Glasgow accused of shooting the shopkeeper, a woman and a policeman. John MacKay reports...

Wednesday 9 June 1993

DIARY: Another TV bulletin tonight. It was a warm, close day and by evening, despite heavy showers, it was very humid. When I went into the studio and turned on the lights, the sweat just poured out because of the heat. It meant that every time we cut pictures I was having to wipe my face with a hanky. When I saw the tape later there was a sweat globule sitting on my jaw throughout – looked like a big plook.

Thursday 24 June 1993

DIARY: Everything overshadowed by announcement that Rosyth has failed to win the refitting contract for nuclear subs, despite Government promises. Blanket coverage – political outrage, workers' despair.

Thursday 1 July 1993

DIARY: The Director General of the BBC, John Birt, was in viewing our operation. I don't like what he's doing to the organisation, putting marketplace management in place of quality and making news so analytical that the national bulletins are getting dull.

Thursday 15 July 1993

BBC Radio News

The Scottish international footballer Duncan Ferguson has signed for Rangers in a deal which is the biggest in the history of British football. Rangers will pay Dundee United a fee which will eventually total £4 million. It ends months of speculation about the player's future. John MacKay reports...

JM: So was announced the biggest deal in the history of British football. A deal for a Scottish internationalist between two Scottish clubs. The Rangers chairman, David Murray, says it demonstrates Rangers ambition to compete with the best in Europe.

DAVID MURRAY: What I've repeatedly said is it's no use reducing your overdraft and making healthy profits if the dividends are not on the park. Our shareholders, I believe, and our supporters want dividends on the park and it's only by bringing in players like Duncan Ferguson we shall continue to do so. There's no point in having no borrowings and no trophies. Rangers is about having a bit of debt, which I'm prepared to continue doing, bringing it down gradually, and attracting the best talent to Rangers.

DUNCAN FERGUSON: It's been my boyhood dream to come and play for the Rangers and it's just starting to sink in.

Duncan Ferguson's time at Rangers was short-lived. It's best remembered for his being charged with assault for headbutting John McStay of Raith Rovers during a game at Ibrox – a charge that ultimately led to him serving a short prison sentence. He established a more successful career in England after being sold to Everton.

David Murray's policy of Rangers carrying debt ultimately overwhelmed the club.

Thursday 22 July 1993

BBC Radio News

Scottish football clubs have been warned that they'll be taken to court if they demand a transfer fee for players who they are no longer paying. The Players Union say it's a gross injustice for a club to seek a fee from another club if the player is out of contract.

NELSON MANDELA IN GLASGOW

Saturday 9 October 1993

BBC TV News

Nelson Mandela today said Scotland had been a source of great strength to him and his comrades during their struggle against apartheid in South Africa. He was speaking in Glasgow where he received the freedom of nine British cities and districts at a special ceremony. John MacKay was there...

NELSON MANDELA, *(speech excerpt from inside Glasgow City Chambers)*: It is a special privilege to be a guest of this great City of Glasgow. It will always enjoy a distinguished place in the records of the international campaign against apartheid. The people of Glasgow were the first in the world to confer on me the Freedom of the City at a time when I and my comrades in the African National Congress (ANC) were imprisoned on Robben Island serving life sentences, which in apartheid South Africa then meant imprisonment until death. Whilst we were physically denied our freedom in the country of our birth, a city, 6,000 miles away, and as removed as Glasgow, refused to accept the legitimacy of the apartheid system, and declared us to be free.'

Sunday 10 October 1993

BBC Radio News

Two Libyans accused of carrying out the Lockerbie Bombing will not be coming to Scotland to stand trial – at least not in the immediate future. The lawyers representing them have advised their clients not to surrender to the Scottish authorities. The two Scottish members of the international defence team have already arrived home. John MacKay reports...

At the end of the year I made my debut presenting *Reporting Scotland*. I was a regular presenter on news bulletins and the sports desks, so in one sense it wasn't a huge leap. But it was the station's flagship news programme and to anchor it was a big step up in prestige.

1994

FERGUS MCCANN TAKEOVER OF CELTIC

Saturday 15 January 1994

DIARY: **Off to Parkhead to cover further demonstrations against the Parkhead board which was straightforward, doing a live two-way into *Sportsound*.**

Wednesday 2 March 1994

BBC Radio News

Celtic may have won 1–0 last night in a Premier League game against Kilmarnock, but the result has probably been lost in the furore surrounding the club's off field activities. The relationship between the board and the club's supporters reached its nadir last night when the lowest crowd for nine years attended Parkhead. A boycott organised by the *Celts For Change* group and the *Supporters' Association* resulted in a crowd of just under 11,000 going to the game, barely a fifth of the ground's capacity. Our reporter John MacKay spent the evening with the Celtic fans and reports now on their increasing frustrations.

JM: This is Baird's Bar in Glasgow's Gallowgate. It's a Celtic pub with memorabilia covering the walls. It's the night of a Celtic game and the place is half empty.

VOX POPS: Usually it's choc-a-bloc in here and the past two or three home games, you can see yourself. Usually you can't move. It's a reflection on what's going on up the road.

I don't want to boycott Celtic, I love Celtic. I want to go out and shout my team on. But if me stopping going and the people like me stopping going gets rid of that shower up there, then I'll do it.

JM: The match kicks off with a Parkhead that isn't as empty as might have been anticipated. The traditional Celtic end is not full, but there is a fair covering of supporters. The away end of the ground is almost totally empty. And the traditional 'Jungle' is perhaps a third full.

VOX POPS: It's the only thing left for the Celtic supporters now, to stay away. I think in the long run they'll go, the board. They've got to go.

JM: These are difficult times at Parkhead. The future direction of the club is unclear and the team on the park is having little success, although tonight they did win 1–0 against Kilmarnock. A last minute goal from John Collins. It was a surreal atmosphere at Celtic Park which turned into the bizarre when, apart from Collins' goal, the highlight of the match was the sight of a fox running the full length of the pitch.

Celtic came within minutes of financial collapse. Their saviour was the Scottish-born, Celtic-supporting Canadian businessman Fergus McCann.

There was a major media presence as he arrived at Glasgow Airport. This drew its own crowd of onlookers, intrigued by the big name who was clearly expected. When McCann walked through international arrivals – a low-key figure with a moustache and bunnet – there was an explosion of light. You could see the bewilderment of the onlookers wondering who he was.

Saturday 5 March 1994

BBC Radio News

Fergus McCann, the man who's taken over Celtic, says he wants the Bank of Scotland – the club's bankers – to explain why they permitted the club to get so close to receivership. He intends to meet bank officials over the next few days. Mr McCann was given a hero's welcome by the Celtic supporters before Celtic's game against St Johnstone in Perth this afternoon. This report from John MacKay...

JM: Mr McCann said his priority now was to stabilise Celtic's financial position, develop a top-class stadium and provide money to build a competitive team.

Fergus McCann put Celtic on a sound financial footing, redeveloped the stadium and finally delivered the league championship. He sold up after five years, exactly what he said he would do.

Thursday 14 April 1994

BBC Radio News

Frederick West, the Gloucester builder who is already facing nine murder charges, has been charged with a tenth, that of his Scottish wife Rena Costello. It follows the discovery of a woman's body in a field at the weekend. Rena Costello, who was originally from Lanarkshire has been missing for 20 years. John MacKay reports...

JM: Rena Costello originally came from Coatbridge. She married Frederick West in the 1960s. Relatives spoke of their sadness. Her cousin Anne Graham said it was a terrible way for her to die. Rena had two daughters by Frederick West. One, Charmaine, has not been seen for several years. Detectives are anxious to trace her.

Eight-year-old Charmaine's remains were found the following month in the Wests' former home in Gloucester.

Thursday 12 May 1994

The Labour leader John Smith died suddenly aged only 55. He was assumed to be the Prime Minister in waiting. I heard the news on radio while on holiday.

Wednesday 23 May 1994

BBC Radio News

Two demonstrators have been arrested following the arrival of Britain's second Trident nuclear submarine on the Clyde. They were among a group of protestors opposed to the arrival of *Victorious* – which is the very latest in Britain's defence firepower. Costing £400 million and with the capacity to carry 16 Trident missiles, the new submarine will be based at Faslane.

Friday 27 May 1994

BBC Radio News

Tonight two pilots leave a Scottish airport at the beginning of a unique flight. Flying microlight aircraft, they will attempt to fly across the North Sea – the first time this has ever been attempted. If they succeed they will then fly their tiny planes around Europe.

The attempt was successful.

COMMENTARY FROM FLIGHT: 'Engines at full blast. We're now going along the runway and that's us up in the air. Very quickly. And going up to some height very quickly as well. You certainly don't get the surge that you might expect from a regular aircraft... we're now turning back towards the airport. A very steep turn... again the craft holding quite steady, very much a surprise to me... dropping now gently towards the runway. Speed still about 45 miles per hour. We're coming down. Just about to drop onto the tarmac. There we go!'

My apparent calmness was betrayed by one of my final lines, 'We're now back on sweet Mother Earth.'

Monday 6 June 1994

BBC Radio News

The popular television series Taggart will continue despite the death this morning of its star Mark McManus. Mr McManus died in his sleep while being treated for pneumonia in Glasgow's Victoria Infirmary. Tributes have been paid to the man who was the epitome of the hard Glasgow detective.

Mark McManus's classic line in the very first 'Taggart' in 1983 – or 'Killer' as it was then known – 'We don't have ligatures in Maryhill,' marked it out as something special. STV did continue the series after his death until 2010.

Wednesday 1 June 1994

BBC Radio News

The Shadow Chancellor, Gordon Brown, has put an end to some of the speculation about the Labour

leadership by announcing that he won't be standing. He said he would be supporting his friend Tony Blair, who's widely tipped as the most likely successor to John Smith. Some of Mr Brown's colleagues have praised his decision, describing it as being in the best interest of the party. But others have expressed disappointment. John MacKay has been gauging reaction...

JM: Gordon Brown said he had taken the decision in the interests of party unity. It now increases the likelihood of his friend and fellow moderniser, Tony Blair, inheriting the mantle of the late John Smith. Mr Brown has been praised for his decision, but not everyone is happy. There was dismay from a fellow Scot, Jimmy Wray, who is the chair of the Scottish Labour backbenchers.

Gordon Brown's stepping aside for Tony Blair became a running sore for Labour. It has been widely recorded how the tension between the two and their supporters undermined what a three term Labour Government might have been able to achieve.

Monday 4 July 1994

DIARY: Met Lorraine Davidson (*STV reporter and former BBC colleague*) on a job today and she repeated what she'd said in her telephone call – that Scottish TV wanted me. Finally phoned their head man, Scott Ferguson. Not in. Thought that was it, but he phoned back soon after and suggested meeting for a beer, 'in the way these things are done.'

I was perfectly happy at the BBC and had

never really considered moving, but I was intrigued by what STV might say.

Tuesday 5 July 1994

DIARY: The Head of Radio Scotland, James Boyle, is showing great interest in my proposed series *Dance Called America*. Called me at home and said he sees it as a big production effort with transmission in the spring. I'm excited about the idea, but the STV approach has thrown that into confusion.

I had pitched the idea of a radio series based on Dr James Hunter's book *Dance Called America* on the Scottish diaspora in the US and Canada. It's a subject that has long fascinated me and the prospect of travelling round North America in the footsteps of the early Scottish settlers thrilled me. It was a real issue for me in deciding whether to move to STV. The series was eventually made by Radio 4.

Thursday 7 July 1994

DIARY: Met Scott Ferguson of STV. They want me as a reporter/presenter. I'd start off reporting, then do some breakfast bulletins and finally a stand-in presenter on Scotland Today, but reporting would be the mainstay.

Friday 8 July 1994

DIARY: I'm more convinced than ever that I'm going to move to Scottish Television. The BBC's Ken Cargill, despite telling me to see him on Friday, was tied up in meetings. When he finally called he said he hadn't really had a chance to think about it and didn't want to make promises he couldn't keep – spoke of attachments, but problems with Equal Opportunities. That's a cop-out. No question who wants me more.

That equivocation was typical BBC management. My decision was made for me. I was happy at the BBC; my only request was to work more in the television newsroom. I had been trained by the BBC and had successfully filled just about every frontline role in the news operation. It was encouraging that my colleagues expressed astonishment that I was allowed to leave. However, it's a move I have never regretted.

Saturday 23 July 1994

DIARY: Usual round of killings and car crashes, but little else. That would all be very different were it someone I knew, but we only get the name and report it. The aftermath is of no interest. It's a sad reality.

Saturday 30 July 1994

DIARY: Covered the first mass outdoor pop/rock festival in Scotland for more than 15 years, 'T'-in-the-Park, at Strathclyde Park – named after the sponsor Tennent's. A relaxed atmosphere. Apart from looking a bit out of place wearing a suit and tie, I enjoyed it.

T-in-the-Park is now a major part of Scotland's festival calendar and a rite of passage for many Scottish teenagers. It moved from Strathclyde Park to Ballado in 1997, expanding to a three day event and attracting tens of thousands each year. It moved to Strathallan in Perthshire in 2015.

Monday 19 September 1994

DIARY: My first day at Scottish Television. I was thrown in at the deep end – which suits me – doing a piece on why a fatal bus crash happened and how it could be prevented. Four people, including two Girl Guides, dead when a double decker hit a bridge. There is none of the fannying about that you have at the BBC as regards editing and getting a crew. It is obviously a smaller, busier operation.

I hadn't even had time to get started on the STV computer system. My first scripts were scribbled on bits of paper.

Tuesday 20 September 1994
STV News

A man who claimed to be Hannibal the Cannibal after biting two people has been jailed for six years at the High Court in Edinburgh.

DIARY: A piece on a guy who's been jailed for six years after being found guilty of biting off part of a woman's ear. Out to Feegie Park in Paisley. Managed to get a neighbour who'd found the woman to speak to me. It's the sort of story the BBC wouldn't touch, but which fascinates people.

The neighbour took a bit of persuasion, but finally invited us into his home. A newspaper photographer tried to follow our cameraman in and the guy said to him, 'No, no photographs.' TV can have that effect on people.

Friday 23 September 1994

DIARY: Covering the funerals in Drumchapel of the two ten-year-old Girl Guides who were killed in Sunday's bus crash. You never get used to white coffins.

Wednesday 28 September 1994

DIARY: Had to be back for 4.00pm to do a studio test for *Scotland Today*. Co-presented with Aasmah Mir. I was relaxed enough. Once I'm more in the style of the programme, that'll help.

Tuesday 4 October 1994
STV News

One of Scotland's biggest ever public inquiries has begun in Ayr. It will recommend whether a 40 mile long line of electricity pylons should be built across the heart of South Ayrshire. For months, Scottish Power have argued that the power line will be a huge economic boost. The STOP campaigners say it will do irreparable damage to the landscape and local economy. The public lobbying is now over as both sides faced each other at the inquiry.

DIARY: Did my first live television link today into lunchtime *Scotland Today*. I had to supply track and rushes (*pictures and voice over*) for a lunchtime package plus cue it live on site, and then do a two-way with Shereen. My radio experience was invaluable there.

The pylons were built.

Wednesday 5 October 1994

DIARY: Presented *Scotland Today* this evening which came as rather a surprise. Spent the morning at a fatal accident inquiry in Linlithgow. When it adjourned for lunch I called in and they told me to come in because I was presenting! It went very well – co-presenter Viv Lumsden was great, as were all the technical staff.

Scott Ferguson (Head of News) said I'd done well, but then told me I'd need to wear a better shirt and tie the next time. My colleague Shereen Nanjiani had a similar experience, being told by another boss not to worry about her first appearance because if she messed up she wouldn't do it again.

Friday 7 October 1994

A new style of police officer will take to the streets of Glasgow tomorrow. Equipped with a new, extendable baton and rigid handcuffs, they are far removed from the traditional bobby, but better able to defend themselves from assault.

Monday 11 October 1994

DIARY: I was presenting the programme – this time with Shereen. It wasn't as smooth as the first one (the second never is) and a lot of chopping and changing. Apart from being caught momentarily at the wrong camera once, it went well enough. Also got my first fan letter requesting a signed photo. Fame!

Wednesday 26 October 1994

DIARY: Pulling together features on problems in rural areas. 'We don't get into the countryside enough.' Spent much of the day in the North Ayrshire village of Dunlop. Problems are low wages, little employment, lack of housing and poor transport. At first I was talking to suits – that's what you get on the phone – and it wasn't really standing up. However, got into the streets and, as ever, when you can persuade locals to speak you get a different perspective.

Wednesday 9 November 1994

DIARY: Out to HCI in Clydebank – the controversial private hospital which today called in the receivers. Did a live link into the programme, one of the lights blowing a minute before going on. We got it sorted with less than ten seconds to go. Big political broo-haha over the story because £30 million of public money pumped into it.

Saturday 19 November 1994

DIARY: The National Lottery, which was launched with much fanfare this week, climaxed tonight. I bought two tickets, but I think only one number came up. There is much soul-searching from the usual sources about it being extra taxation and immoral etc. Personally I see no harm – good causes benefit, and nobody is forced to play.

The National Lottery continues to be a feature of national life.

Saturday 10 December 1994

STV News

The Catholic Church is embroiled in another child sex abuse scandal. It follows Scottish Television's revelations about young boys being abused at a Catholic college. Now it's emerged that another priest has been removed from his parish on the outskirts of Glasgow after admitting he'd interfered with young boys.

DIARY: Another priest exposed as a child abuser. He had been at Milton of Campsie, so up there. I was thoroughly drenched – with the water dripping from my coat into my shoes.

I chapped on one door which was answered by an elderly woman. It was clear she had no idea of the accusations against the priest. When I explained she gasped in shock and slammed the door on me. I was concerned for her wellbeing, but could hardly knock the door again.

1995

Thursday 2 February 1995

STV News

A political storm has blown up over claims that the Labour Party is to consider dropping its commitment to a Scottish Parliament having tax raising powers. Other political parties have reacted strongly. Labour denies there is any change in its position. John MacKay reports.

JM: The storm has been whipped up by an amendment tabled for the party's conference in Inverness next month. The original motion backed 'the rights of the Scottish Parliament to vary levels of taxation within agreed parameters'. The amendment is not so unequivocal. While accepting the right of the Scottish Parliament to have tax raising powers, it recognises there might be constraints. The whole episode underlines Labour's anxiety about not being seen as the party of high taxation. It's held that that was the issue, above any other, which lost the last election for them. And that is why the party is so anxious to dampen any confusion over its policies on tax, either at Westminster or in a Scottish Parliament.

Thursday 9 February 1995

STV News

The campaign against the planned M77 motorway took on a different emphasis today. Until now the thrust of the campaign has been claims about the detrimental effect the road would have on the environment.

Today the concerns of the community were put to the fore. Locals fear having 53,000 vehicles a day passing, almost literally, their back doorstep.

The motorway was constructed and opened in 1997

Friday 10 February 1995

STV News

A fatal accident inquiry (FAI) has heard a medical expert say that taking ecstasy tablets was like playing Russian roulette – it was not the harmless drug its users believe it to be. The inquiry into the deaths of three youths at the *Hanger Thirteen* club in Ayr also heard the manager admit that he couldn't ensure that drugs were not taken into the venue.

And still young people die taking ecstasy.

Monday 27 February 1995

STV News

Politics in Scotland is about to be thrown into turmoil and yet the signs are that most people don't know or don't care. The re-organisation of local government ending the system of two tier councils which has lasted for 20 years will begin in five weeks when the elections for the new single tier authorities take place. The changes will affect us all. In the first of a series of reports John MacKay looks at what's going to happen and why...

JM: Until now district councils have looked after services like housing, cleansing and recreation, parks and sports halls. The regional council has dealt with the larger concerns – the police, education, much of the roads and social work.

As a rough guide the district council is the one to call if you have a problem in your house or on your pathway. As soon as you step into the street, any repairs need to be done by the region. Now, though, all these services will be merged under the one council. Only water and the children's reporters system will not be included. The council map of Scotland will be transformed. Only the three island councils will remain untouched. The existing 53 district and nine regional councils will be replaced by 29 single authorities. Council names like Strathclyde, Lothian and Monklands will disappear. New names like North Ayrshire and North Lanarkshire emerge. The estimated cost of all this ranges from between £100 to £500,000,000... this is one of the biggest pieces of legislation to affect Scotland. It will be a period of upheaval and change – and will have profound implications for the way in which Scotland is run.

Monday 6 March 1995

STV News

A mother and her three-year-old child have had a lucky escape from a blaze in a block of high rise flats in Glasgow. The fire broke out on the second top floor of the Red Road flats, the highest block in Europe. Other residents were also taken to hospital.

DIARY: **The blaze was on the 29th floor of the 30 floor flats. Fortunately the woman and her toddler son escaped, but the flat was gutted. The fire brigade let us in to film and it was quite shocking, everything blackened. They were lucky.**

Wednesday 22 March 1995

DIARY: **Today's news dominated by the collapse of former Rangers star Davie Cooper – a favourite player of mine. He suffered a brain haemorrhage while filming a skills programme for STV. He collapsed as if poleaxed and the others around him thought for up to a minute that he was joking. The prognosis is not good. It's a tragedy.**

Thursday 23 March 1995

STV News

The main news tonight. Football star Davie Cooper loses his fight for life aged only 39. Tributes have been made throughout the day in honour of the man who ranked among the best of Scotland's footballing sons.

The former Rangers and Scotland star had been on a life support machine in Glasgow's Southern General Hospital after suffering a brain haemorrhage. He'd collapsed during the filming of a soccer skills series for Scottish Television in Cumbernauld yesterday. Family and friends kept an all night vigil at his bedside. Early this morning consultants switched off his ventilator after he'd been declared brain dead.

DIARY: **I was presenting tonight's programme with Kirsty (*Kirsty Young*) and was the lead reader. I was very conscious of the fact that there would be hundreds of thousands of people watching the programme to see what we said and hear the tributes. Of any programme I've presented it's probably the one story I've felt most affected by.**

I never met the man, but in the late '70s and '80s he was one of my favourite players. He was a delight to watch. It feels as if a friend has died.

Thursday 6 April 1995

DIARY: Presenting the programme and that was hectic – possibly the most difficult I've done yet. Stories chopped and changed repeatedly, often at the last moment, there was pandemonium in the gallery, I was having to sight read stories, read off autocue and pad out. All part of the job, but rarely so much at once. On with Kirsty and we were both glad to get out of the studio.

Heading out to St Ninian's school in Eastwood for the count for the new East Renfrewshire authority in the local government elections. This one was important because it had been clearly gerrymandered to ensure a Tory authority. However, early on the word was they'd failed to keep control and the late results confirmed that. It was difficult because there were no hard results to go on until late and so there was a limit to what we could say. In the end I think we did well – we got the interviewees that mattered, we called the result early and were confirmed correct.

Monday 1 May 1995

STV News

The poor are getting poorer and the rich are getting richer in Scotland's biggest region, according to a new report. A study of social trends in Strathclyde says the disparity between the well off and those struggling to make ends meet is growing wider. It paints a gloomy picture of long term unemployment, increased homelessness and greater reliance on drugs and alcohol.

This issue never goes away. I have been reporting this story for more than 25 years and nothing, it seems, has changed.

Wednesday 3 May 1995

DIARY: A beautiful day which was just as well because I spent most of it standing in a farm deep in Lanarkshire (Dunsyre). The story surrounds a cheese, Lanark Blue, which is at the centre of a struggle between the producer and the local council which says it's unfit to eat.

The producer of Lanark Blue won his case and it continues to be produced today.

Wednesday 17 May 1995

STV News

An initiative to save the economy of Dunoon from collapse following the departure of the US Navy has been hailed a great success. An independent report released today says that three years on, almost all of the 800 jobs dependent upon the US base have been replaced.

DIARY: Lovely day in Dunoon. Most of it in pleasant sunshine, the piece came together easily and a lovely lunch. Can't complain. Okay it's not frontline reporting, but it's nice to get these wee jobs now and again. At one point I was doing a walking piece to camera up a grassy hill overlooking the town. Inevitably I slipped. One for the Christmas tape I don't doubt.

The programme It'll Be Alright On The Night was once quite lucrative. They paid £250 if something you did was used on the programme. I think there were even repeat fees. It was alleged that some reporters would deliberately mess up a take in the hope of it making its way onto the programme. A standard blooper would be a reporter's reaction if they were doing a piece to camera and some tube beeped their horn as they drove past. When you're against a deadline, you're on your fourth attempt at a complicated piece to camera and some tosser still thinks pressing their horn is original and funny, the reaction in language or gesture is usually spontaneous and heartfelt.

Wednesday 14 June 1995

STV News

One of the biggest rock bands in the world paid an unscheduled visit to Glasgow today, causing the city centre to almost grind to a halt. Thousands turned out to see Bon Jovi play, many of them had travelled from across Scotland and waited for hours to see their heroes.

The event was at Tower Records in Argyle Street. The PR woman instructed us that they were not to be approached and only selected media were to ask questions. The moment they appeared she was swamped by a surge of reporters and crews like a scene from a comedy. The band were fine. At one point I had cameraman Alan Denniston sitting on my shoulders to get a better shot. Good fun.

Wednesday 21 June 1995

STV News

A West Lothian woman has scooped the biggest ever pools win in Scotland. Audrey Grieve from Linlithgow was presented with a cheque for more than £2 million by comedienne Ruby Wax at a ceremony in Glasgow. Mrs Grieve said she hadn't even checked her numbers when the official appeared at her door with the good news.

DIARY: **The pools companies are losing out to the National Lottery so they made a big effort for this.**

Wednesday 5 July 1995

STV News

The sunshine may have gone away, but many people are still making every effort to cultivate that glamourous tanned look on sunbeds. They do so as some of the world's top skin specialists gather for a conference in Glasgow, and one of their main themes is that sunbeds can cause skin cancer.

Rates of skin cancer continue to rise with sunbeds still one of the major causes.

Monday 14 August 1995

STV News

Throughout the country this week, veterans of the Far East campaign against the Japanese will be commemorating the 50th anniversary of VJ Day in mass gatherings. These will be the last. The passage of time has succeeded where the barbarity of the Japanese failed...

JM: The hair may be white or gone, the bearing a little more stooped than it was all those years ago. But the pride still burns fiercely in these men. And the memories. Visions which even now they cannot put words to. This weekend's gathering of the Burma Star will be the last. Caged in cases in the Royal Scots Museum (*a Japanese sword and flag*), these relics of the Japanese war seem almost stately. For the men who saw them in more gruesome circumstances they were the very symbols of evil. But no matter the images created, only those who were there can know of man's inhumanity. And while some of these prisoners of war can enjoy their peaceful surroundings, they can never escape from the past.

JOHN TOMLINSON, Prisoner of War on the Burma Railway:
He was carrying a basket of earth and all of a sudden he dropped. The Japanese guard came along and he said, 'Dead.' There was no such thing as taking him away and burying him, just throw the dirt over the top of him... I never knew there was such a thing as VJ Day because I was that happy with being in hospital and being released and away from the barbarians, you understand? It never even dawned on me that people were celebrating the war had finished or we'd dropped a bomb on Hiroshima. I just thought I'm free.

TOM SCOTT, Japanese Prisoner of War:
I had so many beatings up that it tells a tale on you. I've got a spinal complaint, so you suffer at times with that.

JOE HENRY, Japanese Prisoner of War:
I had a lot of that, bad dreams and what not, waking up with shudders. And that went on for quite a while. And it still happens. The likes of maybe today we're talking about it. Maybe tonight I'll have a wee setback... It always comes back. It

was a bad, bad time. But that's my real thought – mates that I lost (falls to silence).

These old boys – surely all gone now – remain among the most memorable interviewees I have ever met.

Monday 4 September 1995
The premiere of the Mel Gibson film Braveheart – loosely based on the story of William Wallace – was in Stirling. The film was a huge hit and won Oscars for Best Picture and Best Director. It is often cited as being a factor in the resurgence of Scottish nationalism.

STV *News*
MEL GIBSON, Director and Star:
I'm not Scottish and I didn't make the film for those purposes, to be used as some kind of political tool for political gain or loss. I think that whatever happens, the Scottish people will make it happen.

ALEX SALMOND, SNP Leader:
I think the most important thing is the message. The message that comes out of this film is very clear indeed and, hopefully, that's got some relevance to modern day Scotland.

Wednesday 25 October 1995
DIARY: Did a story on a block of flats in Paisley which could have been used to house people, but instead are to be demolished. Got the cameraman to shoot it with the sky in the background until a flash of lightning appeared (there had been several). So my opening line was 'This is the building at the centre of the storm (upsound of thunder over lightning flash).' Very hammy, but livened up the piece.

Monday 30 October 1995

STV News

A new nation could be born tonight when the outcome of the Independence referendum in Quebec is known. Quebecers have been going to the polls to decide whether the French-speaking province should break away from the Canadian Federation. As John MacKay reports, it's an issue which has clear parallels with Scotland...

JM: The results of the Canadian referendum will be known in the early hours of the morning. Pundits are saying it's too close to call. The Quebecois are seeking what many Scottish nationalists seek – Independence for a nation perceived to be smothered by a dominant neighbour and the right to make decisions for themselves. The fabric of the argument presented by Canadian federalists is that the economy would suffer as people fearful of the future took their investment elsewhere, jobs would be lost as industry pulls out to relocate and taxes would increase to pay for Independence. Quebec, it's claimed, earns more from Canada than it puts in. The result is so close that even if it is no to Independence, the issue will not go away.

The parallels with the Scottish Independence referendum nearly 20 years later are very apparent. Quebec voted against Independence by the narrowest of margins.

Friday 3 November 1995

STV News

Scottish children aged as young as seven are suffering from alcoholism. But a conference in Glasgow has been hearing that such problems are being overlooked in the fight to battle drugs. Researchers have been arguing that the political focus is on combatting drug misuse, while the wider issue of underage drinking is being ignored.

Friday 15 December 1995

DIARY: **Final day of camera training. Did some filming in the St Enoch Centre. I've enjoyed the experience, but I hope it's never necessary to use the camera professionally.**

This was one of the various attempts to introduce VJs, or video journalists; reporters who film their own material. The development of simpler, more portable cameras has made VJs a common feature in most TV newsrooms now, but specialist camera operators remain key.

Thursday 28 December 1995

STV News

The freeze has claimed its first homeless victim. 54-year-old John Murphy died in Bathgate after falling. Police say a post mortem has still to be carried out, but say there is no question that the sub-zero temperatures were a key factor. The tragedy has caused outrage among homeless charities and tonight other homeless have been speaking about their fears for their lives.

DIARY: **Very, very cold with the temperatures hitting record lows –**

approaching −20C. When you're walking you don't feel it straight away, but eventually your cheeks begin to pinch and your face feels really frozen.

Some time later a former primary school teacher of mine, Irene Crawford, told me she had seen this report. She had taught both me and one of the homeless people I'd interviewed and it struck her how life can turn out so differently for people. A sobering thought.

1996

Tuesday 9 January 1996

DIARY: Travelled through to Edinburgh to speak to a woman who'd contracted the asbestos condition through cleaning her father's work boots as a child. She's 49 and knows she could die if it advances – just one of the hundreds of lives ruined by asbestos producers.

Thursday 11 January 1996

DIARY: A full day in Leeds. We were going to interview June Hancock – whose compensation victory in the English courts is the basis of our documentary. She grew up beside an asbestos factory, but never worked in it. She's now dying from mesothelioma. It was well worth the journey because she was an excellent interviewee and I couldn't have scripted her answers better. Did some pieces to camera in the Armley district where she grew up – it was real Coronation Street style. While it's better to have more space you can appreciate how these places had a close community spirit.

June Hancock died in 1997. A research fund was established in her name.

Tuesday 12 March 1996

STV News

A Scottish Reporters programme tonight will reveal how doctors are misdiagnosing a disease which will kill hundreds of Scots over the next 30 years. Experts say that mesothelioma, which is contracted from exposure to asbestos, is a health time bomb. Many of its victims have never worked with asbestos and do not know they have the condition.

The fact that their doctors fail to diagnose it also means that they cannot pursue claims for compensation.

Wednesday 21 February 1996

DIARY: Big story was the closure of the Cummins Engineering plant in Shotts with the loss of 700 jobs. A profit making plant where the workers met all their productivity targets. I went out at lunchtime to vox pop the workers. There they were talking about being 'devastated' and what the future held (nothing) and still with mortgages to pay. Not for the first time I feel intrusive – drive in, get the soundbite and away without any real understanding of what these men are going through.

Wednesday 6 March 1996

STV News

Glasgow is to be the focus for a series of initiatives to tackle the city's drug problem. The rate of deaths this year is already matching that of last year when two hundred drug users died. A strategic plan – the first of its kind in Scotland – has been launched to reduce the level of drug abuse. John MacKay reports…

JM: The strategic plan outlines how the various drug agencies can be coordinated to better tackle the city's drug problem. But not all are agreed on the best way forward.

REV RODERICK CAMPBELL, Greater Glasgow Drug Action Team:
There are a lot of strongly and sincerely held views in the drugs world. The role of the DAT is not to favour one or the other, but to try to see the development of both to monitor and evaluate the success of the methodology and try to encourage development.'

MICHAEL FORSYTH, Scottish Secretary: This is a daunting task. Drugs misuse is an enormous and complex problem. There are no easy solutions, although some people seem to think there are and that they have a simple solution. It's vital to be clear about priorities and the aims of services at a local level.

JIM DOHERTY, Gallowgate Family Support Group:
As far as we can find out, it's salaried employees of the health board who're speaking for us parents. We don't need them to speak for us, we can speak for ourselves.

One of the many drugs initiatives over the years. Most involved would concur with Michael Forsyth's observation that drug misuse is an 'enormous and complex' problem. A regular complaint through the years has been that projects would have their funding cut or weren't followed through.

THE DUNBLANE SHOOTINGS

Wednesday 13 March 1996

PA Copy – Central Scotland News Agency – Tim Bugler

Reports are coming in of a shooting at Dunblane Primary School, Perthshire. The Scottish Ambulance Service said 12 CHILDREN ARE BELIEVED DEAD and eight or nine injured. Police have been called from throughout the area and all five doctors from Dunblane Surgery are reported to have been called to the school.

DIARY: Today I worked on what must rank as the most appalling story I've ever been involved in – including Lockerbie. A gunman walked into the gymnasium of Dunblane Primary School and massacred 16 Primary One children and their teacher. He used four handguns and must have picked them off individually. It is incomprehensible why anyone should do this, how they would be capable of it. It seems the killer Thomas Hamilton was rumoured locally as a pervert. Whatever, how could any human being do this? During a quiet moment I cried and wanted to hold my own children.

First word came at the back of 10.00am. I drove up to Dunblane with cameraman Mike Haggerty, holding that PA copy and not convinced it was correct. How could it be? Dunblane? No way. I was fully expecting the car phone to ring and be told to return to base because it was a false alarm. It was only when Mike undertook a police car and it didn't react that I began to realise the truth of the awfulness that lay ahead of us. I will never forget running up to the school amid desperate parents arriving to find out what had happened to their children.

DIARY CONT: We never saw the full horror, but what we did see was heart rending. Parents filled with panic and tears swarming to the school to find out if their child was safe. One spoke of the overwhelming relief of finding hers, immediately followed by the guilt that she felt that way. One father described to me how the parents of those in the class were taken into a room and the wailing coming from it forced him to look away.

We needed to get our filmed material back in time for the lunchtime bulletin and did not have satellite capability at the time. I volunteered because I was to be presenting that night and was not commissioned to do a report. My role was to get a sense of what had happened and write scripts for the evening's live broadcast. I raced back to Glasgow at high speed and then returned immediately to Dunblane.

DOUGIE MCGUIRE
STV News Reporter

The morning of the shootings at Dunblane I killed some time by starting a round of calls – something most reporters do as a routine part of a shift in the quiet hours, when they have nothing else to do, when the desk is pressuring us to come up with something for the programme or just when we need to look busy.

I got through to the Duty Room at Central Scotland Police, and asked if there was anything doing, frankly expecting the usual 'No, all quiet' but this morning was different.

I shouted across the newsroom to Jon Keane (*News Editor*) that there had been a shooting at a school in Dunblane, there were casualties but no details. He looked stunned.

Dave Smith, my cameraman, appeared and we scrambled out into the Cowcaddens car park, heading for one of the distinctive STV Volvos and shouting at the desk that we were going to Dunblane.

Dave was a good, steady cameraman, but not known for his fast driving. At this stage I wasn't too concerned as I was on the phone, trying to find out what had happened. About 15 minutes into the trip as Dave motored sedately along the M80, and with nothing sensible coming out of the calls I was making to the police, I called Ambulance Control, hoping they would be able to help. I can still picture the inside of the car, my tweed jacket sleeve and the notepad on my knee when the girl on the phone said the most devastating words.

'Ambulance are in attendance at Dunblane Primary School. There are 16 children dead, and two adults' she told me.

'Sorry, did you say 16 children?'

'Yes, it's awful.'

She wasn't wrong.

It's strange how, in moments of extreme stress, people revert to behavioural styles which are their natural ones: Dave, if anything seemed to slow down as he heard the conversation and in a slightly military fashion (*Dougie had served in the army*) I imagine, I ordered him to 'Fucking floor it.' We then had an absurd argument about how he wasn't going to speed, with me insisting that the Police had other things on their minds, and fairly shortly we arrived in Dunblane.

Most journalists will admit, I think, that there is a rush of adrenalin and excitement when a story like this breaks, and however appalling it seems now, I was in that state when we got to the school.

Several police cars came out of the school as we were setting up, the officers inside them cradling their sub-machine guns and looking blank. Ambulances were moving about, heading in and out of the playground, and then the screaming hit me.

I could actually hear people – parents obviously – crying, from where we were standing outside the school grounds. When I heard that haunting sound that was the moment this story got real for me, the adrenalin started to fade, and the awful nature of what we, the first TV crew on the scene, were witnessing started to become clear.

There were terribly distressed people – mothers mostly – running past our camera, sobbing hysterically, with other parents reaching for them and trying to slow them down. Everything was confused and we could feel the raw emotion flooding the street. The beat cops who were around looked utterly desolate.

We snatched what we could, and sent off our first tape via a motorbike courier.

Soon the Strathclyde Police media team arrived, and read out the horrible details of what had happened to a small scrum of reporters and camera crews which had assembled. There was an audible gasp from the media when he said, '16, one-six children and their teacher are dead' as this number, the scale of this slaughter were not yet widely known.

Soon, hundreds of crews from across the world would descend on this 'quiet Scottish market town' as Dunblane came to be known.

In all the confusion and with people coming and going I ended up working with Mike Haggerty and it was his memorable vision of the bullet holes in the gym window which led off our coverage for the evening programme, followed by Dave's terribly distressing footage from when we had first arrived.

DIARY CONT: Eventually you become numb to the overwhelming grief around. This evening from our OB position you could see into the gym, although only the policemen/forensics moving around. What horrors they must have seen.

STV News

It's being called 'The Slaughter of the Innocents'. Sixteen small children and their teacher murdered by a gunman in a Dunblane primary school. The killer later shot himself. Tonight, thirteen other children still lie injured in hospital as the sheer scale of the horror unfolds. It happened just after half-past nine this morning as the five and six-year-olds played in the school gymnasium. A man burst in and massacred them with four automatic weapons. We have an hour long programme to report the story that the Prime Minister has called beyond belief. Tonight the town of Dunblane is struggling to comprehend a tragedy beyond words. Sixteen children went happily to school this morning. Tonight they have not come home, their young lives cut short in a moment of appalling brutality.

I had written these words as my opening link for the hour long news special we had prepared. Standing at our position on a hill above the school, I was told that we had technical problems and the programme may have to come from the studio in Glasgow. That was confirmed in the final moments before we went live and I heard Shereen beginning to read my words.

DIARY CONT: The programme was a disaster because we couldn't get our live links to work. Whatever my annoyance at our poor performance it matters nothing. Tonight I can't help but think of the horrors of that gymnasium and the misery in the homes of the dead children.

DOUGIE MCGUIRE, STV News Reporter:

Embarrassingly, our plans to present Scotland Today live from Dunblane on the first night failed due to some technical problems, so while the rest of the broadcasting world spoke to their audiences from Dunblane, STV – the first broadcast media on the scene – couldn't to begin with.

I don't remember a lot more about those days, other than having a persistent headache from constant mobile phone use, the cold weather, and an increasing desire to distance myself from the story. I have always thought it is a disgrace when reporters chase bereaved families who have just lost their beloved son or daughter, but it seemed a tackier and more obviously nasty thing to do in this case and I wanted nothing to do with it.

Something about Dunblane affected me far more than Lockerbie, the only other major disaster I had been intimately involved with, and a desire never to do more reporting of that kind helped steer me towards the world of PR a few months later.

I also remember being embarrassed by the tabloid media (STV included) endlessly repeating film of the piles of flowers which people placed outside the school, and the over written reports about the 'Angels of Dunblane' – a theme generated by one particular wreath.

It might seem odd to be making these points, but I feel that with an event as awful as this, there is little need to over-do the tone of the reporting, the dreadful facts speak eloquently enough for themselves. I think in some ways the journalists who sweep into town and make themselves the story must add further pain to the unimaginable grief that the victims' families are feeling.

But just try telling that to the desk...

Thursday 14 March 1996

STV News

It now seems that Thomas Hamilton's massacre of the children of Dunblane Primary was not a moment's madness, but planned to the last detail. Before going to school to carry out his slaughter, he posted copies of letters about his grievances to a number of outlets.

DIARY: Original intention was that I should return to Dunblane today, but when I arrived in the office we had just received a package of photocopied letters written by killer Thomas Hamilton and I was put to work on

those. We quickly established as best we could that they were genuine (checking with recipients), but it also became apparent from checking the writing that Hamilton had sent them to us himself (+the BBC, *Record* & *Herald*). This made his act all the more appalling because he had clearly planned what he was going to do – it wasn't simply a few moments of madness. It was a sobering thought to realise that the letters in my hands had been photocopied and folded into the envelope by Hamilton; he put stamps on it and sent it to us before setting out to commit the most indescribable outrage. The letters charted a growing grievance spread over the last five or so years. Sent to the local council, his MP and the Queen, they described how his work with children and his whole life was being undermined by rumours of him being a pervert. He mentions Dunblane Primary School where teachers were spreading this 'poison'. By this evening I had put together a four minute 30 second report which is one of the best I've done, but you could hardly fail with the material. I still struggle to comprehend the sheer horror of what happened and what the parents are going through.

Tuesday 9 April 1996

STV News

A tobacco company has failed in its attempt to force a widow to put up a £2,000,000 bond before attempting to sue them. Imperial Tobacco wanted Margaret McTear to put up the money as security to cover their legal costs if her claim against them failed. Mrs McTear is pursuing a test case action begun by her late husband alleging that the tobacco company should have warned him of the health risks when he began smoking as a teenager. The company's petition was rejected by the Court of Session.

Margaret McTear ultimately failed to win the case against Imperial Tobacco.

Tuesday 23 April 1996

DIARY: Covering story of a 12-year-old who drowned in the River Clyde while escaping from a gang. Returned to the area, Carmyle, later, to get a new line. At one point I was in the house of one of the boy's companions, who'd survived. The father was upset and complaining that his son had to go to stay elsewhere because of harassment, including staking out their house and chasing the boy over fences to get a photo. I don't think that's acceptable and it makes me uncomfortable about my profession. The guy said I'd been courteous and fine, but others had acted like scum. We spoke for 20 minutes, but he didn't want to go on camera and that was that. Usually I persuade them, this time I didn't, but I would not have been comfortable adopting the tabloid tactics. Different if it's a crook, but not a victim.

Tuesday 7 May 1996

STV News

A high profile campaign to combat drug use has been launched by the leaders of the four main political parties. The MPs put their differences aside to join a 'battle bus' which is taking the anti-drugs message through the country's major cities. It's in Edinburgh this lunchtime after leaving Aberdeen this morning. Sports stars, the business community, and media personalities have also joined the project. But, as John MacKay reports, some critics say the message being put across will miss its target.

This was the much mocked photo call in which Michael Forsyth, George Robertson, Alex Salmond and Jim Wallace danced very self consciously in sweatshirts with teenagers in a club. The intention was sincere, but it was always going to be open to ridicule.

Monday 13 May 1996

STV News

Britain's last Polaris submarine sailed back into the Firth of Clyde today at the end of its final patrol. The nuclear submarines, first used in the 1960s, have become obsolete with the introduction of Trident. For some it was a sad day, for others a case of good riddance.

DIARY: It's the sort of story you can't really fail – good story, great pictures. Polaris is being replaced by the bigger, even more destructive Trident. It begs the question, how much destructive power do you need? What better uses could the money be put to? However, history teaches that you never should leave yourself totally exposed. My own feeling is that the threat to world peace now is more likely to come from China, or even more likely, the fundamental Muslims.

That question is resurrected again now as the debate intensifies over the replacement of Trident.

Thursday 16 May 1996

STV News

Barbaric, disgusting and abhorrent. The words of a judge after four teenage girls and a 21-year-old man were all found guilty of torturing another woman in a flat in Greenock. A fifth girl had earlier pleaded guilty to lesser charges. There were angry scenes in the High Court in Glasgow as sentences totaling 50 years were handed out. John MacKay reports on today's verdicts and the events surrounding the prolonged attack on the group's victims...

DIARY: Fascinating and highly pressurised day. The Greenock Torture trial which I've been working on, on and off for the past week or so ended late on and I got my piece finished with less than a minute to go, it was that tight. The fascination of seeing people who face serious charges sitting in the dock and the whole tension of waiting for the jury's verdict and then the sentence is intense. The reaction from the accused as they were given sentences ranging from 16 to three and a half years was of much sobbing as their families wailed in the public gallery. Five of them were teenage girls. However, the savagery of the acts meant that you could feel no sympathy.

The public gallery erupted when the sentences were handed down as the families of some of the convicted shouted at each other. Outside people hammered on the prison van as it took the prisoners off to jail, which my cameraman managed to film. I thought the drama in the courtroom was more spectacular as the court officers tried to restore order, so I led my report with that. I had no images of it, though, because there was no camera in the courtroom and so I had to cover it with dull shots of the exterior of the court. My first shots should have been the banging on the prison van because that would immediately draw in the viewer, even although it was not perhaps the strongest line. It was a basic lesson in TV reporting.

Monday 20 May 1996
STV News

Top pop group, Oasis, are at the centre of a row over their summer concerts on Loch Lomondside. 80,000 tickets have been sold for the two day event in August, but people in the local town of Balloch say the tickets have been sold without proper planning permission being granted and without them having been consulted. The town, they claim, will be unable to cope.

JM: Both concerts sold out as soon as the tickets went on sale. Thousands will be spending the night in the makeshift camping areas which, given that Balloch is a one toilet town, could cause problems.

Balloch had one public toilet that I could see, so I couldn't resist that line. I ended my report saying that the townsfolk hoped they 'Don't Look Back in Anger' at the event. There's nothing I can say now in mitigation.

Thursday 23 May 1996
STV News

The largest ever exhibition of the work of Charles Rennie Mackintosh opens tonight in Glasgow. The 350 exhibits will span his entire career and include a reconstruction of one of his celebrated tearooms. There has been no celebration of Mackintosh quite like it and, as John MacKay reports, there never will be again.

I was very pleased with my piece – nice shots, atmospheric music and a minimum of voice. However, I neglected to say where it's being held, so we had a lot of calls saying lovely story, but where is it? Basic.

It was at the McLellan Galleries in Glasgow.

DUNBLANE INQUIRY
Wednesday 29 May 1996
STV News

First tonight, the opening day of the Dunblane Inquiry has heard harrowing accounts of the moment Thomas Hamilton opened fire on a Primary One class. Part time PE teacher Eileen Harrild, who survived the attack, described how she could not comprehend what was happening as the gunman began shooting. Lord Cullen was told that Hamilton had fired one hundred and five shots from one gun before turning a second on himself. Police officers and medical staff have also been describing the scene on their arrival at the school.

JM: The 43-year-old PE teacher described how she was about to start lessons when she became aware of the gym doors opening suddenly. A man in a wooly hat and earmuffs came in, his arms extended, and started firing. She was the first hit, wounded in the arms and chest she stumbled towards a store room in the gym followed by four or five children and another teacher. All had been injured. The shooting continued rapidly as Hamilton continued round the gym. There was a brief lull before the shooting started again. Then Mrs Harrild said there was silence. The shooting and the screaming had stopped. The other teacher to hide in the storeroom gave a written statement. Children were screaming so loudly she said it was as if the noise was inside her head. One child repeatedly said, 'What a bad man.' She tried to pull a mat over them for protection, but she couldn't because of wounds to her head and legs. 'I thought it was the end,' she said. The inquiry heard experts describe how Hamilton had fired 105 bullets in the four minutes of shooting. All came from a Smith and Wesson revolver. He used one bullet from a Browning pistol to shoot himself.

Jack Beattie, one of the first doctors on the scene, described how he had gone from victim to victim checking who could be saved and who was dead. Senior police officer Detective Chief Superintendent John Ogg described how investigations had revealed that Hamilton had worked his way round the gym, left through a fire exit and shot into other classes before returning. He described how difficult it had been to identify some victims. The label on one child's clothes didn't match any of the names on the register. The one person who knew them all so well, Gwen Mayor, was herself dead.

DIARY: **Eileen Harrild's testimony, delivered with little emotion, was gripping and harrowing. The hall was absolutely silent as she spoke. Two images she described were heartbreaking – first of all she said the Primary One children had lined up outside the gym, already in their gym** clothes and very excited. Later she said, '… then there was silence. The shooting and the screaming had stopped.' There could have been no more than ten minutes in between these contrasting images.

To this day the evidence given on the first day of the Cullen Inquiry, and in particular the first eyewitness account by Eileen Harrild, remains the most compelling experience I've ever had as a reporter.

Thursday 30 May 1996

STV News

'It was a scene of unimaginable carnage.' That was head teacher Ron Taylor's description of the moment he entered Dunblane School's gymnasium after Thomas Hamilton had shot dead 16 children and their teacher. Mr Taylor was giving evidence on the second day of Lord Cullen's inquiry into the shootings. Later he said he couldn't understand why anyone should want to keep a weapon at home. He could only imagine they had never seen the effects of a gun – he had. Our reporter John MacKay has been following today's evidence and he joins us now from Stirling…

(*live*) Well here today head teacher Ron Taylor relived events which he described as 'one's worst nightmare'. In remarkably composed testimony, he betrayed little emotion except when asked about when he tended the injured children. (*Into report*)

JM: Mr Taylor first became aware that something was seriously wrong when a teacher came into his room and told him, 'There's a man in the school with a gun. Get down.' He ran to the gym and as he burst through the door he saw a scene which he described as 'unimaginable carnage'.

The air was thick with blue smoke and there was a strong smell of cordite. Some children were crying, but looked to be less injured. Mr Taylor had other teachers remove them. He moved through the gymnasium to establish what had happened. Thomas Hamilton was lying on the floor at the top of the hall. He seemed to be still moving. The school janitor kicked a gun away from him. Asked if he tended to injured children, Mr Taylor replied in a soft voice, 'Yes.'

Another witness, Agnes Awlson, the school's deputy head, said when she had entered the gym she had tried to attend to some children. The janitor told her, 'You can't help them Mrs Awlson, they're gone.'

Later the inquiry heard from 64-year-old Agnes Watt, the mother of Thomas Hamilton, although he had been adopted by his grandparents. She said she saw her son twice a week and he phoned her every night. The day before the killings he had spent the afternoon with her. He'd had a bath and a meal and they talked. Nothing was out of the ordinary, she said. She only found out about what he'd done when she phoned his house and the police answered. The man she considered to be a caring son was the same man who killed the children.

DIARY: It was torrential rain for much of the day which wasn't much fun for poor Mike Haggerty (cameraman) – who has to wait outside. Strong testimony again today from head teacher Ron Taylor and later Hamilton's mother. You couldn't help but feel sorry for her – she was just like any wifey of 60-odd years and was trying to keep some dignity in spite of knowing what her son had become. She was a sympathetic figure.

Friday 31 May 1996

STV News

The Dunblane Inquiry has heard that Thomas Hamilton may have been planning his attack on the school for two years. In written evidence to the inquiry, a member of one of Hamilton's boys' clubs said he was asked to describe the layout of the school and the times that youngsters would be together for assembly.

Hamilton carried enough ammunition to wipe out the entire school. It is believed he had intended shooting them at assembly.

Thursday 27 June 1996

STV News

First tonight, in a total reversal of previous policy, Labour have confirmed they're to hold a referendum on their plans for the Scottish Parliament. Shadow Scottish Secretary George Robertson today admitted he'd got it wrong in the past and he claimed consulting voters before a bill went through Westminster would strengthen the case for Devolution.

My report was a supplementary one on the story.

(*intro*) Mr Blair may have some convincing to do. The reaction from within his party has ranged from muted to unfavourable. Outside the party, the proposal has upset Labour's constitutional convention partners. Indeed, the only people showing any satisfaction are Labour's political opponents.

(*script*) Until today Labour activists believed the the party's position to be clear. As they promised at the last election, Labour would win at Westminster and within a year provide a Scottish parliament with tax raising powers. Now that isn't so clear and many of the faithful feel aggrieved that they haven't been consulted over such a major change in policy.

ARCHIE GRAHAM, former Executive member:
What we are seeing is yet another example of a move towards a democratic centralist system where we elect a leader and then the leader and his office decide everything and then hand down policy to the rest of us.

CAMPBELL CHRISTIE, Scottish TUC:
I have no doubt that when people vote in the General Election in the next few months and they vote Labour, they will be clear that they are voting Labour who will establish a Scottish parliament with tax varying powers. Having got that mandate I see no reason for a further mandate to be achieved.

ALEX SALMOND, SNP Leader:
It's a delaying device, it's a wrecking

tactic as indeed it was in 1979. The only difference is that then the referendum device was played by Labour's backbenchers, now it's the Labour leadership at the highest level who are deploying this wrecking device and delaying tactic.

MICHAEL FORSYTH MP, Scottish Secretary:
They will have to introduce a bill for a referendum and that will have to be closely argued in Parliament. People will want to know what the questions are, all of which is going to take a year. So how can they say they're going to have a referendum to find out what the policy is, and they're going to introduce the policy all within a year? It can't be done.

JM: To discuss today's changes I'm joined by Labour's Chief Whip Donald Dewar. Mr Dewar, hasn't Michael Heseltine got it right (*comments in the House of Commons*), this is more about appeasing Middle England and selling out Scotland?

DONALD DEWAR, Labour Chief Whip:
No. I thought that was tremendous pantomime, but not serious politics. This is a confident move by a confident party. We are constantly told by the carping and criticising Conservatives that we don't have the consent of Scotland, that's there's no support for what we're going to do and what we're saying is we'll call your bluff.

JM: They've been saying that for ages. What has changed?

DD: We've looked at the need to have certainty, we've looked at the way we can implement this. There's absolutely no retreat on the commitment to devolution or the devolution policy, but what we have decided is that the way in which we can build it on sure foundations is to go to Parliament with the impetus and the moral authority that comes from a direct endorsement by the people of Scotland.

Wednesday 3 July 1996

DIARY: I sat in on Scottish Questions in the Commons Chamber. I was sitting above the PM John Major as he announced the return of the Stone of Destiny to Scotland. Just before he spoke he tapped his thumbs on his notes – a very human act. The Employment Secretary Gillian Shepherd sat on the hallowed green benches, shoes off, feet up, absently picking her toes. I did get the impression it was like a big club and there is little doubt the real business of Government does not happen in there.

Tuesday 9 July 1996

STV News

First tonight, the parents of some of the children killed in the Dunblane shooting have been speaking publicly for the first time. They told a news conference that the right of their children to live far outweighs anyone's right to own a gun. They want all guns banned. Facing the cameras for the first time, they spoke of their anger at how Thomas Hamilton was legally entitled to carry a gun and the distress caused by the delay in being told their children had been killed.

DIARY: Their basic message was ban all guns, and certainly in the case of handguns who can argue? They were just such normal people. What else would they be? One read a statement, 'We will never get over it. There will always be a hole in our lives,' she said.

Wednesday 10 July 1996

STV News

It took only a few minutes for Thomas Hamilton to kill the children of Primary One. It has taken six weeks for the inquiry to hear why. It'll take Lord Cullen many weeks more to make recommendations to prevent such a tragedy ever happening again.

DIARY: The final day of the Dunblane Inquiry – it wasn't quite the mad rush I was anticipating. I was beginning to weary of it towards the end. But as the Crown QC said in his closing address, 'We must never lose sight of these little shattered bodies. That is what brought us here.' I doubt I will ever have to work on a more harrowing story in my career. I hope not.

Friday 26 July 1996

DIARY: To Kilmarnock to knock off an interview with the Labour Deputy Leader John Prescott. Very funny – he stumbled over one question three times, ending by stamping his foot and saying, 'Fuck!' Didn't take to him – brusque and rude.

Tuesday 20 August 1996

STV News

Glasgow's image as the 'sick city' of Europe is slowly changing. Fewer people are suffering heart attacks and the cancer rate is falling. But in its local health strategy document the city's health board says more work needs to be done. This is Greater Glasgow Health Board's second strategy plan for improving the city's health into the next millennium.

HARRY BURNS, Director of Public Health:
We've made great strides in Glasgow in improving health. Over the past 20 years the risk of premature death from strokes, heart disease and cancer has decreased substantially. There are other areas that we have not seen such significant improvements. What we're trying to do is point out to the public the initiatives that we feel necessary to bring about these improvements.

Glasgow continues to labour under the 'sick city' label. One in four men in Glasgow won't reach their 65th birthday.

Thursday 29 August 1996

STV News

Scotland's first commercially run wind farm began generating electricity onto the national grid for the first time today. It's one of the first to get through all the planning stages which have prevented similar projects happening in the past. Unlike many similar projects this has had the full backing of the local community.

(*script*) Hagshaw Hill above Douglas in South Lanarkshire. Twenty-six wind turbines producing enough electricity for 17,000 homes. In the new millennium it may be that thousands more will have their power produced by this technology and wind farms will be a common sight.

DIARY: It's the sort of story that on first sight seems dull, but which in actual fact I found fascinating. We had a rush to get something sent away for lunchtime, but we could then spend more time at the site getting good pictures. It was a surreal experience, standing on top of this hill with great views over Lanarkshire, surrounded by these vast turbines swishing through the breeze. Very peculiar and a damn sight better than being stuck in the office.

Windfarms are now a common and often controversial feature across the landscape.

Thursday 5 September 1996

DIARY: An intriguing opportunity has been offered to me. Sky Scottish – a new channel funded by Sky and ourselves will involve a half hour news programme – not dissimilar to *Scotland Today*, but pan-Scottish. Scott (*Scott Ferguson – STV Head of News*) wants me to front it with Andrea Brymer, who's a rising star at STV. He says Andrea is exotic looking, but when she opens her mouth she's a Brechin butcher's daughter. We are 'nineties', he says. The programme would go on satellite and cable an hour later.

Wednesday 9 October 1996

STV News

Seventeen candles burned in Dunblane Cathedral today. Each one in remembrance of the victims of the Dunblane shootings. They were lit during a memorial service, attended by the Prince of Wales. In a moving service during which the parents of each dead child lit a candle with their name on it, the message was 'out of darkness into light'. John MacKay sent this report from Dunblane...

DIARY: We weren't allowed inside – the BBC providing live coverage and pool pictures – so we watched it from the links van. It was very moving. At one point the parents of each child lit a candle for their child as a piper played 'Lament for the Children'. I would have wept if I was on my own.

Friday 18 October 1996

STV News

Scotland needs a nationwide strategy to tackle widespread poverty. The Scottish Anti-Poverty Network has based that claim on what's said to have been the widest consultation on poverty ever undertaken in Scotland. Latest figures show that nearly a fifth of Scottish families are dependent on income support. But the Government says it's spending billions to relieve the problem.

DIARY: Pulled together a piece on an anti-poverty campaign. It's the sort of worthy piece that has to be done on a quiet day and I could almost do it with my eyes shut.

Friday 1 November 1996

DIARY: Sky Scottish was launched today and it all seems to have gone smoothly. I welcomed viewers to the first *Scotland Today* on Sky Scottish and then on we went with the news – about the Government's gun control bill. It went very well except in the first intro I'd read my piece and as Andrea was reading hers there was a panic that the taped report wasn't at the start.

Fortunately it made it, but credit to Andrea for holding her nerve on what was such a big occasion for her.

There was more hassle in production terms today than any of the dry runs (changing ITN pictures to Sky, that sort of thing).

I would regularly present Scotland Today on STV and then essentially the same programme again on Sky Scottish.

Wednesday 27 November 1996

STV News

It's now Britain's worst ever outbreak of the deadly E-coli bug. Six people are dead, more than 100 are being treated and health officials say there could be more deaths to come. Today's toll included three Lanarkshire pensioners and the first suspected case outside the Wishaw area. After a three day delay environmental health experts have revealed thirty outlets across the whole of Central Scotland were supplied by the butcher at the centre of the food poisoning outbreak. Local MPS are now demanding to know why action wasn't taken earlier to trace meat which may have been contaminated.

Twenty-one people died in the outbreak.

1997

Friday 17 January 1997

DIARY: Interviewed the Defence Secretary, Michael Portillo, in Renfrew. He is, some predict, a future leader of the Conservative Party and a possible Prime Minister. He came into the news conference and shook hands with everyone. The only other person I've ever seen do that is the Scottish Office Minister, Lord James Douglas Hamilton. When he does it there is a sense that he is a very nice man – which he is. But with Portillo there was a smarminess which was unappealing.

Michael Portillo never did become the leader of the Conservatives. His defeat in his constituency of Enfield Southgate became one of the defining images of the 1997 election. He has built a new career as a TV presenter and author and comes across as a better fellow for it.

Tuesday 21 January 1997

STV News

There's growing pressure on the leader of the SNP, Alex Salmond, to reveal how his party would vote on any Devolution referendum introduced by a Labour government. An opinion poll for STV shows that almost four-fifths of the electorate think the SNP should explain their intentions. The poll also showed that a large majority of SNP supporters should campaign for a 'Yes' vote in the referendum.

JM: Since Labour revealed their plans to hold a two question referendum on Devolution if they win the Election, the SNP have consistently refused to say how they would urge supporters to vote. The party's view is that yes they support the idea of a referendum, but not the questions proposed by Labour.

JAMES MITCHELL, political analyst: I think the fact that a higher proportion of the SNP's supporters want the SNP to play a full part in the referendum and campaign for a 'Yes' vote – a higher proportion than the public at large – is vitally important.'

IAN LAWSON (SNP activist): 'You can't trust the Labour Party. I've witnessed betrayal after betrayal... Basically, if they can convince me that they've got the support for their own proposals from within the Labour Party in England, then will be the time for the SNP to make their judgement.'

The SNP did campaign for a Yes vote in the Devolution Referendum.

Thursday 6 March 1997

DIARY: The day's main stories – local authority budget cuts and council tax increases, prison officers' association warning of dangerous overcrowding and tonight's Old Firm tie being the game of the season. Laughed with one of my colleagues that this could have been any day over the past few years – the same stories coming round.

GENERAL ELECTION 1997
Thursday 27 March 1997

DIARY: An SNP news conference at 10.00am. The Nats were repeating the line, that rather than Scots being 'subsidy junkies' as the Tories argue, we are in fact net contributors to the UK Treasury. Interviewed Alex Salmond

and that will become a regular. As before, I found him to be very able.

Wednesday 2 April 1997

DIARY: The General Election campaign began properly for me today as I travelled through to Edinburgh for an SNP news conference – I'll be attached to the SNP for the duration. There seems, at this stage, little doubt that Labour will be triumphant.

Thursday 3 April 1997

STV News

Launching Labour's manifesto, Tony Blair unveiled plans to put Devolution on a parliamentary fast track. And he appealed to the public to trust New Labour. But his opponents have attacked the manifesto as a con.

DIARY: Saw Tony Blair, our likely Prime Minister, for the first time in the flesh today – surprisingly more tanned looking than one might have thought. He was visiting Stirling (the one really interesting seat in Scotland – will Michael Forsyth hold on or not?). He was mobbed and it was great to get in amongst it, totally ignoring the pool arrangements as Bobby Whitelaw (*cameraman*) and I leapt fences to get in with the crowd. A real adrenalin buzz, then a sprint to get the pictures sent back by satellite because he was late arriving. People say they can't trust him and on such a short exposure who can say? What did strike me was that he was uncomfortable in the crowd – he did not come across as a 'meet-the-people' kind of man in the way that John Major clearly relishes.

Friday 4 April 1997

DIARY: Big row today was over Tony Blair's visit to Scotland and comments he's made regarding a Scottish Parliament. It's all about detail and semantics and I think much of it is over the head of the electorate. He's been damaged, though, as people have twisted what he said about English parish councils and the Scottish Parliament. His talk of sovereignty remaining with him as an English MP was misjudged. This is where you can get sucked into an election campaign when the Big Picture gets bogged down in a morass of detail.

Monday 7 April 1997

STV News

Promising a sovereign Parliament for a sovereign people, the Scottish National Party have launched their manifesto. They say they'll set up a powerhouse Parliament to create jobs, cut taxes for the low paid and spend more on the Health Service. But the opposition parties have been scathing in their attacks on the Nationalist's plans, describing the manifesto as a Disney World alternative based on polo mint economics. John MacKay has the details of today's launch...

JM: The Scottish National Party's campaign in 1997 is, they say, based on realism. Grand predictions made by the politicians and pundits in 1992 failed to materialise. Slogans like 'Free by '93' have embarrassed the party ever since. They hope that the pledges made in their manifesto will show that the SNP is both sensible and electable.

DIARY: I had my first draft of the script prepared on the train through and although it was a packed news conference with the usual network presence, I got everything done quickly and had it edited in good time for lunchtime despite the editing problems being experienced with the new digital system. I suspect it could be a disappointing election for the SNP, although up to seven to eight seats will please them.

Tuesday 8 April 1997

DIARY: SNP were in Glasgow, but hardly anyone appeared so it was short and sweet. So far I haven't really been asking questions at the news conferences – the sooner they are over the sooner I can do the one-to-ones (*interviews*). On to a church news conference where the church is basically saying none of the parties was offering anything for the poor. To illustrate it I went to a shopping arcade in Drumchapel – all boarded up and graffiti covered. Almost everyone I vox-popped was apathetic and while traditionally they would have been Labour, it's clear that Tony Blair holds nothing for them.

Tuesday 22 April 1997

DIARY: I volunteered to cover parent protests at Renfrewshire District Council over a five pound increase in nursery school charges. Some children have been expelled from other schools in the area because their parents have refused to pay. It turned out to be good stuff with the council meeting disrupted by the parents' protests. The leading Labour group would just not allow it to be discussed, which was stupid. Great pictures in the chamber.

Wednesday 30 April 1997

STV News

JM: A campaign to win hearts and minds. A powerhouse Parliament funded by billions of pounds worth of oil revenues making Scotland the eighth richest nation in the world. That's been the SNP campaign – aimed at overcoming the fear factor, those who doubt Scotland can go it alone. 'Yes we can' has been their cry.

ALEX SALMOND, SNP Leader: We won the economic argument. For the first time in a generation people in Scotland by a majority now believe that Scotland would be better off as an independent country. That's been a major victory for us in the campaign. But y'know tomorrow is going to be about more than just economics. Tomorrow is about national pride, self respect, whether we are a real country or just some sort of English county as London parties, in varying degrees, seem to think we are.

JM: If the SNP end their campaign as the second party in Scotland in terms of parliamentary seats they will consider it a success. Their real chance for power though, would come in any future Scottish Parliament where the proposed PR voting system would give them a bigger say in Scotland's affairs.

Thursday 1 May 1997

ELECTION DAY

DIARY: Back into work at 8.00pm for a long night ahead. I was originally supposed to be at the Glasgow count and ended up cutting hourly wraps because they wanted someone who knew politics and could cut quickly. By midnight it was clear Labour had won.

Friday 2 May 1997

STV News with Shereen Nanjiani

Conservatives in Scotland are adjusting to electoral devastation... with not a single parliamentary seat left north of the border. The high national profile of big names like Michael Forsyth and Malcolm Rifkind didn't save them. They all fell to the Labour landslide. With all the results now in the nation's political map has been dramatically altered – the final pockets of blue north of the border brushed out.

Labour have gone up six to 56 seats, the Liberal Democrats have lost one and gained three to give them a total of ten MPs, the SNP have doubled their number of seats to six and the Tories, of course, have none at all. By share of the vote Labour have 46 per cent, the Nationalists 22, Conservatives 17, Lib Dems 13 and other parties two per cent. John MacKay has the story of the night...

JM: They fell like skittles in a bowling alley. Ten seats from the north to the borders. Conservative after Conservative was toppled. Three men who were among the most powerful in the land yesterday are today out of a job.

MICHAEL FORSYTH: 'There has been a tidal wave against us which is very sad. People clearly wanted a change.'

IAN LANG: 'Scotland is rapidly turning into a one party state and that is bad for politics and very bad for Scotland's future.'

MALCOLM RIFKIND: For my colleagues both North and South of the border this has been a very sad and very worrying evening.'

JM: The attacks came from all sides. From the smallest majority in Ayr to the supposedly safe seat in Eastwood, the Scottish electorate hammered home their rejection. Across the political divide there was joy unconfined as others prepared for government.

GORDON BROWN, Labour MP: The Labour Party is now ready to rebuild the bond of trust between the British people and their Government.

JM: And the SNP doubled their number of seats.

ALEX SALMOND, Leader, SNP: And now we've managed to increase our share of the vote further and double our parliamentary representation, I think we're entitled to a bit of the kudos this evening.

JM: Today Scotland stands as a Conservative free zone. The party controls no councils and it has no Members of Parliament.

DIARY: It's a landslide. Labour have stormed into Government on a massive majority. An historic night. When they look back on politics, 1997 will be up there with the other great events. There are no Conservative MPs in Scotland any more, all ten roundly thumped. It has taken everyone by surprise – even the Labour Party. The country has sent out the clearest message that quite simply it was time for change. The Conservatives have been in power too long and have run out of ideas, their government was pursuing issues out of dogma and not need, eg bureaucratisation of the NHS. I do believe John Major was a decent man and I admire his rise from nothing. I am concerned about Labour's majority being so big and there being no effective opposition. Today was a new dawn for Britain, I wonder what sort of age it will be.

Friday 6 June 1997

DIARY: To Irvine to interview a couple whose premature daughter has been left to die because the doctor said that at 23 weeks she wasn't viable. Raised a number of issues – if the baby is battling to survive, shouldn't they at least try to help it, and if it's a mother's right to have a pregnancy terminated, why doesn't a mother have the right to insist the child be given every chance of survival? It all made a good piece with the tearful testimony from the mother.

Thursday 12 June 1997

DIARY: The Isle of Eigg was today officially handed into the ownership of the islanders themselves. I had good pictures to work with and it's the sort of piece I enjoy doing. My final line was 'As the Hebridean rain fell it was as if years of neglect was being washed away.' Perhaps a bit much, but the piece lent itself to some poetic licence.

Monday 7 July 1997

DIARY: *Scotland Today* is being taken off Sky Scottish from the 1st of August. The official line is that they want to put on more sport and there's not enough room for it all. They want to do a new programme on a Sunday reviewing the Sunday papers and discussing the main Scottish news of the week.

Thursday 24 July 1997

DIARY: Devolution Day – the Government publishing its White Paper for a Scottish Parliament. Much planning had gone into it from our point of view and our programme was very good. Why are hardly any of Labour's 56 MPs going to stand for this Scottish Parliament? Because they know where the power will really be?

Monday 28 July 1997

DIARY: Paul (Paul McKinney, News Editor) revealed to me that a survey of viewers (this is a regular thing) showed that they regard my dress sense to be dull (how dare they!!). I prefer dark clothes because they are more authoritative and I'm not allowed to wear blue.

I could not wear blue because we used a blue backdrop for chromakey. If I wore anything blue, it would pick up what was projected behind me. No-one ever mentioned it over the years we used this set. Quite a contrast later when I regularly wore blue to match the colours of a newer set – the 'Blue Tie MacKay' myth of social networks.

Thursday 31 July 1997

DIARY: So the last *Scotland Today* on Sky Scottish. We played it straight as we signed off, nothing over the top. It's a shame and I enjoyed doing it, but at least I've got my new programme starting on Sunday.

Sky Scottish had pockets of audience all over the place. We got feedback from places like Marbella and Rome and we were particularly chuffed by the fact that, because of Scottish troops, we were big in Bosnia.

Sunday 3 August 1997

DIARY: The new programme, *The Scottish Review*, went out for the first time today. General feeling was that it was good for a first programme. Our review guests Michael Kelly and Susan McGuire (writer/actress). Michael Kelly kept it rolling along.

Wednesday 20 August 1997

DIARY: Labour's launch of the Yes campaign. I wasn't doing the story, but I went to the news conference to get a sense of what they're proposing.

Wednesday 27 August 1997

STV News

While the Devolution campaigners have been appearing in front of cameras, it seems there's been only limited direct contact with the voters themselves. In the latest of our special series of reports on the referendum, John MacKay has visited two of the most fiercely contested seats at May's General Election where he found little evidence of any campaigning on Devolution.

JM: Stirling was one of the most keenly contested seats in Scotland during the General Election. It's a hot-bed of political activity and the scene, three weeks before polling day, of a visit by the prospective Prime Minister. Two weeks before the referendum, which could lead to the biggest upheaval in the political history of the UK, this is the same street.

VOX POPS: During the Election you were getting people coming to your door and to the office. You knew what was going on. This time there's been nothing.

You're the first to approach us.

There's been nothing here.

Absolutely disgraceful. There has been nothing.

I haven't seen any posters.

PAOLO VESTRI, Scotland Forward: The political parties and ourselves took a strategic decision that, rather than have a six week campaign like the General Election and which people got fed up with, it'd be better to have an effective, snappy campaign.

BRIAN MONTEITH, Think Twice: This campaign has been rushed by the Government. There was no need to do that. People are on holiday etc. Both campaigns have suffered. However, over the next two weeks you'll see a far higher profile campaign.'

Sunday 31 August 1997

DIARY: Awoken at 6.35am by the phone going. It was Nicki (*Nicki McGowan, Sunday producer*) with the quite shocking news that Diana, Princess of Wales had been killed in a car crash in Paris. She was only 36. After the initial shock it struck me that there was an awful inevitability about the tragedy. She was the world's most photographed woman, an icon of our time, but by all accounts one who had had an unhappy life despite the unimaginable riches, the glamour and the lifestyle. It has stunned most people and has been an event that united the nation. She was treated badly by the Royal Family, but she was also a manipulator who could not, to my

mind, keep away from the headlines and front pages. Nonetheless, she will now become a tragic figure in history, more so than even Marilyn Monroe, the one figure with whom there are clear parallels.

We had to start from scratch with *The Scottish Review*. I also fronted a special Scottish bulletin at 5.55am for 20 minutes, with a black tie and much gravitas.

The BBC and ITV had blanket coverage – too much by the end of the day I thought, but nonetheless you kept getting drawn back to it.

Above all it can't be forgotten that while Diana has moved into legend, two young boys have lost their mother and you have to feel for them.

STV News
The people of Scotland have been paying tribute to Diana, Princess of Wales. Prayers have been said at services throughout the country. Campaigning in the Devolution Referendum has been suspended. Flowers have been laid by the public at Holyrood Palace and in Glasgow's George Square.

JM: I'm joined by our political correspondent Fiona Ross, Fiona, you mentioned the Devolution Referendum may have to be postponed, is this really feasible?

FIONA ROSS: It is feasible. It's not necessarily likely at the moment, a lot depends on the funeral arrangements. For example, it would not be feasible, obviously, to run a referendum campaign on the future of Scotland on the same day as Princess Diana's funeral. But, of course, politicians really don't want to get into this at the moment, apart from anything else, everybody is quite literally grief stricken. There are also very serious implications here, I mean it's not just as easy as putting a line through it and saying 'och we'll hold it a week later.' They actually have to recall Parliament to do this and re-legislate because it's in the Referendum Act that the referendum is held on the 11th of September. So there is quite a serious problem potentially facing the Government here.

JM: So if we stick with the current timetable how would that affect campaigning, do you think?

FR: Well I don't think there'd be any. I mean there won't be any until after the Princess's funeral. Now I think realistically the funeral isn't going to take place for at least a week. So we may end up with just one or two days campaigning right up against the actual date. I really don't see anybody campaigning between now and the funeral.

Monday 1 September 1997

DIARY: The national mourning of the death of Diana continues unabated. Throughout the country people are laying flowers and signing books of condolence. Queues are stretching for literally miles. More details are emerging too. It's an horrendous story and an awful waste. The funeral will be on Saturday so we've got almost a week more of this to go through. It is clearly something which has touched everyone,

though. My cynicism will not buy into this image of the tragic, fairy tale princess who had finally found true love. Dodi al Fahyed was a playboy she'd been seeing for a couple of months. I suspect that too would have ended in tears. Still a tragic, tragic story.

Saturday 6 September 1997

DIARY: A remarkable day dominated by the funeral of Diana, Princess of Wales. It seems incredible to be writing that of the woman whose image has probably been the one I've been most exposed to for my adult life. You could not fail to be stirred and moved by the theatre of it.

Wednesday 10 September 1997

DIARY: Worked today on a look back over the Devolution Referendum campaign. Frankly, it's been lacklustre and uninspiring. Indeed, it's really only happened in the last 100 hours since Princess Diana's funeral. Plenty of television discussion and newspaper analysis, but nothing like the energy of the General Election campaign. That's probably the reason why it hasn't sparked, everyone used their energies in the Election. And the result of the Election meant that the referendum was a foregone conclusion.

THE DEVOLUTION REFERENDUM
Thursday 11 September 1997

DIARY: Referendum Day. The day Scotland decided whether it wanted to have its own devolved Parliament. By the early hours it was clear that it did. I was at the Clackmannanshire count, the smallest mainland authority and expected to provide the fastest result. It did at around 12.42am – a resounding

'Yes', not entirely unexpected. Finally stood down at 1.30am.

Friday 12 September 1997

STV News

After 300 years, the Scottish people are tonight contemplating the prospect of a Parliament sitting once again in the capital city. The result was a landslide for the Yes campaigners with larger majorities on both referendum questions than many had dared to hope. Seventy-four per cent of voters backed a Scottish Parliament. Sixty-three per cent supported tax varying powers. Just over 60 per cent of the electorate went to the polls.

The Prime Minister wasted no time in heading north to celebrate and congratulate. Alex Salmond and Jim Wallace were also buoyant after a campaign which saw unprecedented levels of co-operation between Labour, the SNP and the Liberal Democrats. John MacKay reports...

JM: Edinburgh. The day the settled will of the Scottish people became known. A good day for Scotland and a good day for the United Kingdom, said the Prime Minister Tony Blair. Scotland had shown the way forward. The politicians had trusted the people, he said, and now the people had shown they trusted themselves

TONY BLAIR, Prime Minister:
Scotland does not need to choose and should not be forced to choose between separation and no change. There is a better, modern way forward. That way is Devolution and today Scotland has shown that's what it wants.

DONALD DEWAR, Scottish Secretary:
The people of Scotland have delivered us their trust and we will deliver for them. The settled will of the Scottish people is there for all to see.

JM: Earlier he had shared a platform with the leaders of the other parties. The question now is how long will that unity continue?

ALEX SALMOND, Scottish National Party:
There's a job of opposition as well. The Labour Party in West Central Scotland suffer the same problems as the Tories at Westminster. They've got to be opposed and the SNP have a responsibility of opposition. That's a responsibility we intend to live up to.

JM: The resounding support for tax varying powers is something the Liberal Democrats are keen to make use of.

JIM WALLACE, Scottish Liberal Democrats:
It'll come as no surprise that we still believe there's a need to invest more in education. To do so we'd maybe wish to use a penny of the tax varying powers, but the important thing is there is a choice.

JM: An historic day. For most a euphoric day. Scotland has decided. The people have celebrated. Now the hard work begins.

DONALD DEWAR, Scottish Secretary:
It was a smashing night, a smashing result. It exceeded my expectations and we outperformed the polls. The important thing is that it gives stability, it gives a tremendous

platform for launching the bill. It gives impetus and moral authority and I think it has cut down the room for argument. The principle is established. Tony Blair was particularly anxious that we should have public endorsement. We took that head on and we have got a remarkable response.

JM: We've seen a great deal of harmony on the political platforms. Does this herald a new era of consensus politics perhaps?

DD: I don't know. I'm neither looking for confrontation, but I'd be cautious about consensus. Consensus is where there is agreement and on this there was agreement. What people were agreeing was that they wanted to come in behind the Labour Government policy, a devolved Parliament within the United Kingdom. And what we've got is evidence of the settled will of the Scottish people. They want that stronger voice, they want to remain within the United Kingdom and that's what we're going to deliver.

JM: And finally, are we looking at the man who could be Scotland's First Minister?

DD: (*chortling*) I don't know who'll be Scotland's First Minister. That's a little way away yet. We've got to elect the Parliament first and then they've got to decide who they want. I don't know, there's a lot of speculation, but my job is to complete the unfinished business. I've got the green light. I've got, I think, the moral authority and impetus from last night's tremendous victory and I'm determined to get that show on the road as quickly as I can.

DIARY: **An historic day and a good one to be a journalist. Scotland has voted overwhelmingly for a Scottish Parliament.**

I had about four hours sleep at home before going back to work and through to Edinburgh where it was all happening. First up, a photo call of Scottish party leaders in Edinburgh City Chambers. Then a sit down interview with the Scottish Secretary Donald Dewar, something rather sprung on me because our people obviously had no idea it was happening. Then Tony Blair made a stage managed visit to Parliament Square. I was co-ordinating three cameras, accessing pool material and fixing interviews. All the while I'm trying to report too. Nonetheless, I wouldn't have missed it – a real sense of occasion, of being a witness to history in the making.

Tuesday 16 September 1997

DIARY: **Back on the road with a vengeance today. Story of yet another child abusing priest – this time in Ayrshire. The church had already hidden him away in an abbey and the crimes stretched back to the '70s. In torrential rain I chapped doors in both his former parishes. No great surprise that no one would speak on camera, although I got some good background material to pad out the piece. Ended up being the lead story too.**

Thursday 9 October 1997

STV News

The Prime Minister's office is refusing to become involved in the row over the proposed transfer of a Scottish murderer to the Maze prison in Belfast. Jason Campbell, who slit the throat of a teenager for wearing a Celtic top, could be moved within days. In Northern Ireland itself, the move has been widely condemned. John MacKay reports...

There was strong opposition to this in Northern Ireland, even among Loyalists. They didn't want Campbell holding the same status as other Loyalist prisoners at the Maze. The leading Unionist newspaper, the Belfast News, had the headline, 'No place for the Scottish Butcher' and asked, 'Will someone in the Northern Ireland Office explain what legitimate political cause Campbell was purporting to represent in perpetrating such a heinous act?'

Wednesday 22 October 1997

DIARY: Did a story about a photographic exhibition in Ayr depicting photos of deformed babies in formaldehyde. It was shocking and tasteless. I can understand why science may need to preserve them, but not for public show. It's wrong.

Thursday 23 October 1997

STV News

Seven children were taken home to their parents in Hamilton last night at the start of a controversial curfew introduced by Strathclyde Police. They were all picked up by police foot patrols who took to the streets after dark. John MacKay reports...

DIARY: Police in Hamilton were setting up what to all intents and purposes was an after dark curfew on young children.

Followed a patrol around and it was farcical with the kids regarding the TV cameras as a magnet. The idea of the media facility wasn't good. You have to ask; what are their parents doing?

Monday 3 November 1997

DIARY: The one thing that always spoils your day as a journalist is when you're assigned to a story that involves local government finance. The gist of the story is that Glasgow City Council is being bailed out of a financial crisis by other, better off councils. At a CoSLA news conference this afternoon to discuss all of this. Most of the points being made were cruising at altitude over my head. Then the desk decided it had to be the lead. I'd be surprised if the viewers understood any of it because I didn't.

Friday 14 November 1997

STV News

Primary school children are to be targeted in a national one million pound drugs awareness campaign. *Scotland Against Drugs* are leading the initiative with the backing of some of the country's largest businesses. The aim is to provide a uniform approach to drugs education across the country.

I wonder how much money has been spent on these campaigns and initiatives over the years and to what end?

DIARY: Paul McKinney (*Head of News*) suggested I could be a parliamentary corr in place of Lorraine (*Lorraine Davidson who was leaving*), but I said 'no.'

Much like my time as sports correspondent, I didn't want to be cut off from regular news.

Monday 24th November 1997

STV News

Britain's new drugs Tsar has caused a storm of protest by backing a controversial treatment programme. Keith Hellawell, on his first visit to Scotland since being appointed to lead the fight against drugs, claims the methadone programme works and he wouldn't rule out people staying on it for life. But tonight some drugs campaigners have criticised his comments, saying methadone kills more addicts than it cures.

Sunday 30 November 1997

DIARY: Scottish Review... discussion was on what it meant to be Scottish. SNP parliamentary candidate Nicola Sturgeon was one of the debaters. She is very sharp.

Thursday 11 December 1997

STV News

One of the greats of Scottish football was cremated today. Billy Bremner, the former captain of Scotland and Leeds United died at the weekend, two days before his 55th birthday. The mourners at his funeral read like a who's who of the footballing heroes from the '60s and '70s.

JOE JORDAN, Ex-Leeds United and Scotland:
To find words to describe him as a player is difficult, but as a friend it's easy because he was always there.

GORDON MCQUEEN, Ex-Leeds United and Scotland:
It just shows you what a high regard Billy was held in, not by just Leeds United players, you've got Alex Ferguson, Nobby Stiles, some of the greats in British football.

DIARY: I remember him well as a player and saw him play for Scotland. Later I found him to be a very pleasant man via telephone conversations I had with him when Radio Scotland's sports corr.

1998

SCOTLAND IN WORLD CUP '98

Monday 9 February 1998

STV News

Glasgow was a city where dreams came true today. The World Cup has begun a tour of the countries competing in this summer's tournament. Scotland was first and everyone from Craig Brown to Govan grannies wanted to touch it.

DIARY: **I held the World Cup today. A dream since childhood. The World Cup sponsors Coca Cola are taking the World Cup on tour and today it was in Glasgow at various locations. From Munich, Buenos Aires, Rome and LA to Ruchill! All the hacks and snappers were like kids getting their photos taken with it – me included. Five kilos of gold, but it was the prestige of it that mattered. In truth I don't believe anyone should have been allowed to touch it – it should have been kept behind a glass case so we could see it. Touching it takes away from its mystique and one fun shot we had of an elderly woman carting it along in her shopping trolley made a mockery of it. I don't believe it was the genuine article whatever they say. Still it was nice to dream.**

Friday 13 February 1998

STV News

An elderly man whose body lay undiscovered in his house for at least a month might have been saved, says his former care warden, if her post hadn't been axed by council cuts. Jimmy Mochan's remains were only discovered in his council flat after neighbours complained of the smell.

Tonight there are warnings it could happen again.

DIARY: **The warden service at the flats had been withdrawn last year. I managed to get a hold of his former warden and she said it will happen again and again. We also had her speaking during a demo last year warning of the dangers of cuts to old folk. It gave us a great line and we wiped the floor with the BBC.**

There is no intense rivalry on the ground between STV and BBC. Many of us have been colleagues at different times and with one or two exceptions will help each other out if possible.

Tuesday 24 February 1998

STV News

More than 200,000 houses need to be built in Scotland in the next decade. As we reported last night, the preference is to use brownfield sites within city boundaries. However, as John MacKay reports tonight, in some places that option is not available and pressure continues to be exerted on the green belt.

Shortage of housing, particularly social housing, is another continuing issue.

Sunday 8 March 1998

DIARY: **Scottish Review. The debate – Old and New Labour was lively – stalwart Janey Buchan dismissing new, young Labour (*Blair McDougall*) as 'ambitious wee creeps'. Lively stuff.**

Monday 16 March 1998

DIARY: **Young boy killed after climbing a tree underneath an electricity pylon. Quiet day, so out to try to make something of it, which in the end I did.**

Got some good local vox pops and spoke to a very articulate wee girl who'd been in the boy's class. I made something out of pretty well nothing and that's professionally satisfying. It proves to me one of the lessons of journalism, don't sit at the desk phoning, always go out to the scene – you get a better feel for the story.

Tuesday 17 March 1998

DIARY: Meeting today about the future of our newsroom ie desktop editing etc. I think it's quite exciting, but my concerns are that it's flawed to believe that all journalists will be able to edit well and that jobs will be lost, not so much in the newsroom, but on the technical side. Training is due to begin in the summer.

Desktop editing is now standard practice for reporters, although specialist craft editors are still an essential element in the newsroom.

Thursday 26 March 1998

DIARY: Today was the sort of day that makes you more inspired by your job – with the feeling that maybe you don't appreciate it enough. I went on a helicopter for the first time over to Kintyre. It was one of those hit the ground running and cram in as much as possible. Story involved work done at the Lord Chancellor Lord Irvine's holiday home. He's been getting a bad press recently for the £650,000 refurbishment of his apartment at the House of Lords. He compounded this by comparing its quality to that of cheap wallpaper at a DIY store. I had a bit of fun with it, including getting the local decorator to show the wallpaper available (£3.50 cheapest to £36.50

dearest). None of the local tradesmen, unsurprisingly, would say anything and it was a struggle to get local reaction. Anyway, finally got it in the can and away. Back at base much unnecessary caution from producer, delay getting into editing and not with the fastest editor and I misjudged the time it would take to cut it, so I missed my hit time. That hurt professionally, but it was a good story.

Monday 30 March 1998

DIARY: At a drugs conference this morning, a further strategy for the next few years – basically saying that once drug abusers are stable they need something meaningful to go on to – a job. The ex-addicts I spoke to, though, talked of wanting to work with other addicts. I'm not so sure how that moves them on – they are still part of that culture and it's not a complete break.

Another drugs strategy.

Friday 3 April 1998

DIARY: Diverted from my original job to a housefire in Kilwinning in which two children died. Looks as though the mother was attempting suicide. Tragic, but because there was no real sign of damage – it was all smoke – there was a strange air about the place. There was no great sense of emotion from bystanders.

Monday 20 April 1998

DIARY: Started off with a meeting for the new programme – to be titled *Seven Days*. New team in place, Lorraine Weber being my main cohort. It all sounds quite good – if not hugely changed from the initial outline. Denis Mooney (*Executive Producer*) said,

'This could either be nothing or something very good.' I'm fairly confident it'll be the latter.

Tuesday 28 April 1998

DIARY: Launch of a new sport strategy for Scotland. Set at the new Hampden Park which is rapidly taking shape. It looks very impressive, although they had space for a running track which they decided not to do – short sighted SFA? Surely not. It's good to have such a national stadium, but frankly it should not have been built where it was – inner city stadia are of the 19th century. For the 21st century they should be built out of town with good access – not necessarily a greenfield site, but say somewhere like Ravenscraig. The problem is that would require vision and lack of self-interest.

Hampden had to be closed during and after the Commonwealth Games in 2014 to install and then remove a running track.

Sunday 3 May 1998

DIARY: So the new programme *Seven Days* aired for the first time today – the best day of the year, which won't do much for ratings. The paper review was fine – Dorothy Paul her usual self and David Hayman very good indeed.

The final part was an 11 minute set piece interview with the Scottish Secretary Donald Dewar. It was supposed to be relaxed and conversational and it was. I pushed him on the threat from the SNP and later I thought I should have pushed him more on the personality issue between him and Alex Salmond. I like Dewar. I've always found him pleasant and unpretentious.

Monday 11 May 1998

STV News

A major part of Scotland's build up to the World Cup began today – the filming of the video for the World Cup song – 'Don't Come Home Too Soon' by Del Amitri. The Tartan Army invaded Prestwick Airport to star behind potential 'Mel Gibsons' like Colin Hendry and Gordon Durie.

DIARY: Sent out to Prestwick Airport because 'we think Del Amitri are filming their World Cup video there.' I was thoroughly pissed off, but as sometimes happens it turned out to be fine. Hung around for a while getting shots, vox pops, disappeared to the seafront for lunch and returned to get the players etc. Colin Hendry, the Scottish captain, seemed a decent bloke, as did Justin Currie of Del Amitri.

Big story was the resignation of the Celtic coach Wim Jansen over disputes with Fergus McCann and Jack Brown. Celtic have an incredible knack of creating a fiasco from success. The fans, understandably, are raging.

Wednesday 13 May 1998

DIARY: There is renewed talk of a *Scottish News at Ten*.

A 'Scottish Six' – replacing the network news with a programme produced and presented in Scotland covering international, UK and Scottish news – has been discussed often over the years.

Monday 18 May 1998

STV News

And finally, as we're always told, the Scottish diet is terrible. Deep fried Mars Bars plumbed our culinary depths. There have been attempts to expand our horizons – alligator burgers and frogs legs to name a couple. But as John MacKay reports, something new could be about to save the nation's health…

DIARY: Today it was about a chippy in Dunblane selling ostrich haggis! It's a bit of a gimmick but it seems to be selling, and people who sampled it thought it was good. Ended up at the ostrich farm near Thornhill in Stirlingshire. The farmer took us into their enclosure and they were right up at my face, pecking my watch and shoes. They were young ones – apparently fully grown they can reach up to eight feet high and then I'd have been really uncomfortable. Got a good wee piece out of it and it passed a pleasant afternoon in the country.

Tuesday 9 June 1998

DIARY: The World Cup begins tomorrow with Scotland taking on World Champions Brazil in the opening match. For Scotland it doesn't come much better than that. The build up has reached a crescendo now and it's what everyone is talking about – where are you watching it? What's your prediction? Everyone is up for it. I reported on the options available – pub, house, big tents in Glasgow Green and even churches.

Scotland lost 2–1, but performed creditably. The image of John Collins equalising from the penalty spot is now part of Scottish football's iconography.

Tuesday 23 June 1998

STV News

An entire nation will grind to a halt in about an hour from now when Scotland take on Morocco for a place in the next round of the World Cup finals. Roads have been jammed as people try to get home in time for the game and energy companies are expecting power surges during breaks. And the nation is confident – bookies say punters are pouring money onto a Scotland victory.

Scotland were gubbed 3–0 and went out of the World Cup in France.

Sunday 21 June 1998

DIARY: Folk singer Dick Gaughan was on and he was a smashing bloke. He played for us and was extremely good – the first time we've done something like that.

Sunday 28 June 1998

DIARY: *Seven Days* is a good wee programme. Newspaper reviewers Dorothy-Grace Elder and Michael Kelly were good value. We had a jazz guitarist Martin Taylor, of whom I'd never heard, but is a man of international stature based in Ayrshire. Good guy. I don't like jazz, but I'm in awe of his virtuosity.

Tuesday 4 August 1998

STV News

A mother who killed her twin children by poisoning their juice and then setting fire to their bedroom has been sent to Carstairs. Thirty-one-year-old Janice Miller pleaded guilty to culpable homicide on the grounds of diminished responsibility. The High Court in Glasgow heard she'd tried to take her own life after taking those of her children. On being revived by doctors she told them, 'If I'd known I'd be alive I wouldn't have done it. I told them we'd be together.'

DIARY: Tragic story today following on from a story I covered on the 3 April about a mother who killed her two children, but failed to kill herself. She's to remain in Carstairs. The details were awful, how she crushed tablets (painkillers) into their night time juice. She'd tried it a couple of times before, but couldn't go through with it. Goodness knows what drives someone to kill her children.

Monday 10 August 1998

Reporting on a meeting of Glasgow social workers. There were a lot of politically motivated activists around and much ill feeling towards the media.

DIARY: At one point myself and cameraman Ross Armstrong were in a circle surrounded by people, whom I'm sure were Trots, chanting 'Scum! Scum!' I can't say I felt intimidated, although it was uncomfortable for a few seconds. Dealt with it by ignoring them and getting on with the job.

Thursday 13 August 1998

DIARY: I spent the whole day working on a piece on NHS waiting lists, which seem to have peaked after lengthening consistently despite Labour's pledge to bring them down. We focused on the fact that although nationally down, figures for individual health boards, eg Glasgow, are still up.

NHS waiting lists are another regular for the reporters. They were then and they still are. However, unlike some hardly annuals, people really do care about this.

Wednesday 26 August 1998

DIARY: Paul (*Paul McKinney, Head of News*) told me that he wanted me to

co-anchor the 6.30pm with Shereen now that Viv is going. The slight downside is that he'd want me to do it five nights a week and give up *Seven Days*. My priority has always been to do the 6.30pm and if it came down to a choice there is no doubt what I'd do.

Monday 14 September 1998

DIARY: Celtic's AGM was expected to be a stormy affair and it was, but it never came near the disorder that some suggested might happen. Despite Celtic winning the championship last year, the fans are angry that Wim Jansen left, are unconvinced by Dr Josef Venglos and, also, that there have been no new signings. Reporters were allowed to be present and I have to say that Fergus McCann and Jock Brown (the two targets for the anger, especially the latter) handled it no problem. I was amazed at how poor so many of the questions were.

Wednesday 16 September 1998

DIARY: Tonight's programme was hectic. The first two stories didn't make, the satellite link failed, the autocue packed in, tapes were late starting and another one was spat out mid-story. It was pandemonium. It really was a case of not knowing what's coming next, but that's what we're paid for and the viewers would only have noticed the obvious, eg a tape clock appearing at one point.

Thursday 17 September 1998

DIARY: Last day working exclusively as a reporter. Back on the caretakers' strike – lots of flats damaged because concierges were off duty. Some kids alleged to me that the caretakers had put them up to it, which gave me a strong line.

Monday 21 September 1998

DIARY: For now into the foreseeable future I'll be the main co-anchor on the 6.30pm – presentation will be my priority, not a reporter who fills in.

I had reservations about coming off the road as a reporter, but I enjoyed presentation and the buzz of live broadcasting. I also liked having an overview of the day's events. Before the instant alerts of social media, reporters would often be unaware of what was happening outside of their own story.

Tuesday 22 September 1998

STV News

Trams could soon be reintroduced to Edinburgh after a 40-year absence. A company in the capital is proposing to bring them back as a way of combatting traffic pollution and congestion in the city.

(*Liz Monaghan script*) – running from Haymarket along the length of Princes Street, down Leith Walk to the docks, the company behind the project say commuters would benefit greatly.

This was the start of a long, expensive and tortuous episode for Edinburgh.

Tuesday 20 October 1998

DIARY: Started on Editstar (*desktop editing*) today and it looks fascinating. While I'm dubious about the principle of journalists doing the editing, because it leaves less time for actual reporting – which is what we're supposed to do. However, that concern aside, I think I'll enjoy it – it's closer to my time in radio when you had complete control over the work you did.

Tuesday 24 November 1998

DIARY: So the new age has dawned – we began broadcasting using the new system. And it was a disaster! Camera shots were wrong, over-the-shoulders (*onscreen images*) covered my face, soengs (*taped reports*) were late. It was just an unacceptable mess. Most of it was caused not by human error, but by equipment just not doing what it's supposed to do.

Walking down Sauchiehall Street just after that, some wise guy came up to me with a newspaper held over his face and said, 'A'right big man!' There were a few similar episodes.

Monday 30 November 1998

DIARY: *Scotland Today* fell off the air – the first time that has happened to my knowledge. It was a humiliation, nothing less. We went on-air knowing that there would be a problem with a live link to Fiona Ross, but otherwise no indication of the fiasco to follow. Supposed to start on a two-shot to camera three, but I was punched up on a single to cam one. The story wasn't on autocue either. Fiona couldn't hear us properly, but did manage to cue her own package. Then a two-way with her failed – she didn't hear. Next package had a sound problem, as did the next and other pieces seemed to have disappeared altogether. The gallery was pandemonium, but there's no director anymore so no one was really telling us what to do. All I could hear was swearing and 'We're going to crash off air!' said repeatedly. All the while Shereen and I are having to apologise for the problems – often with the cameras actually shifting while we were in shot. Had a breathing space in sport, most of which was on tape, which clarified the decision that we were going to have to come off. Had a final headline sequence which was also a fiasco and then I had to fill for a minute or so, apologising for the chaos and saying we'd fallen below our 'high standards'. In the great scheme of things it's not important, but it was professionally humiliating. There was a short meeting afterwards, but everyone too shattered to say much.

As fate would have it, we were wearing sprigs of lucky white heather because it was St Andrew's Day. To fill the time left, our continuity had put on an excerpt of a classic STV series 'Edge of the Land', which featured stunning views of Scotland's coastline from the air. The phones were lighting up as the shattered team returned to the newsroom. We answered them with some trepidation, apologies at the ready. So many of the calls, however, were to say that 'Edge of the Land' was brilliant.

Thursday 3 December 1998

DIARY: I presented the inevitable fiasco in the 11.00am bulletin and was so pissed off that I went for a walk (soengs froze etc, stills (*photos*) flashed up at the wrong time). An elderly woman stopped me (turns out her name was MacKay too and recently widowed and she ended up kissing my hand). She told me she'd be thinking of me.

Thursday 10 December 1998

DIARY: The BBC Governors today ruled, mistakenly, that there could be no Scottish *Six O'Clock News* on the Beeb. I have long been convinced of the need

for such a thing with the Scottish Parliament on the horizon. The London news is often irrelevant here. The focus has been on the BBC as the public broadcaster, but in a classic BBC fudge, Scotland is to be given an extra £10 million to cover the Holyrood Parliament. There is also a persuasive argument that our strength is our local identity and it may be diluted by doing international, UK and local stuff. Interesting times.

Wednesday 23 December 1998

DIARY: During tonight's 6.30pm, David Tanner mentioned Rangers would be signing new goalie Stefan Klos tomorrow and I made the crack about when we can expect to hear about his knee injury (*which seems to affect every Rangers signing*). Inevitably it lit up the phone lines with one caller calling me a 'snidey Fenian bastard'. Funny if it wasn't so sad.

1999

Friday 15 January 1999

DIARY: I had to take on a pre-arranged set piece interview with Cardinal Thomas Winning – Scotland's leading Roman Catholic (RC). He's marking 50 years as a priest with a special mass on Sunday. Interview was good – he spoke of a permissive society that has 'gone sick' and the objective of 'one church' in Scotland in the next 50 years. He stands for something and does so unwaveringly. As a man he's pleasant enough, but you would never get too close to him.

TONY BLAIR ON POVERTY AND SOCIAL EXCLUSION

Friday 5 February 1999

DIARY: I interviewed the Prime Minister today – the first time I've done so. In this job you soon lose the thrill of meeting famous people, but there's no doubt that meeting the Prime Minister had more impact than most. He met me, shook my hand, did the interview, but there was no chit-chat. He sat on a bed to pose for a photograph for a snapper and cracked a joke about checking what was behind him, but I could never say there was a glimpse of the real man. He certainly did not have any sort of aura, but he's good at what he does. He was up here to do some 'Nat bashing' but *Seven Days* got a last minute chance to speak to him and asked me to interview him, specifically on poverty and social exclusion.

TONY BLAIR, Prime Minister: The real purpose of the new social exclusion unit is to bring together the various bits of Government so that money for the New Deal and for young people to get jobs, the extra money on housing and their education and health all comes together, so that we're trying to revitalise a whole area. But, of course, it takes a lot of time because we're dealing with some very deep-seated, deep-rooted problems.

JM: The Scottish National Party is making much of social exclusion. You're talking about time. There are 90 days until the elections to the Scottish Parliament. Are you concerned this is an area where the SNP can make inroads?

TB: The only party that has a policy for youth unemployment is us. The New Deal is the biggest youth unemployment scheme there's ever been. And the costs of Independence in terms of taxes and jobs and industry will far outweigh anything they can put into issues like social exclusion, so people have got a choice about this. If you're going to put that extra money into schools and hospitals then that's one thing, but if Scotland really did decide that it wanted to go independent, the costs of Independence would far outweigh any of these investments.

JM: Prime Minister, thank you.

Thursday 11 February 1999

DIARY: Doing some promos for the programme next week with a view to our moving time to 6.00pm in March. The theme is 'First in Scotland' because we'll now be on ahead of Rep Scot.

Monday 1 March 1999

DIARY: 1999 is the year everyone is ignoring and it's rattling by quickly.

Monday 8 March 1999

DIARY: So we went on at the earlier time tonight – 6.00pm, with a little tinkering to the format of the show. It was a good programme – very pacy and completely clean. We were helped by having a good lead – the sacking of SFA chief executive Jim Farry. The half hour less didn't make much difference with people making their hit times (*deadline*).

Friday 12 March 1999

DIARY: Woke up to hear that the SNP had decided to forego the penny income tax cut proposed by the Chancellor this week ie, it'll cost more to stay in Scotland than it would in England (or at least that's how it's being played). As soon as I heard it I thought that's the Scottish Parliament election campaign over already.

Thursday 19 March 1999

STV News

The two men charged with the Lockerbie Bombing will be handed over for trial within three weeks. The Libyan leader Colonel Gaddafi agreed to the surrender of the two after talks with the South African President Nelson Mandela. He gave the Libyans guarantees about the men's future and they'll now be handed over to the United Nations.

Thursday 22 April 1999

DIARY: Polls showing the SNP vote in free fall. Much is being made of this election failing to come to life and I think that is true.

Friday 23 April 1999

DIARY: There was a fiasco over the appearance of SNP Leader Alex Salmond on our phone-in. Main problem was his shirt which was blue and keying against our blue background. I had to make the dash to the changing room to grab a selection of shirts. I then had to stand in a small room with an understandably irate Salmond trying to calm him down as he stripped off his shirt and tried on other ones. He was fuming.

SCOTTISH PARLIAMENT ELECTIONS 1999

Wednesday 5 May 1999

DIARY: A final frantic day of campaigning. Asked to go out to do what was effectively a public information piece on the ballot papers and what to do with them. Tomorrow is an historic day for Scotland and yet there is no sense of that.

Thursday 6 May 1999

DIARY: The historic day dawns. Scots vote for their own Parliament for the first time in nearly 300 years; ordinary Scots for the first time ever. Yet, there has been no sense of history either in the build-up or today. I was at the Glasgow SECC. The big question was Glasgow Govan – could the SNP take it from Labour (*they couldn't*). Also, could Tommy Sheridan (*Scottish Socialist*) get in under the list system? Yes he did.

Frustrating night for me because of communications problems; they couldn't pick us up at Glasgow for the first hour and a half, so all my preparation work was a waste of time.

Got Gordon Jackson, Govan winner, first and Tommy Sheridan.

Friday 7 May 1999

STV News – live from Edinburgh with Shereen Nanjiani

Good evening. The first Scottish Government for 300 years will be a Labour–Liberal Democrat coalition after the Scottish people refused to give any party enough seats to run the country on their own. Labour will be the single largest party in the new parliament by some distance. With the final results now in, Labour have won 56 seats, their likely coalition partners, the Lib Dems, have won 17. The Conservatives won no first-past-the-post seats, but picked up 18 top-up seats. And the SNP become the official opposition with 35 seats. Independent Denis Canavan, Socialist leader Tommy Sheridan and Britain's first Green Party parliamentarian, Robin Harper, make up the 129 member parliament.

JOHN MACKAY: We're joined now by the leader of the SNP and now the leader of the official opposition in the new parliament, Alex Salmond. Congratulations on becoming a member of the new parliament.

ALEX SALMOND, Leader, SNP: Thank you very much.

JM: Are you disappointed you didn't make the 40 threshold?

AS: Well that's your threshold. I mean this is the biggest parliamentary group in the SNP's history and the largest number of parliamentarians we've ever had before is 11. Now

we're going to have 35 in this new parliament; that's tremendously exciting. We're going to be a real opposition for Scotland's parliament and that role as a vibrant, innovative opposition is in many way just as important as the administration.

JM: You didn't make the breakthrough in the Central Belt that perhaps you would have hoped for, particularly in places like Glasgow Govan. That must surely be a disappointment?

AS: We had huge swings, I mean we had a 16 per cent swing in Glasgow Baillieston for example and right across Central Scotland, in areas where we used to be a mile behind Labour, we're breathing down their necks.

DIARY: A new day dawns on a new Scotland. So those of us involved would like to portray it. The truth is that there seems to be a remarkable indifference. The turnout was about 58 per cent – so not far off half the population didn't bother. Left the SECC at 5.30am. I'd made much of the fact that the programme had to come from Edinburgh, so Shereen and I travelled there. By the end of the programme Edinburgh Castle was shrouded in mist. Alex Salmond seemed relatively okay and was certainly not bowing to suggestions that by failing to get what some regarded as a 40-seat threshold he would quit. Labour will be the dominant party, but they don't have an overall majority, so a Lib–Lab pact is likely. There has been much talk of a new style of politics. My suspicion is that it'll mirror Westminster. Give it time.

Monday 10 May 1999

DIARY: The Labour and Lib Dems have started discussions on a possible coalition, but Labour have been acting shamelessly. In this promised era of new politics, they have been at their usual cloak and dagger routine and Donald Dewar is coming over all powerful and presidential, doing minimal talking in front of the cameras. Changed days.

Wednesday 12 May 1999

DIARY: With the words, 'The Scottish Parliament, adjourned on the 25th day of March 1707, is hereby reconvened,' the Scottish Parliament became a reality. I have to say that for the first time during the whole process since the referendum, I felt that I was witnessing history being made. There was a definite sense of occasion. The whole tone coming through was of a different, more relaxed Parliament, less constrained by tradition.

DONALD DEWAR BECOMES SCOTLAND'S FIRST MINISTER

Thursday 13 May 1999

STV News

Donald Dewar is Scotland's First Minister. He was finally voted into the post at a special session of the Edinburgh Parliament this afternoon. Within the last few minutes the Labour group in the Parliament has ratified a coalition deal with the Liberal Democrats.

DONALD DEWAR, First Minister: Scotland's Parliament is no longer a political pamphlet, a campaign trail, a waving flag. It is here. It is real.

Donald Dewar's first TV interview as First Minister

JM: We're joined live from Edinburgh by Scotland's First Minister Donald Dewar. First of all, congratulations on your appointment.

DONALD DEWAR, First Minister: Thank you very much indeed. I'm obviously very thrilled and very conscious of the responsibilities.

JM: You have come from a meeting where the Labour group has ratified the coalition deal. Can you tell us what the details are?

DD: No. I'm waiting, of course, for the outcome of the other meeting, which is with the Liberal Democrats. What I can say is that the essence of any good agreement is that both sides are satisfied with it and both sides see advantages, not just for themselves, but for good government in Scotland. It gives stability, it means we'll have an administration that can deliver priorities that Scotland voted for.

JM: Can you understand why people might see it as a stitch up? They may see that this is something agreed in a back room and this is not the spirit of the new politics.

DD: All I can say to you is that there were long and detailed negotiations in which a large number of Liberal Democrats took part and we reached an agreement which both of us felt we could recommend to our parliamentary groups. And if you're talking about a willingness to look beyond narrow party bands in order to reach agreements that are in the interests of the people of Scotland, I would have thought there would be a widespread welcome for this flexibility and for the ability to put together two programmes to get the best possible deal for Scotland.

DIARY: Apart from congratulating him, the main issue was the coalition deal agreed between Labour and the Lib Dems. He was standing outside the Parliament hearing me on an ear-piece, so it would have been unfair to keep interrupting him, meaning that maybe it wasn't as hard an interview as I'd have liked.

Friday 14 May 1999

DIARY: A deal between Labour and the Lib Dems to form a coalition government. The Lib Dems will be undermined by negotiating on their insistence on the abolition of tuition fees. 'Not negotiable,' they said. They'll be slaughtered for this and rightly so.

Friday 28 May 1999

DIARY: The programme went fine, although we had a light-hearted report on men crying, showing their true emotion. I, obviously jokingly, said 'bunch of sissies'. The phones were ringing by the time I got down to the newsroom. I think some people just sit waiting to be offended.

This has become even more apparent since the rise of social media. There are people who wait trembling in anticipation of being offended. This goes hand in hand with demands for apologies.

Monday 31 May 1999

DIARY: Very, very sad news this morning of the death of my former BBC colleague Kenny Macintyre. He died yesterday evening having suffered a heart attack while out running. His tie was still on his desk. Kenny was something of a professional father figure. He was also, unquestionably, the best reporter I've ever worked with. There were tributes from the Prime Minister, the First Minister etc which said something about the standing of the man. It is remarkable how many people regarded him as a confidant – me included. I'll miss him.

Kenny Macintyre was a phenomenon. He was Radio Scotland's political correspondent and his contacts were extraordinary. It seemed that absolutely anyone would take his calls. He worked all the hours of the week and would go home to Mull at the weekend. His drive to and from the ferry in Oban defied the basic laws of distance and time, but he always made it. There are more anecdotes about Kenny Macintyre than anyone else I've ever known and all of us who knew him will have one of our own. His death at 54 was a shock.

OPENING OF SCOTTISH PARLIAMENT

The Queen's address to the Scottish Parliament:

It is our solemn duty in this chamber with the eyes of the country upon us to mark the point when this new Parliament assumes its full powers in the service of the Scottish people. It is a moment, rare in the life of any nation, when we step across the threshold of a new constitutional age.

Thursday 1 July 1999

STV News – live from Edinburgh Castle with Shereen Nanjiani

1 July 1999. The day Edinburgh was able to call itself a capital again. A Scottish Parliament is opened after 300 years.

Good evening and welcome to Edinburgh. You join us from the castle, high above the city which today has truly witnessed history in the making.

We were told: There shall be a Scottish Parliament. Now there IS a Scottish Parliament. Opened by the Queen in a ceremony that mixed all the grandeur of a state occasion.

An emotional day too. The expectations are high. More than anyone else, the man charged with making a success of this parliament is the First Minister Donald Dewar. I spoke to him and asked him for reflections on the day...

DONALD DEWAR, First Minister: I thought it was just a happy day. Everyone was enjoying themselves. There was a tremendous buzz, a real atmosphere. And the most outstanding heroes of the day was the crowd. They were there in enormous numbers, people from all over Scotland. It wasn't just Edinburgh, I met people from all different parts of Scotland and there was a genuine warmth and enthusiasm which I just found enormously encouraging.

JM: There has been criticism of the early days of the Parliament, MSPs working out salaries, working out hours. You've said the reason for that was the Parliament didn't have the powers to do anything more. It now does have, so what can we expect to see?

DD: Well obviously there is a legislative programme we've got to get underway. We've got to start the

hearings and the pre-legislative scrutiny, but, you know, the whole point of the six weeks period was to get all these housekeeping matters behind us. But we also looked at, for example, freedom of information, very important, we also looked at tuition fees and higher education. We had an important statement about the way we're going to handle the Education Bill. Macintosh, which is going to affect really radically our whole local government system, was previewed and we're going to have some announcements tomorrow. There's a lot been happening. I mean, at the end of the day, the power of the press is to set the agenda. Now that has got to be a selective process, but the fact that they highlight certain things doesn't mean that there is not a lot of other things going on.

JM: The Queen said in her speech that it was your obligation to set lasting standards. Is this Parliament capable of that?

DD: Well they are fallible human beings like everyone else and they're open to the pressures of public opinion. What we are doing is that we are setting high standards and we're setting out to try and hold to them.

JM: Finally Mr Dewar, is this it, or do you think there is maybe a sense that what we've seen today might push the Scottish people to take that extra step towards Independence?

DD: There is, I think, always an attraction about simple solutions, but the trouble about simple solutions is they usually leave the problems behind them and I think that what we've got to do is make sure that government serves Scotland, listens to Scotland and deals with the real priorities of Scotland. And if we do that I think we can work effectively and happily and democratically within the partnership which is our United Kingdom. But that's a continuing argument. Let's get on in the meantime with actually dealing with the issues that are central to the everyday lives of the people in Scotland.

JM: First Minister, thank you very much.

DIARY: Another of this year's historical days – the official opening of the Scottish Parliament by the Queen and the formal handover of powers from Westminster. Watched the ceremony on TV, but what really made it special for me was when Concorde and nine Red Arrows staged a fly past over Edinburgh Castle. Less than ten minutes later in the west I was in the car with my young son when Concorde and the Red Arrows flew low directly over us. It was a wonderful moment. I must have been quite excited because after they passed he asked, 'Why were you shouting, Daddy?' My youngest in his nursery said he'd heard a 'big noise.'

We did the programme from the western defences of the Castle and a wonderful location it was too, if a bit breezy. Interviewed Donald Dewar and told him, for what it was worth, that his speech hit the mark.

Friday 30 July 1999
DIARY: *Tall Ships Race* at Greenock.

The weather was good, probably too good because there wasn't enough wind for the ships to use their sails which would have been very impressive. Still, it was impressive enough.

Friday 3 September 1999
STV News – live from Glasgow Airport
Eight people are dead and three are seriously injured in a plane crash near Glasgow Airport. The Cessna light aircraft was on an internal flight to Aberdeen when it appears to have lost power and come down in some farmland. The plane, operated by Edinburgh Air Charter, had taken off from Glasgow Airport at 12.25pm. It made a normal ascent, but crashed in flames less than twelve minutes later at 12.37pm. The plane was carrying air crew from the Airtours company and full investigation into the tragedy is due to begin later this evening.

A Fatal Accident Inquiry concluded that an engine had malfunctioned and the pilot had closed the wrong engine, his judgement possibly hampered by the fact that a bang had been heard from the good engine soon after take-off.

SCOTLAND V ENGLAND
EUROPEAN CHAMPIONSHIP
QUALIFIERS
Friday 12 November 1999
STV News – live from Hampden with Jane Lewis
Good evening from Hampden. In just under 20 hours the game we've all been waiting for will be under way. The atmosphere is already building here as the Scots get set to face the Auld Enemy for the first time in three

years. In the next half-hour we'll have all the team news. We'll hear from players past and present and talk to the fans with tickets and those without.

DIARY: I've been watching how people have been getting wound up for the match and I can't. I've been cutting packages of nostalgia all week, including the memorable '77 win at Wembley, when I remember being so excited, and the '74 win at Hampden, which I attended. Great wallowing in it, but no expectation of achieving anything like it tomorrow. If we get a draw to make a game of it at Wembley that's all we can ask.

Scotland lost 2–0.

Wednesday 17 November 1999

STV News – live from Wembley with Kirstin Gove

Good evening. In two hours time Scotland will take to this field of dreams, in the hope of overcoming the 2–0 deficit from Saturday's first match.

Here at Wembley the waiting is almost over. In the words of our national side's captain and talisman, Colin Hendry, Scotland need a ridiculously impressive performance to beat the English. If they're looking for inspiration for their mission impossible, we'll leave you tonight with some of the images from past glories and of the Tartan Army gathering in hope of a win against all the odds. From all of us here, good night and good luck Scotland.

DIARY: Scotland beat England 1–0 at Wembley. We still go out over two legs,
but we won the last international to be played at the old Wembley and I was there, although it was a close thing. Wembley was odd in that, trackside, the legendary large pitch wasn't so big, the tunnel wasn't so long and the terraces not so impressive, but later looking down from high up in the Olympic Gallery there was a sense of grandeur – it was greater than the sum of its parts. Scotland thoroughly deserved their win through a Don Hutchinson goal and almost got the vital second, minutes from the end. Another heroic failure.

We were live behind the goal immediately in front of the tunnel and it all went to plan. We hung around after that but it became quickly clear that we were going to get moved and any hope of hanging around trackside was not on (there had been an oversight in getting us tickets to see the actual game). Ended up spending an hour going from pillar to post, finally blagging our way into the ITV area. Jane, Kirstin and I sitting amongst English fans and barely able to contain ourselves. Grabbed vox pops afterwards, eventually back to hotel by 11.30pm and a few drinks. Good end to what I will reflect on as a memorable day.

Scotland came so close to getting the second goal that would have extended the tie, when a Christian Dailly header was wonderfully saved by David Seaman in the last ten minutes.

Monday 22 November 1999

DIARY: Annoyed with myself when I neglected to move a script that had been read and also drifted away. Next thing I found myself on camera, ignoring the autocue and reading from script, exactly what had been read before. I apologised and moved on, but it was sloppy.

Wednesday 22 December 1999

DIARY: Straight out to Lanarkshire on a tragic story. A family of four killed when their home was ripped apart by a gas explosion in the middle of the night. They had no chance. These tragic stories always seem to happen at this time of year. When I got there it was a shock to see how the house was literally flattened to rubble. A terrible tragedy.

2000

Monday 17 January 2000

DIARY: Did an on-the-hoof interview with Cardinal Thomas Winning about the ongoing Section 28 row. It was a strong interview with references to 'the perversion' of homosexuality. Led tonight's programme.

I didn't flag this up to the newsdesk as anything significant when I returned with the interview because, although it was hard hitting, I thought Cardinal Winning had said the same thing before. Apparently not in these words.

STV News

The leader of Scotland's Roman Catholics is tonight under fire for speaking out against what he called 'the perversion of homosexuality'. Cardinal Winning made his controversial comments as he weighed into the debate over the proposed scrapping of Section 28. That's the legislation which prohibits local authorities from promoting the acceptability of homosexuality. The Cardinal told *Scotland Today* that the Scottish Executive should concentrate its efforts on issues of greater importance.

CARDINAL THOMAS WINNING: 'The Catholic Church doesn't have any concern about people who are homosexual. It's the homosexual acts that we object to very much. I hesitate to use the word perversion, but let's face up to the truth of this situation, that's what it is. Are we now being asked to say what was wrong before is now right and they can go ahead and do it?'

TIM HOPKINS, Equality Network: 'I'm appalled by it. Cardinal Winning seems to be calling for a return to the old days when gay people were treated like burglars and locked up. It's appalling prejudice and I think that most people in Scotland will feel the same way.'

WENDY ALEXANDER, Communities Minister:
I think we're hoping that in the new Scotland we'll perhaps understand a little more and condemn a little less. The First Minister earlier today talked about a tolerance for a new century and for a new Scotland. I think that's the spirit of the Executive's proposals.

FIONA ROSS, Political Correspondent: Public opinion is difficult to judge. A survey of Scottish Television viewers last week showed that 82 per cent want Section 28 to stay. Brian Souter (*the businessman who funded a private referendum on the issue and characterised his campaign with the quote, 'We didnae vote for it and we're no' havin' it.'*) may have touched a nerve. This was hailed as a great reforming, liberal measure heralding the dawn of a new Scotland. But it may just be that Scotland isn't quite as tolerant as some people would like to think.

Friday 25 February 2000

DIARY: Last programme under the old, blue 'chromakey' system. It will be no loss to see it go. It was a cold, dated set. The new set looks to be a significant improvement.

Thursday 16 March 2000

DIARY: Volunteered to go with a camera to film the departure of Romanian 'economic' refugees from houses in Sighthill. They've been begging and apparently shouldn't have been sent here in the first place. Got some good footage out of it and ended up with the lead piece. The women especially dressed so differently and gold teeth are prominent. I was struck, though, by the smell from them and their belongings – it's a smell I've noticed in some houses in Glasgow – it's the smell of poverty; musty and stale.

Thursday 11 May 2000

DIARY: All became hectic just before we went on-air after a fairly routine day. The Government announced what is effectively a climb-down on their plans to repeal the anti-homosexual Section 28. I had a good interview with Education Minister Sam Galbraith, a wily politician, in which it was apparent that he couldn't admit the obvious.

STV News

A dramatic turn of events after months of campaigning between pro and anti clause campaigners. The Government saying that they won't move on the issue. Well to explain now why they have, we're joined by the Education Minister Sam Galbraith. Mr Galbraith, nothing but a climbdown surely?

SAM GALBRAITH, Education Minister: Och now now, you shouldn't use that language. What we've done is, my Education Committee asked me to consider this question of some underpinning statutory guidance.

We've been listening to the mums and dads and we've responded to that and that's what we've done today.

JM: Why didn't you listen to them months ago when they were all saying this?

SG: We've been listening to them for some time, so we have.

JM: So why did it take you so long to react?

SG: These are matters that need careful consideration. I think we've done the right thing, we have been listening to the mums and dads and we've responded to them. This is a listening government and we've done the right thing by them.

Section 28 (or Clause 28 or Section 2a as it was variously known) was repealed by a vote in the Scottish Parliament.

Wednesday 28 June 2000

DIARY: Through to Edinburgh for the first anniversary of the Parliament (general opinion is that it could do more and has squandered time on trivial issues like Section 28). It gave me an idea of the geography of the temporary Parliament, where our offices are and, of course, the now very familiar black and white corridor.

The Scottish Parliament was based in the Church of Scotland's General Assembly Hall on The Mound in Edinburgh for the first four years of its existence. Interviews with politicians and political reporters were conducted in a corridor in the main entrance floored with black and white tiles – the black and white corridor.

Wednesday 2 August 2000

DIARY: A surprise announcement that the Chancellor Gordon Brown is marrying in Fife tomorrow. I pulled together a 50' piece, but five minutes before going on-air the studio reported that there was a serious sound problem. It was perfectly good on the computer, but there was a technical fault between there and the server. Anyway, I got them to play it mute while I read my script live. Pleased to pull it off – professional satisfaction.

Wednesday 6 September 2000

DIARY: Sitting in on my first debate at the Scottish Parliament. Back into the chamber to watch the beginning of a debate on education – the political subject of the moment because of the exams fiasco. No consensus politics here – very much in the Westminster yah-boo style. Also like Westminster, the chamber is much smaller than you'd expect.

FUEL STRIKE

Tuesday 12 September 2000

STV News

Scotland is facing the prospect of paralysis tonight as the fuel crisis hits home. More than half of the country's petrol stations closed today leaving many areas without supply. But significantly, public support still seems to be with the protestors, who have again brought chaos to the streets.

Hauliers and farmers were campaigning about the high taxation of fuel. The hauliers took convoys of hundreds into Edinburgh and Aberdeen, and crawled slowly through the streets to bring them to a halt. An STV phone poll showed 96 per cent backing for the truckers. At the time unleaded petrol was typically around

79 pence per litre and diesel was 81 pence per litre.

VOX POPS: I support the guys who are blockading. The price of petrol is outrageous.

The French have got it right, haven't they? (*French truckers had been successful in a similar campaign*) That's what's wrong here, we all give in too easily.

TONY BLAIR, Prime Minister: I do not in any way minimise the plight of some of the hauliers and farmers who are genuinely suffering, but the way to help them is not to harm the rest of the country. I regret deeply the inconvenience and difficulty caused to the public, but the consequences of giving in to this type of blockade would be infinitely worse. For that reason let me assure the public that the action required to get the situation back to normal will be taken. It will take some time to get everything back working as it should be, but it will be done.'

TRUCKERS: It cripples us standing at the side of the road, but it's at the stage that we've got to stand up and say, right we've got to do something. Everybody has to stand up and do something.

This Government will have to listen. That's all we're asking for a reduction in the fuel cost.'

DIARY: Fuel crisis is overwhelming everything. Some people are struggling with most petrol stations closed. Everyone is talking about it. Our programme tonight was almost entirely given over to it. It's been the first real test of Tony Blair's government.

Wednesday 13 September 2000

DIARY: More fuel crisis – tankers not leaving refineries and now real fears of food shortages. What is so interesting is that people still widely support the protestors and that must be worrying for the Government. Tony Blair is coming out of it all very badly – the first time he's really been getting an all-round kicking. It seems that the Government is too arrogant. We've been performing well and the audience have been turning to us in huge numbers.

The blockades ended because the protestors did not want to lose public support, which might have happened if warnings about threats to essential services became a reality. They gave the Government a 60-day deadline to reduce fuel duty. The Chancellor Gordon Brown made some concessions in his pre-budget report in November.

FIRST MINISTER DONALD DEWAR'S DEATH

Tuesday 10 October 2000
First news approx 5.45pm

PA SNAP: Scottish First Minister Donald Dewar has been taken to Edinburgh Royal Infirmary after a fall, a spokesman said tonight.

PA SNAP: Scottish First Minister Donald Dewar is 'seriously ill', a spokesman said tonight.

PA: Scottish First Minister Donald Dewar has died at Edinburgh's Western General Hospital, medical staff said.

Wednesday 11 October 2000

STV News

JOHN: The First Minister is dead.

SHEREEN: Tonight, Scotland is a nation in mourning.

JOHN: The man regarded as the Father of the Nation passed away shortly after midday at Edinburgh's Western General Hospital, where he was being treated after suffering a brain haemorrhage.

SHEREEN: In this special edition of Scotland Today, we'll be paying tribute to Donald Dewar and assessing the legacy of the man who did more than anyone to make the dream of a Scottish Parliament a reality.

DIARY: We carried a report in last night's programme saying he had been taken to hospital as a precaution following a fall. That developed with a brain haemorrhage and, although not officially declared dead until 12.18pm today, they knew last night there was no hope.

It dominated today of course and we put out a good programme tonight, including tributes. It wasn't a frantic day because it was well planned and everything came together well. What was cause for more thought was getting the tone right.

His death was sudden and unexpected (despite open heart surgery earlier this year) and it leaves a gaping hole in Scottish politics with no one capable of filling his shoes. He had always pursued a Scottish Parliament and it is fitting that he saw it happen.

One can get carried away on sentiment – he was a ditherer, the first year of the Parliament has been embroiled unnecessarily on issues like Section 28 etc – but his public persona was of a decent man who could not fully come to terms with the gloss of modern politics. For the little I know of him, I liked him. He had a sense of humour and that distinctive 'umm aah' delivery.

Bernard Ponsonby, our reporter, said that in a hundred years when the history of this time in Scotland is written, Donald Dewar's name will stand out. I think that is true.

Wednesday 18 October 2000

STV News

A man you could trust. A man of vision and integrity. Gordon Brown summed up the feelings of the country this afternoon as Scotland said farewell to its First Minister. The funeral service was a fitting tribute to the man who devoted his life to the ideals of equality and social justice. The most powerful in the land were there, including most of the cabinet and the Prince of Wales. But there were no divisions inside Glasgow's great Cathedral. Civic leaders sat beside shop workers and pensioners – all united in grief for the nation's lost leader.

GORDON BROWN, Chancellor: Donald Dewar would have been the last to acknowledge the true scale of his achievement. But the friend we lost only seven days ago was one of only a handful of people across the centuries of whom it could be said, he founded a new Parliament. What was special about Donald as a politician was that he consistently and tirelessly pushed the logic of his decency and worked for a more just and equal society.

VOX POPS: I just came because I just felt... I felt it was appropriate to come.

I respected the man. He was all for Scotland and so am I.

He was a great leader of the Scots. One of the true political heroes of the time. He's going to be missed a lot.

FIONA ROSS, STV political correspondent and close friend of Donald Dewar:
Donald wasn't interested in clothes, he wasn't interested in how he looked, he walked about looking like a complete tip. It doesn't matter what you tried to do about it. I tried bullying, I tried threats, intimidation. None of it worked. D'you know I bought him a tie once? He used it to wipe the windscreen of his car...
Donald Dewar was many things to many people. He was a proud father, he was loyal to his party, he was loyal to his country. He was a true Scot. He loved the culture, the people, the history. Sadly, he's now part of Scotland's history.

DIARY: The funeral of First Minister Donald Dewar, the closest Scotland has had, or will have, to a 'State' funeral for many a year. We had built a proper studio in Cathedral Square looking onto the Cathedral doors. Our special programme began at 2.00pm and almost immediately I had to talk over the arrival of the Prime Minister,

describing it live. The great and the good were all there and perhaps the best part of it all was the applause from the watching crowd as Donald Dewar's cortege drove through the city. The playing of 'A Man's A Man' on the fiddle at the end was very moving.

HENRY MCLEISH BECOMES FIRST MINISTER
Henry McLeish was elected by an internal vote of the Scottish Labour Party to become the second First Minister.

Friday 20 October 2000
STV News
HENRY MCLEISH, speech to Labour Party:
Colleagues it's a very, very, very great privilege. Thanks for the honour. Let me say, I won't let you down.

He was formally appointed by the Scottish Parliament on Thursday 26 October.

Thursday 26 October 2000
STV News
HENRY MCLEISH, First Minister:
I will speak up for Scotland on every occasion, for every part of Scotland and for everyone in this country.

Henry McLeish in interview with Shereen Nanjiani
It was a historic moment, it was a moment of high emotion for me. A great honour. Obviously great challenges and opportunities ahead and I very much welcome that. Nevertheless, today has been a consuming day and I was very, very proud indeed.

Friday 27 October 2000

STV News

Henry McLeish was officially installed as Scotland's new First Minister this afternoon. The Queen handed Mr McLeish a Royal Warrant of Appointment at Holyrood Palace in Edinburgh. He then took a series of oaths confirming his appointment at the Court of Session.

Friday 1 December 2000

DIARY: Today is World AIDS Day and the lunchtime team wore AIDS ribbons. No other station did. I phoned in to say that I would not be wearing one and if it came to a confrontation they'd be better to get someone else to do the programme. Anyway, they accepted it and I didn't wear one – indeed none of us did. My argument was one of consistency – we don't wear them for breast cancer or the multitude of other deserving conditions.

FIRST MINISTER IN ROME TO MEET THE POPE

Sunday 3 December 2000

DIARY: Tonight I'm in Rome which was dark by the time we got there. A hire car had been arranged for us, which we'd both been dubious about – justifiably as it turned out. We got into Rome easily, but we had two maps – one showing us how to get into Rome, the other a more detailed one of where our hotel was, but neither showed how they linked. It took us three hours until we finally chanced upon the street we were looking for, having previously driven so far north we were into the red light district and then suburbs. A most frustrating evening. Even asked for directions in 'MacKay's' Scottish theme pub, but they couldn't help.

We could not for the life of us find our hotel. When I saw 'MacKay's Pub' my spirits soared, but quickly sagged. They didn't know where the hotel was. When I shared my enthusiasm about having the same name as the bar, they could not have cared less. Later as our spirits flagged further, I told Fraser Cleland – the cameraman with me – that we would stop at the very next person we saw. Sure enough we saw a figure under a street light. As we coasted towards her, I was struck by her pose and the shortness of her skirt. It took a moment for my sluggish brain to interpret these signals. There followed frantic exhortations to Fraser to 'go on, go on!' I don't think the '... asking for directions' defence would have worked.

Monday 4 December 2000

DIARY: Today could not have gone any better, especially given our total lack of planning. The Vatican is beautiful. Apparently Rome has been cleaned up significantly for this Millennium year. My worry was getting in to get shots of the First Minister actually meeting the Pope. We had two breaks – first a Scottish Television religious programme, *Eikon*, was being filmed by an independent production company who'd arranged passes some time ago. I knew some of them and had a promise that I could get whatever they shot. However, my former colleague Ronnie Convery was there with Cardinal Winning (he's his PR man) and his ability to speak Italian smoothed some corners. We chanced our arm and managed to blag our way right into the Vatican. We were in a gallery in the hall where the audience was taking place and I suspect that if Fraser had worn a tie we'd have got onto the dais itself. Anyway, with our own camera and *Eikon*'s close-ups I had every shot I needed. At the end, the Scottish contingent sang 'Flower of Scotland' which gave me my closing line for my piece to camera. I'd already organised to meet Henry McLeish and Cardinal Winning outside. It really worked wonderfully well. We fed from APTV and it was all smooth.

It was fascinating being so close to the Pope. He's old – 80 now and clearly failing – but there is an aura. I sat yards from him and was struck by how weary he seemed to be, but the influence the man has on the world is remarkable.

STV News

A chorus of 'Flower of Scotland' rang round the unlikely setting of the Vatican today after the First Minister had an historic meeting with the Pope. Henry McLeish is there along with other prominent Scots to celebrate the 400th anniversary of the founding of the college which trains Scottish priests. *Scotland Today*'s John MacKay is in Rome and he sent this report...

JM: Here in Rome, the Eternal City, the leader of the historic Catholic Church meets the leader of the fledgling Scottish Parliament.

POPE JOHN PAUL II: A warm greeting to the Secretary of State for Scotland and the First Minister, as well as distinguished visitors and benefactors who are honouring this occasion with their presence.

HENRY MCLEISH, First Minister: It was wonderful to represent Scotland on your first trip abroad with a visit to the Vatican and an audience with His Holiness the Pope. But I think it is also significant for Scotland because I think it is absolutely vital that we have a very inclusive society, we have a very tolerant society and also a society that speaks to each other and listens to each other. So, all in all it's been a wonderful day.

CARDINAL THOMAS WINNING: The contrast between the Scotland of the 17th Century and Scotland of the Year 2000 is quite extraordinary. The Scottish Parliament outlawed the Catholic Church in 1560. And today we have the First Minister of a new Parliament in Scotland (in Rome), which for me and for the Catholic community is a very important presence.

It might have been a December night, but Rome was still glorious. We wandered through the piazzas and Christmas markets and dined and drank wine under the stars at the Panthenon. Had I not been looking at a hairy-faced cameraman it could have been seductively romantic.

Friday 8 December 2000

STV News

Chaos. Shambles. Fiasco. Just some of the words used by MSPs to describe the summer's exams crisis as they revealed today there were very nearly no results at all this year. The Scottish Parliament's Education Committee made 56 recommendations in a damning report and warned there were no guarantees for next year's exams.

A new exam system had been introduced in 2000. It was plagued with problems and the SQA (Scottish Qualifications Authority) had to admit that some students received incorrect exam results. Some didn't receive any.

MADONNA'S WEDDING

Thursday 21 December 2000

DIARY: Dornoch is a media village now. The area outside the cathedral was a forest of snappers' ladders. Wandered about getting a feel for things and speaking to some locals. They were all quite thrilled by it. Every other station had built platforms, but I was stuck on the ground and squashed by the crowd. It worked out rather well. We were part of the atmosphere. Tonight's event was the christening of Madonna's son Rocco – significant because it was likely to be the only photo opportunity we'd get. We were live as the cars began arriving with various celebrities and they kept throwing to me to describe what was going on. Unfortunately, Madonna didn't arrive until after we'd gone off air, but it was good stuff nonetheless. It was a carnival atmosphere in Dornoch and enjoyable to be there.

I found myself spouting the following. It went against every professional instinct, talking with little knowledge of the subject and, worse, no confirmation. Having said that, it was great fun.

JM: We have seen Stella McCartney, the leading designer at the Chloe fashion group. She, of course, was expected to design Madonna's wedding dress. Stories here that there are, in fact, going to be three wedding dresses. One is going to be worn at the actual ceremony, one is going to be worn at a dinner – that will be designed by Donatella Versace – and there is also going to be a gown in the evening, which is also going to be designed by Donatella Versace.

We've got a big Mercedes at the back. That may indeed be her. Yes, that's Madonna arriving. Arriving for the christening of her son Rocco. There's the car pulling up. She's sitting in the passenger seat at the back and we'll see her come out in a moment. (*Sting emerges*). It's not, it's Trudie Tyler (*actually Styler – Sting's wife*). It's not Madonna. It's Sting and his wife Trudie Tyler (*still wrong*), who, of course, brought the couple, Guy Ritchie and Madonna together (*I had to be up on my celebrity gossip for this sort of insight*).

One photographer was arrested after hiding in the church organ in Dornoch Cathedral.

Friday 22 December 2000

DIARY: Today was a contrast to last night's fun. Scores of media crews standing outside the entrance to Skibo Castle waiting in vain for something to happen or to be confirmed. A couple of cars arrived later in the day and a couple of photographers were ejected. Apart from that there was nothing.

I spent my day doing two-ways into our programmes saying nothing was happening. My lunchtime stuff was very light-hearted and I had a couple of interviewees, including NBC's correspondent. In the evening I had the same light heartedness, but made the point that it was another classic example of Madonna's manipulation of the media.

I even did a two-way with _Canada_ AM – Canada's national breakfast programme – and heard later that my sister-in-law and nephew had seen it.

The media lock out for the wedding was very effective. The following excerpts from some of my live reports show my failure to hide the tedium we were all feeling.

JM: Another Land Rover has just gone in, we've all got terribly excited, nobody in it. And that's been the story of the event so far. I was asked last night what Madonna was wearing and I said a yellow dress. Apparently, that doesn't suffice. So, my understanding is that it is a cream silk creation by Stella McCartney. Her £49,000 diamond bracelet has got 19 carats of diamonds and is designed to go with the Gothic dress she will be wearing. I thought I had to get that right. That's it. Now you know.

We know for sure that Gwyneth Paltrow is here, we saw her at the christening last night. Rupert Everett is here. Sting and his wife Trudie Tyler (_still wrong_) is here, so we know these people are here for definite. Now as for the rest; Brad Pitt was apparently spotted buying a packet of fags down in Inverness and was pursued. Nobody has seen him since, so we don't know if he's going to be here either. Whether his girlfriend Jennifer Aniston is going to be with him or not, we don't know.

Gwyneth Paltrow is Brad Pitt's ex and, of course, there might be a bit of tension there between her and Jennifer Aniston. The suspicion is, therefore, that Jennifer Aniston may not come. George Clooney apparently stayed very quietly in Bonar Bridge. Nobody recognised him until after he'd gone. Apparently he was buying a packet of fags as well, so there's going to be a lot of smoking going on as far as we can understand.

2001

Tuesday 30 January 2001

DIARY: Big surprise in the newsroom today was the announcement by the judges at the Lockerbie trial that they will return their verdict tomorrow. At the end of the evidence they said they would return on the 30th to announce when they'd give their verdict. Everyone expected a date next week, but they've surprised us all by saying they'll announce it tomorrow. This has led to the suspicion that they want as few relatives there as possible because they've got a not proven/not guilty verdict.

Wednesday 31 January 2001

STV News

A Libyan intelligence agent is tonight starting a life sentence for the Lockerbie Bombing. The decision by judges at the unique Scottish court in the Netherlands to convict Abdel Basset al-Megrahi and to free his co-accused is having a worldwide impact.

Martin Geissler's report said after nine years under suspicion and nine months on trial, Megrahi's conviction made him the biggest mass murder in British criminal history.

DIARY: This morning one of the two Libyans accused of the Lockerbie bombing – Megrahi – was found guilty. The other – Fahaima – not guilty. The verdict surprised most of us. The prosecution case was almost entirely circumstantial. It dominated all our news. Most of the work was done by David Cowan and Martin Geissler in the Netherlands.

Wednesday 28 February 2001

DIARY: *Scotland Today* is the best regional news programme in Britain – official. We won the award at tonight's Royal Television Society presentation and it is great news. Amongst the tributes paid to it was that it was 'well-presented.' It's a real boost. We had an inkling that we might have won from the positioning of our table near the front. It was great when a shot of me and Sarah (*Sarah Heaney co-presenter*) was flashed up. When I later watched some of the war reporting and investigative reporting that were up for prizes, it was a bit humbling. But this is a great achievement. The schmoozing that went on was a bit much for me, but otherwise an enjoyable night. Eventually crashed into my bed about 4.00am.

As we sat among the news media glitterati, I studied the award. When I leaned forward to put it back on the table it slipped from my hand and smashed some glasses very loudly. There was a momentary pause in the proceedings before it dawned on them that the breaking glass was just the Scots, so they carried on.

FOOT AND MOUTH OUTBREAK

Thursday 1 March 2001

DIARY: Home after only about four hours sleep. Went for a kip before returning to work.

Woken by a phone call from Norman Corbett (*News Producer*) asking me to go down to Lockerbie to present the programme live, because the foot and mouth outbreak has hit Scotland at a farm there. I thought he was taking the piss, but no.

STV News – live from Lockerbie

Good evening, live from Lockerbie where earlier today the first case of the Foot and Mouth outbreak in Scotland was confirmed. Tests at a farm at Canonbie, just 15 miles from here, later also proved positive. The news is devastating for Scotland's farmers and, indeed, for the industry as a whole. And tonight, with tests being carried out at a third farm, the entire country is beginning to feel the impact. Whole swathes of the countryside are being cut off from the public.

The Foot and Mouth outbreak resulted in the culling of millions of livestock. Many farmers left the industry. The National Audit Office estimated it cost the country £8 billion.

Tuesday 13 March 2001

STV News

60 years ago tonight was the first night of the Clydebank Blitz. Planes of the German Luftwaffe targetted the Clydeside town and dropped tons of high explosives. A thousand people died. Thousands more were injured and many more left homeless. Tonight the town begins a series of commemorative events to remember that dreadful time. John MacKay is there…

DIARY: Some of the testimony was very moving, especially from a woman named Helen McNeil who very vividly recalled the devastation.

Tuesday 24 April 2001

STV News – live from Bathgate

Good evening from Bathgate. It was the news that the workforce here had dreaded, yet expected. Motorola today confirmed the closure of its giant complex in West Lothian leaving more than 3,000 workers to face the dole. The problem is simple – not enough people want to buy the mobile phones that are made here. But the consequences for the workforce are devastating.

DIARY: The loss of 3,200 jobs at Motorola in Bathgate, West Lothian – the single biggest job announcement in at least a decade, possibly more. We did the programme live from there. I'm rather struck by the lack of as much gloom as one might expect – perhaps because there are other opportunities in the area. Still, a terrible blow.

CARDINAL THOMAS WINNING'S FUNERAL

Monday 25 June 2001

DIARY: The funeral of Cardinal Thomas Winning in Glasgow. I was presenting the lunchtime programme from the site, aided by Father Patrick Burke who was interpreting what was happening. All the pomp and ceremony is impressive, and although some would like to do away with it, for my part such spectacles are important and a connection with the past.

Tuesday 11 September 2001

Along with the rest of the world, we watched in horror as the hijacked planes flew into the Twin Towers at the World Trade Centre in New York City.

DIARY: We were reduced to shorter bulletins and nobody had any issue with that. We focused on the American's trapped here because of the air restrictions and Scots with family over there. It's really all we could do.

Friday 12 October 2001

STV News with Shereen

A man described as 'a serial killer in the making' is tonight starting a life sentence for the murder of Kilmarnock teenager Barry Wallace. After the verdict it was revealed that William Beggs has killed before and has a history of horrifying violence against young men in England and Scotland. Barry Wallace's parents said this afternoon, 'We are glad this devil's trail of destruction has been halted.'

DIARY: **It is a gruesome story involving Beggs picking up Wallace – who was trying to get home after a works night out – taking him to his flat, handcuffing him, raping him, killing him and then chopping up his body, later disposing of the pieces in Loch Lomond – the head being discovered on Troon beach. Horrifying. Much of the case was circumstantial and there was a real fear he might get off with it.**

THE RESIGNATION OF HENRY McLEISH AS FIRST MINISTER

Friday 2 November 2001

STV News

Scotland's First Minister is facing the biggest crisis of his political career over the 'Officegate' affair. Henry McLeish has refused to answer questions on 11 years worth of rent earned by sub-letting his Glenrothes constituency offices after paying back £9,000 to Westminster last week.

Henry McLeish had sublet part of his constituency office to a legal firm, which was against the rules. He had repaid the money he had received, but an admission that there had been further sublets since 1987 which he could not account for had created a political crisis.

Thursday 8 November 2001

STV News – live from The Mound in Edinburgh

Good evening from Edinburgh on a day of high drama that has sent shock waves through Scottish politics and reverberated across the nation. For the second time in little more than a year the country is looking for a new First Minister.

HENRY MCLEISH, (Statement to Parliament):

What is important is that I take full, personal responsibility. Others who work with me and for me have been criticised, but the ultimate responsibility is mine and mine alone. I will continue with my duties as MSP for Central Fife, serving the people I know and grew up with. Sir David (*Sir David Steel, Presiding Officer*) that, in itself, is and remains an enormous privilege for me. Thank you, Sir David and colleagues for the courtesy.

With Political Editor Bernard Ponsonby

JM: Bernard, it's not so much a case of what Henry McLeish did, but how he handled it.

BERNARD PONSONBY: It's how he handled it because there is a golden rule in politics for a major politician; if there are any questions over your probity or over your competence and managerial skills, what you have to do is that you have to get everything out in the open on day one. But he didn't do that. As a consequence he's been hounded. As a consequence, information has been drip fed into the public domain and it's all created the impression that events were driving Henry McLeish rather than Henry McLeish taking control of events. And that's always suicide for a politician and when it comes to questioning his competence I think he realised that it had the consequences of destabilising the Executive and destabilising Labour ahead of the next elections in 2003.

JM: I'm joined here in Edinburgh by some of the main players in the events over the past few days.

DAVID MCLETCHIE, Scottish Conservative Leader:
We said that Henry McLeish should resign because his conduct was unbecoming of the First Minister of Scotland. He has come to the same conclusion in tendering his resignation. He did so in a dignified manner this afternoon in the Scottish Parliament and now we have to draw a veil over that and move on.

JOHN SWINNEY, SNP Leader:
It's obviously been a sad day for Henry McLeish personally and we all feel for that, but it was quite clear that this issue was not going away. The First Minister, by not coming clean about the issue a long time ago, had undermined the trust that has to exist between the public and the First Minister. Now what we've seen is the Scottish Parliament having to oversee a mess created at Westminster, and it's been the Scottish Parliament's openness and transparency that's brought this to light and it demonstrates to everyone, particularly the Labour Party, that these things have got to be brought to the surface.

CATHY JAMIESON, Deputy Leader of Scottish Labour:
I think it's important to recognise that the whole of the parliamentary Labour Party accepted Henry's resignation with some regret. We believe that he did a good job in the time that he was First Minister for Scotland. He had a clear commitment to the Parliament. And now what we want to do is to move on, to deliver our programme by having an election; open, transparent and above board with all sections of the party to ensure that we select a leader.

JM: Henry McLeish said it was time for others to lead in his resignation speech. The Officegate affair has now been played out, the next act begins. Who will be Scotland's new leader? Good night.

DIARY: It took everyone by surprise. Had he said right at the beginning, 'Here's what happened, I'm sorry,' it would have blown over. However, it was complete and utter incompetence and that is how his time in the post has come across. He wept when he was appointed First Minister and I was rather taken by the fact that it meant something to him, but he's been a disappointment.

Tuesday 6 November 2001

DIARY: Charity premiere of 'Harry Potter and the Philosopher's Stone' at the Ocean Terminal in Leith. Harry Potter has been a publishing phenomenon for the past five years and the film is expected to be just as big.

It was and all the sequels thereafter.

JACK MCCONNELL BECOMES FIRST MINISTER

Thursday 22 November 2001

STV News

Scotland Tonight has a new First Minister. Jack McConnell was installed as the leader of the nation and promised, 'I'll listen to the people.' Mr McConnell pledges to deliver on public services and act on the priorities that matter to real people.

Speech to Parliament

JACK MCCONNELL, First Minister: Politics and public service are about nothing if they're not based on principles, focused on improving lives and dedicated to a better world. We come from different places, those of us who are here serving in this Parliament. We've all been in different circumstances, but the greatest challenge that we all face is to leave a better world to those who follow us.

JM: The First Minister joins us now live from Edinburgh. First of all, Mr McConnell, congratulations on your appointment.

JMC: Thank you very much, John.

JM: Hundreds of thousands of people are watching you just now. What difference are you going to make to their lives?

JMC: I want to do three things as First Minister. Firstly, I want to ensure that we are focused in the Scottish Parliament on the delivery of vital public services that really matter, the people's priorities – education, health, transport, jobs and crime. Secondly, I want to make sure that we build confidence in the Parliament by being open and transparent in all that we do. And thirdly, and by far the most important, I want to make sure that every child in Scotland has the sort of opportunities that I've had in life and that we close that opportunity gap, so that those who have the worst possible start in life do not then have the worst possible adulthood.

JM: Your election has been described by some as a coronation, by others as a stitch-up, and you were Labour's only candidate for office. Does that undermine your authority?

JMC: I think it's great to have such confidence from my colleagues that they are prepared to support me in that way, and I now want to make sure that we move quickly to make the sort of improvement in public services to deal with the issue of public confidence in the Parliament and to make sure that our budgets, our decisions and our actions are skewed in favour of new opportunities for those who need them most. And if we get the chance to do that over the next few weeks and months, I believe

2002 can see the hopes and ambitions of the people of Scotland for that Parliament, now start to be realised.

2002

Monday 14 January 2002

DIARY: Produced my first programme at STV today – the lunchtime opt out. Proved to be something of a baptism of fire with one piece not playing and having to be dropped down.

I enjoyed producing news programmes, but ultimately producing the evening news and presenting it was not practical. Trying to make production decisions while on-air in the studio was fraught.

SCOTLAND'S WOMEN CURLING TEAM WIN GOLD AT THE WINTER OLYMPICS

Tuesday 26 February 2002

DIARY: Live into the programme from Glasgow Airport on the arrival home of our gold medal winning curling team from the Winter Olympics. It's one of those good news stories that gives everyone a lift and they are nice people. I was in the middle of a media scrum and had to link two packages and do a live with team skip Rona Martin.

STV News – live from Glasgow Airport
Five days after their success, Scotland's Golden Girls are home. Before the Winter Olympics few people would have known who they were. Now they're national heroines, their arrival today greeted by bagpipes, by well wishers and, of course, the usual media scrum.

RONA MARTIN, Team Skip:
I can't quite take it in yet. We went away to play curling, we won the competition, came back, but all of this is a lot to take in.

LOCKERBIE BOMBER'S APPEAL

Wednesday 13 March 2002

DIARY: To Camp Zeist. Steve (*Steve Kydd – cameraman*) and Craig (*Craig Millar – reporter*) had both been there before so they told me what to do – cars searched, everything searched. Our camera position is in the 'shooting gallery' especially built across from the special court. I'd managed to speak to lawyers from both sides and was prepared for my two-way into the 6.00pm.

Thursday 14 March 2002

STV News

This is not a time for celebration or despair, but a time to think about how we prevent it ever happening again.' The words of Jim Swire, whose daughter died when Pan Am Flight 103 blew up over Lockerbie. Tonight the man responsible for Britain's biggest mass murder is heading to Scotland to serve his life sentence after five judges rejected Abdel Basset al-Megrahi's appeal at the Scottish Court in the Netherlands.

SARAH HEANEY: John MacKay is in Camp Zeist and was in court for today's verdict. John, can you describe first what it was like in the courtroom?

JOHN MACKAY: Very dramatic, Sarah. In the moments just before Lord Cullen announced the judgement, the tension was palpable. He was expected to speak for about ten to fifteen minutes. In the end he spoke for a lot less than that and seemed to take people by surprise by how quickly he announced the appeal was

not being upheld. It took a moment or two for that to sink in. When it did, al-Megrahi's wife stood up wailing and started to run towards the back of the court. Relatives tried to hold her back. Al-Megrahi's brother put his hands to his face. Al-Megrahi himself looked forlornly at his wife, his face ashen. Just feet away, the relatives of the victims hugged each other, applauding. Somebody shouted 'Yes!' A contrast of emotions. And in the midst of all of this, al-Megrahi was taken away from the court almost unnoticed.

SH: John, where is al-Megrahi and what happens now?

JM: He is in this compound behind me, in the jail where he has been for the last three years. He will be removed, we believe, this evening in a joint operation between Scottish Police, the Scottish Prison Service and Dutch authorities. He is a high security prisoner, so no details are being released at all about what his movements will be... An area is being prepared for what we believe will be a helicopter landing and at some point will be taken off to his ultimate destination – Barlinnie Jail in Glasgow.

One lighter moment in a generally sombre day happened later in the afternoon when I went for a wander during a lull in proceedings. Camp Zeist was a former airbase for the Dutch military and included an outdoor aircraft museum. Although it was deserted, it occurred to me that there must be a toilet there and I could use the facilities. As I walked about I suddenly heard the screech and scrunch of a car skidding on the stones behind me. Startled, I looked round and saw one police officer behind the open car door with a drawn weapon and another walking towards me. He demanded to see my ID, which I fumbled to show him, all the time watching the guy with the gun. They quickly realised this was not some saboteur of the trial, but an eejit who'd meandered away from the right zone. Interestingly, the officer pronounced my surname correctly. The Netherlands is the only place that ever happens because my clan has historical ties with the Dutch. Anyway, I explained rather sheepishly that I'd been looking for a toilet. The officer, with some incredulity, swept his hand towards the thick forest that surrounded the entire base. 'The toilet is everywhere,' he said.

Thursday 21 March 2002

DIARY: Scottish skier Alain Baxter formally stripped of his Winter Olympics bronze medal. He's been harshly dealt with. He took a Vick's nasal spray in the US, not realising it was made up differently from the one in the UK that he's been taking since childhood. It seems very unfair – no one doubts him.

CHAMPIONS LEAGUE FINAL
Wednesday 15 May 2002

STV News – live from Hampden Park with Jane Lewis

Tonight's the night. The arena is set. The prize is waiting to be claimed. The best in Europe compete before the eyes of the world. Glasgow is transformed into a carnival city. But can tonight's game match the glories of the past?

Good evening from Hampden Park for tonight's Champions League Final. The stage is set for a European showdown between Real Madrid and Bayer Leverkusen. With kick off less than two hours away, fans are already pouring into the stadium and the atmosphere is building. Glasgow has been transformed into a festival city. Thousands of fans are creating a carnival atmosphere

DIARY: It was some spectacle. We were seated right up at the back of the South Stand and with a great view. The Real Madrid fans created a good atmosphere. It felt a privilege to be there. Real scored quickly through Raul. The Germans came back into it with an equaliser and really took a grip on the game before Zinedine Zidane scored a wonderful goal just before half time – a volley from just inside the box. Normally a goal produces a mass exhalation – a roar – but this was a mass inhalation – a gasp – before the crowd went crazy. An incredible moment. Much comparison with the classic 1960 final beforehand, but it didn't come close. However, Zidane's goal will live on in the memory.

Thursday 27 June 2002

DIARY: Started the day as a producer in Glasgow and ended it in a motel outside Dijon in East Central France. The lead story was the news of a coach crash involving schoolchildren from Largs Academy. One 15-year-old girl died.

Friday 28 June 2002

DIARY: Found the hospital in Dijon no problem. However, most of the action was taking place about 45 minutes drive back the way at Semur–en–Auxois. More people were waiting there in hospital and that's where we based ourselves all day. Basically just got whatever we could, a couple of interviews etc, but mostly sitting around.

Did two lives into the lunchtime programme and then had to do an 'as live' and a track and rushes for the back of 3.00pm. However, round about then some of the children were released from the hospital, some in ambulances, some in taxis. Got some good shots, a couple of snatched sound bites and an interview with the school head teacher. Had to dump everything I had prepared before. After that we heard the driver was being charged with involuntary manslaughter. In the 15 minutes before our feed time it was quite pressurised, but that's the sort of pressure I can deal with.

Much of the material we got was down to the sharpness of my cameraman Bobby Whitelaw, who spotted activity at the hospital as we hacks were shooting the breeze to pass the time. The reporter and camera operator have to work as a team and feed off each other. Bobby is one of the very best.

Wednesday 13 November 2002

DIARY: The start of a 48-hour strike by firefighters. They were walking out bang on 6.00pm just as we were going on-air, so we decided to do the programme live from Cowcaddens fire station, just up the road. There were a lot of technical problems, eg a camera failing and no communication between the satellite truck and the gallery. As we were into the on-air countdown my ear piece separated and I only got it sorted with less than ten seconds to go. All

very hairy, but it's when the job is most enjoyable. The firefighters were actually walking out as I began speaking.

Friday 29 November 2002

DIARY: After work drinks. Conversed with young colleagues Ewan Petrie and Lesley Colquhoun. Discussed how they would change the programme. Lesley thinks we should make it 'more cool' and I asked her how she would make me 'cooler'. She candidly said I wouldn't do it because I was 'too old.'

Lesley continues to be a colleague and we've never spoken of it again.

Monday 9 December 2002

DIARY: Spent all day through in Edinburgh. A huge fire – which was only finally dampened down this evening – has gutted buildings in the Cowgate in the Old Town. I was to anchor there after lunchtime and this evening. Not much for me to do other than answer some questions, introduce packages etc and do a couple of interviews.

Wednesday 11 December 2002

DIARY: An unfortunate first tonight. I couldn't remain in the studio until the end of the programme because I had to dash to the loo to be sick. It was very unpleasant. The only part I was missing for was the goodbye, but I was clearly missing. I'd begun to feel uncomfortable soon after we went on-air, but it was only as we got onto the sport that I was having problems. In the end, there was only once choice I could make.

The programme ended with Shereen saying goodnight and the camera pulling out to reveal my empty chair.

DIARY CONT: **Out to interview Archbishop Mario Conti of Glasgow about Catholic schools. There is an ongoing debate about sectarianism in Scotland and how best to tackle it. Voices have been raised again about the existence of Catholic schools with state support.**

STV News

Scotland's Catholic Bishops say they are dismayed and angered at attempts to link denominational schools and sectarianism. Critics claim separating pupils because of their faith reinforces divisions in the community, and does nothing for religious tolerance.

FRED FORRESTER, Former Deputy General Secretary, EIS:
Catholic schools are implicated in it and really ought to accept that fact. They are not the cause of it, I would concede that readily, but their existence is implicated in prolonging sectarianism.

MARIO CONTI, Archbishop of Glasgow:
The suggestion that somehow or other these schools are the cause of, the origin of, or the continuation of sectarianism within the community is quite unfair and really quite offensive. It's almost as bad as saying, as was said in the '20s of the last century, we've got a problem here with sectarianism, we've got a problem of bigotry, let's send the Irish back to Ireland.

JM: But surely one way to tackle sectarianism is greater understanding, and if children are brought up separately then that understanding isn't going to be there.

MC: You give that as an analysis, but I'm not sure that analysis is correct. To blame, first of all, religion for sectarianism, for the bigotry that is in the country, for the divisions which are in Glasgow, and then to pinpoint Catholic schools as somehow a contributory factor to it is an unfair analysis and is offensive to the Catholic community. I want to say that as strongly as possible at this point because I don't want anybody to be under the impression that somehow or other we're going to sit down, listen to all this and gradually see something that we think is important being whittled away or undermined.

The issue of state funded denominational schools continues to surface periodically.

GEORGE IS SCOTLAND'S CHAMPION WHISTLER

A WEEK or two ago, a letter appeared in our Readers' Page asking why nobody seems to whistle any more.

It brought several letters from readers in the Falkirk area telling us about a man with a crutch who's always whistling.

Indeed, they say, he must be Scotland's champion whistler.

Well, we did a bit of detective work and found he's George Cruickshank, of Eastburn Tower, Falkirk.

George, who's 78, has been whistling since he was a boy.

He has to use a crutch because of a childhood illness.

The other week he was walking along Falkirk High Street when a car drew up alongside him.

The driver asked George if he used to work as a gateman at the Walker Hunter Iron Works.

He'd recognised him because of his whistling—even though they last worked together in 1936.

George has no musical knowledge at all. He can't play an instrument or read music, but when he hears a tune he likes, it sticks in his mind.

His tunes range from favourite Scots songs to international classics.

"The Road To The Isles" and "The Northern Lights Of Old Aberdeen" are among his favourites, though he's also been known to whistle the odd bit of opera.

He's lost count of the number of times he's been stopped by strangers who just want to tell him how cheered they are by his whistling.

1986 · One of my early headlines.

1988 · BBC Radio Orkney
I was nervous as I flicked open the microphone
for my first ever live broadcast.

JM

1988 · My notes from the first phone call about the Lockerbie Bombing.

1991 · BBC Radio Scotland
This was news as it was happening, or as close as it could be for the time.
BBC

JOHN MacKAY

1994 · First time presenting *Scotland Today*. I was told to wear a better shirt and tie the next time.
STV

1995 · Joe Henry, one of the Old Boys. 'It always comes back. It was a bad, bad time.'
STV

```
                  _fine printed
13/03/96 10:52 pmk ?:?? !36-.. HHH
.. HHH
PAH5784 6 MRC 8192 MERCURY WIRE
1 SHOOTING
CENTRAL SCOTLAND NEWS AGENCY
Copy from TIM BUGLER, CENTRAL SCOTLAND NEWS AGENCY,


        Date: 13.3.96
tim bugler/central/shooting/flash..1
REPORTS are coming in of a shooting at Dunblane Primary School,
Perthshire. The Scottish Ambulance Service said 12 CHILDREN ARE BELIEVED
DEAD, and eight or nine injured.
     Police have been called in from throughout the area, and
all five doctors from Dunblane Surgery are reported to have
been called to the school.
ends....
MMMM
```

1996 · The first report on the Dunblane shootings.

1997 · They fell like skittles in a bowling alley. STV

1997 · 'A good day for Scotland and a good day for the United Kingdom,' said the Prime Minister.
STV

1997 · 'The settled will of the Scottish people is there for all to see.' Donald Dewar.
STV

1998 · I held the World Cup today. A dream since childhood.

JM

1999 · Scotland's Parliament is no longer a political pamphlet, a campaign trail, a waving flag. It is here. It is real.

STV

1999 · 'We're joined by the leader of the SNP and now the leader of the official opposition in the new parliament.'
STV

2000 · Madonna's Wedding – It went against every professional instinct, talking with little knowledge of the subject and, worse, no confirmation. It was great fun.
STV

2000 · In a hundred years when the history of this time in Scotland is written, Donald Dewar's name will stand out.
STV

2003 · Seville – A bottle came out of the darkness and hit me on the back of the head. I just buckled and went down.

JM

2004 · To my eye the Parliament building looks like an attempt to do up some 1960s new town council flats.

STV

2007 · Within the last half hour, at the last count of the last region to declare, the SNP secured victory.
STV

2007 · The Blair era is over. The Brown era has begun.
STV

2008 · Barlinnie Special – The prisoners started shouting and hammering the doors when I made reference to 'murderers and rapists' among them.
STV

2011 · Our eyes are on the future and the dreams that can be realised.
STV

2011 · *Scotland Tonight* launched.

JM

2012 · Kevin Bridges – Just a funny, funny guy. His resurrection of the exclamation 'Yaldy' is just one of many delights for me.

JM

2012 · Andy Murray – He was so lean. If I hadn't known better I'd have thought he needed a good feed.
JM

2012 · Olympic Homecoming – Sir Chris Hoy 6x Gold Medallist.
JM

2013 · A Friday night drink and a helicopter crashes into the pub. How random and how awful.

STV

Alistair Darling – You can get the change you want with a stronger, more secure Scottish Parliament by staying in the UK.

JM

2014 · Alex Salmond's last interview before the referendum – We know we want to be a more equal and just society, so vote for that future, vote Yes tomorrow.
JM

As Big Ben chimed and I delivered that line to the nation about two capitals waiting, the hairs stood on the back of my neck.
STV

2015 General Election – Nicola Sturgeon. She'd been
up all night and was saying she wasn't sure she could
remember her own name.

JM   STV

2003

Friday 3 January 2003

DIARY: Saw the new set for the programme. We are making quite a radical departure away from sitting behind a desk to sitting on a 'news bench' (sofa). I had strong reservations, but it looks excellent on camera and the colours and lighting are good. We're provided with a variety of new shots and we move about the set more. The downside, the only one, is the sig tune which is insipid.

Friday 7 March 2003

DIARY: Big debate in work this afternoon. Potentially good *Scotland Today* story in the verdict on a child minder accused of murder. 'Not Proven'. Or the latest report from Hans Blix, the UN Weapons Inspector on the situation in Iraq. We also had the chance of a live from Martin Geissler in Kuwait with the British troops. Do we effectively ignore the war and stick with our usual agenda? Today my view was that we should go with the latest developments and we did it very well. Others, though, were not convinced.

Monday 17 March 2003

STV News

Britain and America appear to be just hours away from going to war with Iraq as moves towards military action in the Gulf claimed the first high profile political casualty. Robin Cook resigned as leader of the Commons in protest after Tony Blair and George Bush abandoned diplomatic efforts to resolve the crisis through the United Nations. Today's events appear to signal that war is now inevitable. The UN failed to reach consensus on a new resolution authorising war. Following an emergency cabinet meeting the Foreign Secretary Jack Straw will address MPs in the next hour. And President Bush is to address the American people at 1.00am our time.

Thursday 20 March 2003

STV News

Thousands of Scottish servicemen and women are tonight steeling themselves to take part in an invasion of Iraq. Infantrymen and tank crews are waiting for orders in Kuwait. RAF Tornados from Scottish bases are on standby to join the aerial bombardment. At home their families are waiting for news from the front. Meanwhile, anti-war protests continued across the country

Friday 21 March 2003

STV News

Scottish soldiers are tonight reported to be advancing towards Basra, Iraq's second city. The Ministry of Defence says *The Black Watch* are taking part in a joint British and American offensive. Lead elements of the force are said to be on the outskirts of Basra, which is a key strategic objective of the allies.

Monday 14 April 2003

DIARY: The Scottish Parliament Election campaign is well underway, although it's unlikely most people have noticed. We led with it for the first time tonight – a row over NHS waiting lists.

SCOTTISH PARLIAMENTARY
ELECTIONS 2003

Thursday 1 May 2003

DIARY: Not a night of glory for me. I
was to do the late bulletin and then
dash off to Hamilton for the first result.
It was always cutting it fine, but when I
got lost it became impossible. I arrived
as the winning candidate –Tom
McCabe – made his acceptance speech.
It wasn't actually that big a deal. We
didn't have our own election programme
and were really just doing inserts into
the ITV News channel. I did an interview
with McCabe and that was my night.

Friday 2 May 2003

STV News – with Shereen Nanjiani
(Headline Sequence)

TONIGHT'S TOP STORIES

**The Joy of Six. Voters shake up Scottish
politics as the biggest winners are the
smaller parties.**

**Jack's back for four more years and set
for coalition talks.**

**Poor show as more than half the
electorate don't vote.**

Good evening. Scotland's
parliamentary elections have seen a
night of stunning success for the
underdogs. Labour may be returning
to power, but with the narrowest of
margins. Election 2003 will be
remembered for the rise of the
Greens, the Scottish Socialists and
single issue candidates – the pensioner
and the hospital campaigner who will
take their seats alongside the
established parties in the chamber.

So how does the chamber look?
Labour on 50 seats, down five from

the last Parliament. The Lib Dems on
17, that's up one. It brings the
coalition partners two seats more
than the decisive 65 seats needed for
a majority. The SNP are on 27, down
six, and the Tories are on 18, down
one. And there are the big changes.
The Greens on seven, the Scottish
Socialist Party on six and the
independents on four.

JACK MCCONNELL, Leader, Scottish
Labour:
Yesterday's votes gave Labour in
Scotland the honour of being the
largest party in the Scottish
Parliament. I believe people across
Scotland did that because Scottish
Labour put forward the ideas and the
policies to tackle directly the
priorities the people of Scotland have.

JIM WALLACE, Leader, Scottish Liberal
Democrats:
We actually held our position whilst
the Labour Party, which has been
senior party in the Coalition, actually
fell back. That must strengthen our
position, it changes the balance if
there was to be a coalition, if we were
to go into negotiation.

DAVID MCLETCHIE, Leader, Scottish
Conservatives:
If any of you wish to eat your words
in private, take a wee serving of
humble pie, we'll be available at the
conclusion of this press conference.

JM: For the Scottish National Party it
might have been a slick campaign,
but it didn't translate into the
breakthrough to Government. For a
time they were ahead in the polls, but
finished up losing six MSPs. The party

leader John Swinney joins us now live from Edinburgh. Mr Swinney, you said earlier on today that you had moved from being a party of protest, but were not yet accepted as a party of government. What do you do now?

JOHN SWINNEY, Leader SNP: Well I think that's an inaccurate reflection of what happened last night. We were vulnerable on the regional list vote. We had most of our members elected by that system four years ago and obviously there were new faces, new parties came onto the scene this time round and it made us vulnerable. What I recognise is that the SNP, in wanting to deliver Scottish Independence, has got to have leadership of the first-past-the-post constituencies in Scotland and that's what I'm equipping the party to do... What the election leaves us with is a necessity to make sure the SNP completes the transition that I've set it on, of moving from being a party of protest vote into a party of government; of alternative government.

DIARY: Should make for a more interesting Parliament and it's no bad thing that the big parties have lost. It has been a singularly uninspiring election. Aside from how the politicians fared, the big story of the election is voter apathy with fewer than half of the electorate deciding to vote.

CELTIC IN THE UEFA CUP FINAL IN SEVILLE

Tuesday 20 May 2003

DIARY: I travelled with the satellite to a nice setting on the waterfront of the Guadalcivir, with the Torro Del Orro (*Tower of Gold*) as our backdrop. Very picturesque. A lot of Celtic fans around, but by no means swamping the city. I was required to do various links and insets from the sat truck through the day so I couldn't wander too far away. Took myself for a walk up to the Cathedral, around which was the largest gathering of Celtic fans. It meant when I went on-air at lunchtime, I knew something of what was going on. Anchored the programme this evening from our location and it went well. Big day ahead tomorrow. Seville, from what I've seen, is a lovely city. Some of the buildings are stunning. It is very hot in the afternoon though, baking hot in the mid to high 30s.

STV News – live from Seville with Jane Lewis

Good evening from Seville with just 24 hours to go until the big kick off. The temperatures and the tension are high here in the build up to tomorrow's UEFA Cup Final. Tens of thousands of Celtic fans are already here, desperate not to miss the biggest game for their club in a generation.

The heat was intense and as we prepared to go on-air I was perspiring a lot. One effect of this, bizarrely, was the dye from the dark suede shoes I was wearing began to stain the trouser leg of my light chinos. As I was getting the countdown to going on-air, one of the Celtic fans watching shouted, 'Haw big man, you've pished yersel'!' I uttered 'Good evening' with that alarming thought in my head.

Wednesday 21 May 2003

DIARY: Everything focused on today and it went very well until much later when I was hit on the head by a thrown bottle.

Broadcasting for most of the day. At first we were in a square near to the Cathedral that was heaving with Celtic fans, perhaps 15–20,000. I had to do the 11.00am bulletin standing on a camera box with them pushing on to me, hitting me with a rubber mallet and draping Celtic scarves on me. By 12.50pm (1.50pm Seville time) the *Daily Record* bus arrived and I did much of the programme from on top of that with Celtic fans in the background. I anchored the 2.00pm from there, the first half with Jane and then a phone-in and texts with Jim Delahunt for the second half. The humour of the Celtic fans was very good. By this time (3.30pm local time) it was absolutely baking.

STV News – live from Seville with Jane Lewis

Good evening and welcome to Seville for this special edition of *Scotland Today*. With the kick-off approaching, the waiting is nearly over. It's more than 30 years since Celtic enjoyed European success and the 75,000 fans here and the hundreds of thousands of fans at home believe that that European dream could come true tonight. The excitement and tension has been building in this city throughout the day ahead of the UEFA Cup Final – and let's just give you a taste of that just now (upsound of thousands of Celtic fans singing).

MARTIN O'NEIL, Manager, Celtic:
We have reached a final now and we've done it with some terrifically gifted players that people seem to forget. And we've done it with a terrific spirit, the sort of spirit that I think was typical of the 1967 team.

JOSE MOURINHO, Coach, Porto:
I have a lot of respect for Celtic. I have more than respect for Celtic, I respect football and to respect football is to understand that the big final is 50–50.

JM: Well this is the Spanish city of Seville, but you wouldn't believe it (upsound of Celtic fans cheering). Celtic fans often sing that if you know their history it's enough to make your heart go. Another chapter will be written in that history tonight and there's no doubt their hearts will be going. From *Scotland Today* in Seville, good night and good luck to Celtic.

DIARY: The bus and us moved to another site near the stadium for the evening. It was at one of the big screens available for fans without tickets. By now though, the *Daily Record* bus had been required to leave because of abuse from fans – who regard it as the Daily Ranger. Anyway, we got on to the Scottish Sun bus and Jane and I anchored the 6.00pm from there. No denying it was a triumph – all going smoothly and capturing the atmosphere perfectly. Back in Glasgow they were raving about it.

I remained on the bus to watch the match, but as time passed a handful of scumbags began to have a go – some resentment over *The Sun* this time. As the match progressed some missiles began to get thrown, glass tumblers, fags and I got spat on. Then Larsson equalised for a second time. Shortly after a bottle came out of the darkness and hit me towards the back of my head above the right ear. I just buckled and went down, although I never lost consciousness. I was very dizzy, though, and decided to go straight back to the hotel, fortunately getting a taxi quickly.

The Spanish police grabbed the halfwits responsible and gestured as if to ask what I wanted done with them. I wanted them punished, but the thought of getting involved in a foreign legal system and perhaps having to attend a court hearing wasn't something I wanted to do, so I gestured to let them go. I've never understood what their problem was. The Celtic fans were in great form during our time in Seville. The incident happened immediately after Henrik Larsson had brought Celtic back into the game again. Rather than enjoy the moment, these morons preferred to focus on some trivial grievance about a bus.

DIARY: I sat in my room watching Celtic lose 3–2 in extra time, but I remember little of it. When I did try to go to sleep, I couldn't. Every time I was about to fall over something in my system forced me awake. My colleagues Raman Bhardwaj and later Jim Delahunt called at different times to check on me and evidently weren't happy with what they saw. Jane Lewis got the hotel to order a doctor for me. In a mixture of broken English and sign language he diagnosed shock, I think. Anyway, he gave me a shot of something and only then did I sleep, after about 4.30am.

When my son was very young, his gran had knitted him a superhero figure and he would ask me to take it away with me and keep it on my bed. I continued to do so long after he'd grown out of it, almost as a tradition. I'd always be careful to put it in my case in the morning to avoid strange looks from the hotel maids. On the day of the game I had forgotten to do that and returned to see the figure placed prominently on top of my pillow. Later, when the doctor came to see me, he was accompanied by an assistant, a member of the hotel staff, Jane, Raman, Jim, my editor Paul McKinney and possibly a couple of others. They all left as the doctor prepared to give me a jag. The last thing I remember seeing before drifting off was the superhero figure still proudly on top of my pillow. They would all have seen it. I drifted into oblivion thinking, 'Nooooo!' It has never been mentioned, but I know they know.

Thursday 22 May 2003

DIARY: Rather a lost day after last night's incident.

Monday 27 October 2003

STV News reported on the history of the Scottish Parliament project. Initially proposed at a budget of £40 million, in 1998 Donald Dewar had announced the new Scottish Parliament would be built on the site of an old brewery next to Holyrood Palace. The architect Enrique Miralles was chosen, in part because his company had a track record of completing projects on time and on budget. By June 1999 the cost had risen to £109 million and MPs were calling for a review. By April 2000 it was £195 million and again assurances were given that it wouldn't cost any more. By December 2001 it had reached £260 million and a year later, it was £325 million. The final bill was £414 million. And it was three years late.

Wednesday 12 November 2003

STV News

Nobody likes to talk about it, but

maybe that's part of the problem. Sex was top of the agenda for politicians and doctors alike today as they unveiled a new plan to improve our health by tackling a national culture of shyness on the subject. The strategy aims to remove Scotland's unenviable record of the having the highest teenage pregnancy rate in Europe. A new national Sex Tsar will be appointed to coordinate the project. He or she will try to reduce the number of unwanted pregnancies and stem the dramatic rise in sexually transmitted infections. And parents will be encouraged to be more open when talking about sex to their children.

Wednesday 19 November 2003

Holland v Scotland for a place in the Euro 2004 finals. Scotland had won the first leg in Glasgow 1–0.

STV News – live from the Amsterdam Arena with Jane Lewis

Good evening. *Scotland Today* comes to you live from the spectacular Amsterdam Arena. Could this be where Bertie's Bravehearts become national heroes? The Tartan Army are, of course, over here and they're hoping for a night to remember.

The roof of the Amsterdam Arena is open and the crowd is beginning to fill in to this spectacular stadium. Will it be another near miss for Scotland or will it be a night of glory? One thing is certain – an entire nation is behind them. From all of us at the Amsterdam Arena, it's good night and come on Scotland!

It wasn't a near miss; Scotland were hammered 6–0. My hotel was several miles out of Amsterdam because it was a late decision to send me. I had been dismayed that I would probably miss out on an after match beer with my colleagues. When the time came, I was only too glad to slip away from the game early.

It was a bad night all round. A misunderstanding with Dutch security at the stadium meant that later on they wouldn't let us return to the trackside where our camera was positioned. With less than ten minutes to on-air, I was reduced to saying to the armed security on the gate, 'I'm begging you.' It worked. Maybe I should have tried it more often.

Wednesday 26 November 2003

STV News

The number of people stabbed to death in Scotland is at its highest level for a decade. Shocking figures released today also show that our country has the third highest murder rate in the European Union with Glasgow being one of the most dangerous cities in Britain. Ministers blame a blade and booze culture, but say they are confident they can change things.

Knife crime dropped significantly following a determined campaign, including the introduction of jail sentences for carrying a knife.

2004

Saturday 31 January 2004

STV News – live from Rosepark Care Home

Good evening from the Rosepark Care Home in Uddingston in Lanarkshire where today ten elderly residents died. Many of the pensioners are thought to have been overcome by smoke as they slept. The fire began at 4.40am this morning in a storage cupboard. The Queen has led messages of sympathy to the relatives of those who died. Tonight three elderly people are still critically ill in hospital. Another four remain in hospital for further treatment.

MARYHILL FACTORY EXPLOSION

Tuesday 11 May 2004

STV News – live from Maryhill with Shereen Nanjiani

Several people remain trapped under the rubble of this Glasgow plastics factory. They've been there for six hours after the building collapsed like a house of cards. In the last few minutes it's been confirmed that three people have been killed, 24 are still being treated in hospital, 16 of them are in a serious condition. The emergency services have been working through the day here to rescue those under the rubble. It's understood firefighters have been talking to at least one of those trapped beneath the debris.

The final toll of the ICL Plastics Factory (sometimes known as Stockline) explosion was nine dead and 33 injured. It was caused by gas leaking from corroded underground pipes.

SHARON FREW
STV Reporter

I admit I froze when I first saw all the debris and rubble, the woman sitting on the kerb with an oxygen mask on her face, the man lying on the road, who was being treated by a doctor. I later learned that he and his staff had run from a nearby GP surgery when they heard the blast. Another woman was being told to keep breathing into a paper bag by a nurse. Then I spotted a girl being helped from the wreckage, covered in dust. She was calling out for someone to help find her sister. My cameraman, Gary shouted at me, 'Come on' or something like that. His words made me snap back and focus. Medical staff were here helping the walking wounded. My job was to find out what had happened.

Nothing I had done before had prepared me for the major disaster now in front of me.

When I took the call from the newsdesk, all the producer told me was, 'head to Grovepark Street, there's a report of an explosion at a factory.' By coincidence, we were minutes away from the scene. We arrived as the first emergency crews did, before any police cordon had been set up. We walked down the street with firefighters and paramedics running past us to the devastated building.

Filming as we went, I knew I had to find eyewitnesses, but I was surrounded by people who were unable to talk. Then I noticed a small

135

crowd that had gathered. The men, wearing overalls, were covered in dust. One had a bandage on his head to stem the bleeding. Both were clearly in shock, but they agreed to speak to me and described how they'd been working in the factory when suddenly, there was a bang and everything went black. They crawled through the darkness to safety.

Even after ten more years experience as a reporter, I'm not sure you're ever really prepared for what faces you when you first arrive at the scene of a major disaster. I've covered many more in the decade that followed. What I do know is that the news footage and interviews gathered in those first minutes are vital. These are images that could be shown, as with the Maryhill explosion, for years to come. It's important to try and get to the heart of what happened, to keep your eyes and ears open, to find eyewitnesses, but above all, report calmly and with care and compassion.

JOAN COLLINS
Thursday 6 May 2004
STV News
JOAN COLLINS: Clean (*laughs*). Always wear lipstick, but not on your teeth. And powder. I don't think shiny faces are very attractive. And be groomed.

I'd asked her for make-up advice for my colleagues.

JOHN SWINNEY RESIGNS AS LEADER OF THE SNP
Tuesday 22 June 2004
STV News
John Swinney is giving up the leadership of the SNP, blaming back biting and constant criticism from within the party. His decision follows mounting pressure after poor results at the European elections.

JOHN SWINNEY, Leader SNP:
It has become clear to me over the last few days that the constant and relentless speculation over my position is obscuring and, crucially in my judgement, will continue to obscure the political objectives of the SNP... No member of the SNP should ever underestimate the damage that is caused to our movement by the loose and dangerous talk of the few.

I first remembered John Swinney coming into the BBC for interviews and was always struck by the evident decency of the man. I thought his party had treated him poorly.

Friday 3 September 2004
STV News
'It's good to be back.' The words of Alex Salmond as he secured the leadership of the SNP for the second time. The Banff and Buchan MP defeated Mike Russell and Roseanna Cunningham winning more than 75 per cent of the vote. Mr Salmond's running mate Nicola Sturgeon was elected deputy leader.

HOLYROOD INQUIRY

Wednesday 15 September 2004

STV News – live from Holyrood

Good evening and welcome to the heart of the Capital where tonight the eyes of the nation are on the building behind me and their thoughts are concentrated on the pronouncements of one man. Lord Fraser of Carmyllie was given the task of working out how our country's finest minds managed to make such an unholy mess of providing a building from which the Scottish Parliament could run the country. It's three years late and ten times over budget and when you hear Lord Fraser's findings you might have trouble trusting some of those involved to run a raffle.

We'll be looking at who was blamed in Lord Fraser's report. In differing degrees; the civil servants who were managing the project, but withheld key information from ministers about costs and the risk to the tax payer; the politicians who were supposed to be in charge, but never seemed to get a grip; the Spanish architects who showed scant regard for costs. And the Father of Devolution himself, Donald Dewar, who didn't knowingly mislead Parliament, but who rushed the whole thing through and failed to spot how it was going so disastrously wrong.

LORD FRASER OF CARMYLLIE: 'I have a number of sharp criticisms and recommendations to make on matters which ought to have been better understood. Nevertheless, there is no single villain of the peace.'

JM: It's worth noting that in all the months of this inquiry when the great and the good appeared before Lord Fraser, rarely, if ever, was there a word of apology. Indeed, Lord Fraser himself said that the walls of the Canongate echoed to the cries of, 'It wisnae me.' Some of these people will be uncomfortable tonight.

JM: We're joined now by Margo MacDonald MSP, a long term critic of the project. You said you hoped this report would decide who would get MBEs and who would get P45s. Are you happy that's been achieved?

MARGO MacDONALD: Unfortunately, I think some of the latter have managed to escape to other jobs. But it's a very detailed report and I don't think that Peter Fraser has actually missed anybody and hit the wall... Everybody who trooped into the witness box to give evidence said 'oh it wisnae me.' And they were still at it today.

JM: The Scottish Parliament is now open for business and in full operation. The inquiry into the fiasco surrounding its construction is now complete. History will judge this building by what happens inside and that will depend on the people we elect to represent us there. Good night.

To my eye the Parliament building looks like an attempt to do up some 1960s council flats. The interior is impressive, but the exterior does not proclaim the building to be the seat of the Scottish Government.

MICHAEL CROW
STV Political Correspondent
As Westminster Correspondent I

reported on the referendum and subsequent Scotland Bill going through the Houses of Parliament. I then moved home to Scotland to cover the birth of the new Scottish Parliament. It was an exciting time to be a political journalist.

Donald Dewar, Alex Salmond, Jim Wallace and David McLetchie were the leaders of the main political parties – all big political beasts. The election of a Green MSP, Robin Harper, and Tommy Sheridan from the SSP, was hugely symbolic as it promised a new type of politics in the UK. The electoral arithmetic also led to a coalition government – something not seen in peacetime British politics since the 1930s. All the media coverage was of a new political dawn for Scotland.

For me, Donald Dewar's brilliant speech at the opening of the Parliament best captured this historic time:

'Today, we look forward to the time when this moment will be seen as a turning point: the day when democracy was renewed in Scotland, when we revitalised our place in this our United Kingdom. This is about more than our politics and our laws. This is about who we are, how we carry ourselves.'

Unfortunately the Parliament did not carry itself as well as people had hoped and, perhaps unsurprisingly, MSPs struggled to live up to the huge burden of expectation that had been placed upon them. Within a short period of time the positive coverage gave way to negative stories about commemorative medals, lobbying, pay and allowances.

And nothing epitomised the fall from grace as keenly as the building of the new Scottish Parliament. Huge cost over-runs, a lack of accountability and a complete lack of sensitivity at how damaging the story could be, ensured it dominated political coverage for years. Westminster created the Scottish Parliament, but then delivered a hospital pass in the form of the Holyrood building contract. But as an institution the Parliament, for its part, failed its first real test in managing the fallout.

All this served to switch the focus of political coverage from Westminster to the Scottish Parliament. MPs, much to their annoyance, rarely got a look in to the stories of the day. MSPs were more accessible and more newsworthy and the political dynamic in Scotland was changed forever. While the Parliament may now be a permanent and constructive part of the Scottish political landscape, its early days promised much, but struggled to live up to the high expectations placed upon it. A new political dawn was ushered in – but perhaps not the one that people had anticipated.

OPENING OF NEW SCOTTISH PARLIAMENT
Saturday 9 October 2004
Opening ceremony

JACK MCCONNELL, First Minister: This chamber... at the heart of our new Scottish Parliament building. It is a heart that should beat with the pulse of the nation and resound with the passion of Scotland. This chamber – a triumph of design and engineering – is the place Scotland's Parliament can now call home...

After five years our young Parliament can now take up occupation of this, the permanent address. This is a building to which we have come amid debate and controversy...

It is now accepted without dispute that this is the permanent home for the nation's final discussion on matters that affect the way we live and the way we shape the lives of future generations...

Five years ago Scotland found a new voice. Today we celebrate a new confidence. A permanent parliament with which to announce our ambitions, encourage our enterprise and fight for fairness. We have a new building that will be the envy of many the world over. But today more than anything we have a Parliament that has come of age in a country whose time has come.'

Thursday 4 November 2004

STV News

Three Black Watch soldiers have been killed in a bomb blast at their base near Baghdad. Reports are coming in that one interpreter has also been killed and there are eight others injured.

Monday 22 November 2004

STV News

It's been described as football's game of hate. The Old Firm showdown at the weekend was one of the most explosive in recent years. Today the First Minister slammed both Rangers and Celtic. Jack McConnell said the scenes were unacceptable and a step back in time.

Even by Old Firm standards this was an intense game, including sendings-off, incidents that should have resulted in more sendings-off, accusations of provocation by various players towards the crowd, police involvement and more.

2005

The concentration camps at Auschwitz Birkenau were liberated in January 1945. Of the six million who died in the Holocaust, one and a half million had perished there.

To mark the 60th anniversary, I travelled to Poland with producer Howard Simpson and cameraman Neil McLaren. Despite being very sunny, it was bitterly cold and the three of us were chilled to the bone. And to the soul.

We produced three reports. The images Neil filmed, the survivors Howard had found and the melancholic music of Arvo Part's 'Spiegel im Spiegel', all made my words superfluous.

Monday 24 January 2005

STV News

This Thursday is Holocaust Memorial Day when the world remembers the millions who died in the Nazi extermination camps. This year also commemorates the 60th anniversary of the liberation of Auschwitz. More than any other death camp, Auschwitz symbolises the horror of the Holocaust. For *Scotland Today*, I visited the camp in Southern Poland.

DAY 1

JM: (*shot of Polish road sign with the name Oswiecim*) The southern Polish town of Oswiecim is rather nondescript. Houses, a railway and some factories (*shot of sign saying Auschwitz*). But when it's given its German name it takes on a much greater significance.

ERNEST LEVY, Auschwitz Survivor: One simply did not want to believe it that things like that are happening. You don't want to believe it. Like my late father, who perished in Buchenwald, always said, 'It'll be alright, y'know. Just one more dance. We will move.' But we didn't move. We got caught in the tragedy.

TERESA WONTOR-CICHY, Auschwitz Historian: It's a cemetery. The biggest cemetery in the world.

JM: (*shots of museum displays*) This is human hair. Some pleats remain in place. It was used to make carpets and nets. There are shoes. Personal items. Other remains (*shot of children's clothes and toys*), like so much at Auschwitz, are beyond words.

MARIANNE GRANT, Auschwitz Survivor: Most of the children were taken away. Of course the babies they took away right away. The children were gassed and, for work, only the adults were allowed to live.

JM: (*at the gas chamber*) The dying was neither quick. Nor quiet.

ERNEST LEVY: You couldn't breathe from the stench. It was lying on my chest the smell. The terrible, terrible stench. Och, it is indescribable.

JM: Some survivors found sanctuary in Scotland. We'll hear their stories tomorrow.

DAY 2

In this second report we hear from those who survived and found refuge here in Scotland.

JM: 60 years ago the Third Reich was facing collapse and the Nazis had failed in their attempt to wipe out the Jews from Europe. In time many of these displaced people, who had lost everything, found sanctuary in the UK. For some, Scotland became home. They brought with them vivid testimony of the horrors of the death camps.

ERNEST LEVY, 40 years in Scotland: They didn't look at you, practically. Life and death, but for them it was absolutely nothing. Just, you go there, you go there. I looked reasonably well and young and so I was sent to the left. But there was no real thought in it, who is going to the right, who is going to live, who is going to die.

MARIANNE GRANT, 40 years in Scotland: When Mengele (*Josef Mengele, the notorious Nazi doctor at Auschwitz, known as the Angel of Death*) called you, well I tell you, I was trembling. And he said, 'You draw me this.' And I did that and I knew if I made a blob this was me finished. I actually painted for my life.

BOB KUTNER, Jewish Refugee and allied interrogator – 50 years in Scotland: He was a young man about 19. SS, I think he was an officer. But when I interrogated him – I had the documentation lying there – and I said that it said here that he'd killed nine Jews in a cellar. And he said, 'No I didn't, it was only eight.' He kept giving me an argument and then he said, 'Ah well, what's one Jew more or less?'

JM: Every victim had a story. One of particular resonance for Scotland was that of Stefan Jasieński, a Polish soldier who trained here before returning to aid the resistance.

TERESA WONTOR-CICHY, Auschwitz Historian: He was captured and brought here to Auschwitz and to different cells. But in one of them he stayed and he left some drawings. In January '45, so a few days before the liberation, Stefan Jasieński was executed here in Auschwitz.

JM: These are carvings that Stefan Jasieński made on his cell door here in Auschwitz. It's mostly biographical detail and happier moments from his life. For instance, here's his family crest. And here he is parachuting back into Poland. Of particular interest to us, though, is this one here – a greyhound dog from Glasgow. When Jasieński and his comrades were training in Scotland they enjoyed nothing more than going to the greyhound racing in Glasgow. And night after night they saw this dog, number four, coming in last. One evening Jasieński had a good feeling about the dog, bet on it and sure enough the dog won. It's rather moving to think that this greyhound from Glasgow brought some light to Jasieński in his last, dark, desperate hours here in Auschwitz.

JM: Why do you think you survived when so many others didn't?

ERNEST LEVY: In the back of your mind there is always a little hope left, a little hope. Maybe I'll survive and I will tell the world what happened. It's that incentive, you know? And that's always at the back of your mind, maybe I will survive. I will fight on. Fight on and fight on 'til the last moment. Don't give in.

DAY 3

JM: (*Walking through Auschwitz*) What's very disconcerting about Auschwitz is that it is not exactly as you expect it to appear. This apparent avenue, for example, is almost unthreatening. (*Turning to reveal prison wire*) It's only when you see it from a different perspective and you see the barbed wire and the watchtower that you realise this was a place of horror. Block 11 was the Death Block and at the Death Wall literally thousands and thousands of men, women and children were executed.

MARIANNE GRANT, Auschwitz Survivor:
Anything can happen again, anywhere. You can see people are hating each other and killing each other all over the world today, which is horrendous. That's why we can't forget, we must never forget. We've got to bring it up again and again and again.

JM: This pond is a deep, gloomy, grey colour. That may be explained by the fact that it lies adjacent to what was once a gas chamber and crematorium here at Birkenau. The ashes of countless thousands of people were dumped in this water.

ERNEST LEVY, Auschwitz Survivor:
We can't turn the clock back. We have to learn to co-exist. We have to learn from the past and it is a very important anniversary. Because here we are, the last Mohicans, who can tell you the first hand experiences. There are very few left. And with every survivor who dies and every day that passes, to remember what happened to the world, becomes more and more important.

BOB KUTNER, Jewish Refugee:
The evil of those days can be repeated and repeated and repeated if it isn't stopped. It's a bit late to stop it now, but it's not too late to teach oncoming generations what that evil was. And you can only hope that most young people will appreciate that what happened then was the most unbelievable blot on humanity.

JM: More visitors of all ages are coming here than ever before. Perhaps they recognise the pleas in the memorial here, 'Forever let this place be a cry of despair and a warning to humanity.'

Ernest Levy died in 2009, aged 84.

Marianne Grant died in 2007, aged 86.

MAKE POVERTY HISTORY MARCH
Monday 6 June 2005

DIARY: Interview with Bob Geldof, who is the focus of the anti-poverty protestors ahead of the G8 summit. I pressed him on the point of concerns about his call for a million to converge on Edinburgh. His point was – and he said it openly – that the question was silly given the scale of poverty in Africa.

I made the case that the message of poverty was being overshadowed by security concerns – precisely the points that were being made in the Scottish Parliament today. He was a strange interviewee, either monosyllabic or verbose, but not unpleasant.

Saturday 2 July 2005

STV News – live from The Meadows in Edinburgh

This is *Scotland Today* live from Edinburgh and one of the biggest demonstrations this country has ever seen. An estimated 225,000 people have marched through the streets of the capital and formed a human ring around the city centre. Their message to the world leaders arriving in Gleneagles next week is clear – Make Poverty History. They hope that message will be heard.

VOX POPS WITH MARCHERS:

I think all these amounts of people can make a difference, even if it's a small one.

If you don't do anything you won't get anything. Join in and make your voice heard.

I hope it'll make a difference. I'm not full of confidence, but I hope it will. Damn well should because there's an awful lot of people here saying what they think and I hope someone's listening.

JM: The build up to this rally was, arguably, almost as much about the possibility of trouble as it was about the actual message itself. Thankfully, despite the huge turnout, there were no arrests.

The rally has heard from very powerful speakers with very powerful messages, among them comic and actor Eddie Izzard and *Lord of the Rings* star Billy Boyd. They both join us now.

JM: Billy Boyd from *Lord of the Rings*, you're a Scot, have you ever seen anything like this here?

BILLY BOYD: No, I don't think we have in Scotland. I mean this is huge. Someone was just saying it's over 200,000 people. I think at one point they were expecting 40–50,000 people, so it's huge. In fact it's so huge that me and Eddie tried to get on the march at one point and we couldn't even get on. We had to do our own.

JM: That attitude is there, but do you think that in the reality it will happen, something will change?

EDDIE IZZARD: They've made political investment in this and if this week goes off and nothing happens they're going to feel rather foolish. And people do want to leave a legacy, there's egos involved here and so there is political agendas and whatever, but I think leaving a legacy of we made slavery history now let's make poverty history, it can be done.

JM: Eddie Izzard and Billy Boyd, thanks for joining us.

JM: Today's rally here in Edinburgh, a huge rally, is the beginning of a series of events building up to and through the G8 Summit at Gleneagles. A very powerful message has been sent to world leaders. This time next week we will know if they have listened.

G8 SUMMIT AT GLEANEAGLES
Wednesday 6 July 2005

STV News at Six – live from Gleneagles
Good evening, live from Gleneagles where behind us eight of the world's most powerful men over the next three days will hold talks aimed at ending poverty in Africa and tackling climate change. But for the second time this week there have been shocking scenes of violence. More than 100 demonstrators have been arrested and up to 30 police officers have been badly injured, some of them requiring hospital treatment...

JM: I'm joined by our Political Editor Bernard Ponsonby. Bernard, again the politics of policing is going to be crucial today. What have you made of today's events?

BERNARD PONSONBY: Well I think we should state a number of things. First of all there was trouble here today, John, because a number of people were hell bent on creating trouble, particularly those anarchists who were at that eco-camp based in Stirling. Now the police would make the point that at the end of the day the world leaders arrived at Prestwick, they were transported by helicopter onto the lawn just here behind us and they're safe and sound. But we also have to bear in mind a number of people have been injured. It took us three hours to get in, it took some of our colleagues four hours to get in and at one point we were held up when literally half a dozen people were dancing in the middle of the road. The police, it appeared, were quite happy to simply watch them dance.

JM: So should the police have been more firm with the anarchists?

BP: That's one of the questions they're going to have to ask themselves overnight. Right from day one they have used this word 'proportionate', proportionate policing, but let's just look at a number of issues. A couple of thousand people who wanted to go to Auchterarder to that G8 alternative march couldn't get there because Gleneagles was cut off because of the activity of these anarchists. These were the people who were hell bent on all of the disruption. Their activities, which were by and large away from Gleneagles, cut across the civil liberties of many people in Central Scotland who couldn't go to work. It cut across the civil liberties of those people who wanted to go to a legitimate protest and couldn't get there. That's a question which I think the police are going to have to reflect on this evening.

I remember returning to the impressive media village and having to go through security check points, showing a special pass. One of the people ahead of me was the First Minister of Scotland, Jack McConnell. This was Scotland and national leaders and their entourages were being flown right onto the hotel grounds, but Scotland's First Minister was obliged to go through the same security as the rest of us. I thought it was demeaning.

The G8 Summit was overtaken on its second day, the 7 July, by the bombings in London. Word began to filter through in the morning to the media centre. At first it was reported as an electrical fault on the underground. When the true scale of the horror became apparent, the Summit became secondary on the news agenda.

Friday 8 July 2005

STV News – Live from Gleneagles

Good evening from Gleneagles. Poverty has not been made history. The G8 summit, so overshadowed by events in London yesterday, has now broken up with assurances from Tony Blair that big progress has been made on Africa. Now they have agreed to double aid to $50 billion, but some charities are saying tonight that the world's richest countries have turned their backs on the world's poor.

TONY BLAIR, Prime Minister:
It's in the nature of politics that you do not achieve absolutely everything you want to achieve, but nonetheless I believe we have made very substantial progress indeed. As I said to you earlier today, we did not simply, by this communiqué, 'make poverty history', but we did show how it can be done.

SIR BOB GELDOF, Live8 organiser:
Africa and the poor of that continent have got more out of the last three days than they have ever got in any previous summit, let's be clear. And they got that because three billion people demanded that it should be so.

The biggest entourage I saw at the whole event was that fussing around U2 singer Bono. He came onto the media platform and moved from one network news outlet to another, repeating the same pompous line about adapting Churchill's quote of it not being the end of poverty, but the beginning of the end. But he – or one of his many minders – refused to do STV, despite the fact that we had done so much to promote his Live 8 concert at Murrayfield. Had I not been live on air at the time I would have made my views known to him. It's perhaps best that I never got the chance.

On the final afternoon of the summit, I stood on my own at our position on the TV platform looking onto Gleneagles Hotel, just clarifying my thoughts for our *Six O'Clock News*. A big limousine purred away and the occupant in the rear seat waved as he passed by. It was only at the last moment I realised it was the Russian President Vladimir Putin. I looked around me and couldn't see anyone else. He must have been waving at the lone figure he saw watching him and I hadn't responded. I watched my back for a few days after that.

Thursday 22 September 2005

STV News

Mike Watson, the Labour Lord and former Glasgow MSP, is spending his first night in a prison cell after being sentenced to 16 months for starting a fire and endangering lives at an upmarket hotel. The sheriff said jail was the only option for the disgraced politician who'd admitted setting curtains alight after an awards dinner for the country's top politicians.

Monday 31 October 2005

STV News

The leader of the Scottish Conservatives, David McLetchie, has resigned over the row about the taxi expenses he charged to the Scottish Parliament. The circumstances of his departure are ironically similar to those which saw the departure of the former First Minister Henry McLeish. Mr McLetchie had led the attack at the time and now he himself has been brought down.

The row had been about the use of taxis for party political rather than parliamentary purposes, which is against the rules. Mr McLetchie said the claims had been made in good faith, but recognised the damage done to the Scottish Conservatives. Annabel Goldie took over as leader unopposed.

Tuesday 20 December 2005

STV News

Just as thousands of people do every year, they promised to love, honour and respect each other in sickness and in health, for richer, for richer, for poorer, for better, for worse. John Maguire and Laurence Scott-Mackay became the first couple in Scotland to exchange vows in what has been called a 'gay wedding', or to give it its official name, a civil partnership ceremony.

2006

Thursday 26 January 2006

DIARY: Met Ronnie Burgess, a former newspaper snapper, who took the classic image of serial killer Peter Manuel smiling with a curl of hair falling forward. He snatched the photo despite Manuel's warning (*Manuel was not a suspect at this point*) and Manuel told him he would get him. He said it wasn't a threat, it was a promise. 'The man who crossed mass murderer Peter Manuel and lived.' Makes the piece. Burgess was also sitting in the High Court in Glasgow when Manuel was sentenced to death.

Friday 27 January 2006

STV News

Fifty years ago this month the body of a young woman (*Anne Knielands*) was found in East Kilbride. Her murder was the first of a number of killings that would terrorise Glasgow and Lanarkshire. A mass murderer was on the loose, killing indiscriminately. Young women never returned home from nights out and families died in their beds. The terror ended only when Peter Manuel went to the gallows at Barlinnie Prison.

JM: Peter Manuel was a career criminal. A nocturnal creature who ranged across Lanarkshire and Glasgow from his family home in Birkenshaw. But the murder of Anne Knielands made him a killer, a killer who couldn't stop.

RONNIE BURGESS, Photographer: He was talking to the police officer and I thought this is my opportunity to get a picture of him. Put the camera up, took his picture and he said, 'I'll get you for that.' And the policeman said, 'Are you threatening him?' He says, 'No,' he says, 'I'm promising him.' And then the next day he came into the newspaper office looking for me... I saw him next when I was sitting in the press box at the High Court in Glasgow when Lord Cameron passed his judgement on him – 'Hang by the neck until you are dead.' And that was Peter Manuel for me.

Wednesday 1 February 2006

STV News

Anti-war vigils are taking place across *Scotland Tonight* protesting the mounting human cost of Britain's engagement in Iraq. It follows the death yesterday of Gordon Pritchard, the 100th British soldier to die since the conflict began. It emerged today that the Edinburgh corporal met the Prime Minister during his service in Iraq. Tony Blair is coming under ever increasing pressure to bring the troops home.

Wednesday 15 February 2006

DIARY: Shereen, Jane and Sarah are all leaving the company, their voluntary redundancies accepted. Alan Saunby is another one going. Shereen is the most popular face and her loss will be a blow.

The STV audience adored Shereen. She had a warmth that came through the screen and everywhere I went people would ask where she was. We came through a lot together, presented many big programmes, laughed, squabbled and made a good team. She called herself my 'other, other half' and that just about sums it up. It was my pleasure to work with her. Her departure genuinely was the end of an era at STV.

I always looked like the bodyguard next to the glamour of Shereen, Sarah and Jane. It was a role that came easily to me and I was happy with it. I could have gone on-air wearing a vest and nobody would really have noticed, provided I had a tie on. It's only ever about the ties for men. For women it's much more complicated.

Friday 17 March 2006

STV News

Good evening. Thousands of people turned out today to pay their final respects to Jimmy Johnstone. The Celtic legend died on Monday after a long battle with Motor Neurone Disease. His former Lisbon Lion teammates, current Old Firm managers and players, joined mourners to say goodbye to a football great.

JM: They came in their thousands for the last time to cheer Jimmy Johnstone at Parkhead. They paid tribute to a man whose footballing talent brings colour to the black and white footage of the time. And his team mates remembered too. Together they bestrode the football fields of Scotland and of Europe as Champions.

BILLY MCNEILL, Lisbon Lion: The first time I laid eyes on Jimmy Johnstone was whilst playing in a first team game at Celtic Park as a young player and when the ball went behind the goals at the Rangers end at Celtic Park this wee ballboy with a mass of red curly hair used to get the ball and start flicking it up. He was flicking it up 20–30 times. The team wasn't particularly sparkling then, not as good as the team today. Wee Neilie Mauchin saw him and shouted, 'quick get that ball off that wee fella before he embarrasses us further!'

WILLIE HAUGHEY, Family Friend: Could I read a telegram that the family received this morning that would have meant so much to Jimmy? It's actually from his hero, it says 'On behalf of all the members of this club, our deepest condolences at the death of Jimmy Johnstone… 'from Alfredo Di Stefano and everyone at Real Madrid.'

JM: At Parkhead the wind twisted and tormented a flag. Just as Jimmy Johnstone had done to defenders throughout the years.

SMOKING BAN

Friday 24 March 2006

STV News – live from a Glasgow pub
A new page in Scotland's history will be written this Sunday, 26 March 2006, when it becomes illegal to smoke in indoor public places. Tonight is the last Friday night smokers will be able to light-up while enjoying a night out. The measures will be enforced with a determination to halt Scotland's unenviable health record. Some killer facts. 13,000 people die every year in Scotland from using tobacco. Around 1,000 Scots who have never smoked die every year from passive smoking. It's estimated this ban will prevent 219

deaths a year from lung cancer and heart disease, and up to 187 from stroke and respiratory diseases. Of course not everyone is in favour of the ban. There are those who argue bars could be forced to close, jobs could go, and the ban will signal the end of social culture as we know it.

JACK MCCONNELL, First Minister: I think Scotland is a law abiding country, I think we are law abiding people, I think people understand the arguments. The reality is that more than two thirds of Scots are not smokers, more than two thirds of those who do smoke want to give up and I think we will see widespread compliance for the ban, enthusiastic support for it and eventually those are particularly unhappy realising that they need to go with the majority.

The ban was introduced without too many problems. It is now a common sight across the country to see people standing outside pubs and offices having a fag.

Thursday 6th April 2006

STV News – live from Fife
Good evening. The deadly H5N1 bird flu virus is here in Cellardyke in Fife. A dead swan found here in the harbour just at the slipway behind me there has tested positive. That was confirmed this afternoon. Tonight the Executive has announced sweeping measures to contain the virus, but already there are 14 other birds across the country being tested. A huge area from Fife, moving north through Perth to Dundee to Angus, has been declared a wild bird risk

area. A quarter of a million birds need to be taken indoors to prevent the spread of the disease.

If contracted by humans, bird flu can be lethal. Under normal circumstances humans are unlikely to be infected, but the threat of a pandemic caused by a cross-species virus remains very real. No humans were infected in Scotland and the restrictions were lifted that same month.

I was despatched to Cellardyke at short notice without knowing much about bird flu. At the back of my mind there was a slight concern about travelling to the place where this virus was potentially lurking. As I walked down the picturesque cobbled streets of the village, I was disconcerted to see two separate splashes of vomit. This was ramped up even further when a downy feather blew into my face as the street opened up to reveal the harbour. Then on the final countdown to going on-air, I glanced down at my script as a prompt and saw streaks of blood on it. I managed to control the panic as I went live. Just.

It turned out the blood had come from a paper cut on my finger. One specialist later told me, you'd have had to boil that swan down into soup and drink it before you'd even have been at risk. I didn't know that at the time, though.

STV MOVES TO PACIFIC QUAY

In July 2006, STV moved from our old studios at Cowcaddens to new premises on the south bank of the River Clyde at Pacific Quay. It was the start of a new era. A key part of that was the move to single presentation. We took an entirely new approach and changed the role from one of presenter to that of an anchor who was the focal point for live links to reporters/ interviewees at other locations.

The new era was a success on every level. The newer studio allowed us to make Scotland Today look so much better. Our audience climbed significantly and there was widespread critical praise.

This was when the 'I'm John MacKay' took on a life of its own as a catchphrase. I had said it often enough before in programmes with other presenters, but maybe it stood out more when I was on my own. It is repeated back to me constantly. Indeed, I've been told more than once that a child's first words have been 'Ohn A-Kay.'

Friday 11 August 2006

STV News

Scotland remains on red alert this evening after the news of a terrorist plot to blow up passenger planes. EasyJet has warned customers that all its London–bound flights from Glasgow, Edinburgh and Aberdeen have been cancelled today. Air travellers have been told to expect further disruption throughout the weekend.

Tuesday 22 August 2006

STV News

One in ten immigrants who has come to the UK in the past two years from Europe, has settled in Scotland. The majority of the 32,000 people who've arrived here are working in the hospitality industry. Both Glasgow and Edinburgh already have large Polish communities, but other nationalities are now establishing their identities.

Monday 2 October 2006

STV News

A police investigation is underway tonight into perjury allegations arising from the Tommy Sheridan defamation trial. It was just two months ago that Mr Sheridan won an action against the News of the World, which had printed sex claims about him. But yesterday the Sunday newspaper published video footage which allegedly show the MSP admitting a number of the claims.

Wednesday 1 November 2006

STV News

According to a new poll, more than half of the electorate now want an end to the Union. In the ICM poll, 51 per cent said they are for an Independent Scotland, 39 per cent against and ten per cent said they didn't know. The findings have also handed a boost to the SNP, as 32 per cent said they would vote nationalist compared to 30 per cent for Labour on the constituency vote in next year's Scottish elections.

2007

Monday 8 January 2007

DIARY: **The launch of our split news operation, where we split the programme mid-way through for five or six minutes and the east coast gets news more local to them and same for the west.**

Tuesday 23 January 2007

STV News

The First Minister Jack McConnell says he's disappointed to have been dragged into the cash for peerages controversy. Scotland's Labour leader was questioned by police on a nomination he made to the House of Lords as part of their ten-month long inquiry into the alleged sale of honours for money by leading politicians.

The Cash for Honours scandal had begun the previous year after complaints by the SNP MP Angus MacNeil that wealthy donors to the Labour Party had been offered peerages. No one was charged after an investigation lasting more than a year. Tony Blair was the first serving Prime Minister to be interviewed (as a witness) during a police investigation.

Wednesday 24 January 2007

STV News

Over the last four years thousands of youngsters have been taking part in one of the biggest ever studies into family life. Its initial findings reveal step-families will soon outnumber any other. Single parents now raise one in five children and grandparents play an even greater role in their upbringing.

Thursday 1 March 2007

STV News

The Royal Bank of Scotland has announced the biggest profit ever made by a Scottish company. Edinburgh-based RBS made 9.2 billion, 16 per cent more than the previous year. Thousands of its Scottish staff are to receive bonuses for the ninth year in a row.

SCOTTISH PARLIAMENT ELECTIONS 2007

Wednesday 2 May 2007

STV News

The campaigning is almost over. Early tomorrow morning the polling stations open for what is expected to be one of the most dramatic elections in recent history. The polls show the gap between the two leading parties is the closest in more than 30 years.

And our Political Editor Bernard Ponsonby joins us now. Your thoughts on the campaign and Labour prospects?

BERNARD PONSONBY: Since last year, John, Labour have fought this election on the policy of their principal opponents – Independence. Yes they believe they have a responsibility to say to voters this will lead to chaos and you will end up paying. Jack McConnell admits it's negative. Is that negativity born out of desperation? Is it better ground than fighting on your record and defending a lame duck Prime Minister? Well the polls are showing that Labour are clawing their way back – if they are to be the largest

party on Friday the strategy will be vindicated. If not, perhaps recrimination and even resignation will be the order of the day. You simply can't lose and expect to lead. The stakes are high for Jack McConnell tomorrow. I think he personally has had a good campaign, but has he done enough to hold onto power and to his job? Over to the voters.

Our Political Correspondent Michael Crow is outside the SNP headquarters in Edinburgh: Michael are we on the verge of political history?

MICHAEL CROW: It is just too close to call. There are a number of important factors which could determine whether the SNP win this election. Firstly, have they done enough to attract the undecided voters? Secondly, will disaffected Labour voters switch to the SNP or stay at home? There is no doubt that the core SNP vote will turn out. They are enthused, they feel their time has come. The question is has Alex Salmond done enough to persuade people who haven't voted SNP before to vote for him tomorrow? They've spent over a million pounds on the campaign. They are ahead in the polls. If they can't win this election then one wonders if their time will ever come.

Friday 4 May 2007

STV News – live from the Scottish Parliament with Andrea Brymer

Good evening from the Capital and welcome to this 60 minute special, live from the Scottish Parliament. The Scottish National Party have won the Scottish Elections, by the narrowest of margins. Within the last half hour, at the last count, of the last region to declare, the SNP secured victory by 47 seats to Labour's 46. But how, here at the heart of Scottish democracy, could things gone so wrong? How were 150,000 voters written off? How could so many ballot papers have been spoiled?

Just to confirm the total results – the SNP on 47 seats, Labour on 46, the Conservatives on 17, the Liberal Democrats on 16, the Greens on two and an independent, Margo MacDonald.

JM: So the SNP have won the Election by one seat. Nicola Sturgeon of the party joins us now at the Scottish Parliament. Congratulations on your success.

NICOLA STURGEON, Deputy Leader, SNP
It's a tremendous achievement, John, the people of Scotland have today chosen a new political path. They've opted to put the SNP in the driving seat of Scotland's new Government. It's an enormous responsibility and it's one we're determined to discharge with humility, with imagination and with a great deal of passion.

JM: But it's not quite the margin you would have wished.

NS: We are in a PR system and, of course, narrow margins are to be expected, but we've not only won the largest number of seats, we're

significantly ahead in terms of the popular vote. I think the SNP have resoundingly won this election. Labour have lost it. The people of Scotland want now a new political direction and it's for the SNP to lead them in that new direction.

JM: On this, the most controversial of elections, it was an extremely tense night at polling stations across the whole country. Every vote has been hard fought for, in one of the closest ever battles between Labour and the SNP. Here's the story of the night.

(*Michael Crow script*) It was meant to be the most exciting election for a generation. It has ended up being a national embarrassment and a democratic farce. Up to 150,000 people have had their votes rejected because of a catalogue of problems. Confusion over how to fill in the ballot papers has rendered many invalid. People have been putting crosses in the wrong place and numbers where they shouldn't have. This has led to problems with the new electronic counting system, delayed results and left democracy in chaos.

JM: Our Political Editor Bernard Ponsonby joins us now. Bernard we have talked about the chaos, what about the politics of election 2007?

BP: Labour's vote didn't collapse, you know, but the SNP's shot ahead so much that we have to say that Labour's 50 year dominance of Scottish politics is at an end. The battle between Labour and the SNP was so fierce it has squeezed minor parties right out of our political system. Although that Labour vote didn't collapse, they have lost this election. There is now a question mark tonight over Jack McConnell's future because they were kicked more brutally in their heartlands than ever before. The Tories have flatlined and the Lib Dems, I think, will be largely disappointed by their showing.

ALEX SALMOND, Leader, SNP
Scotland wants a change of Government, they want the SNP to be given the opportunity to show what we can do. That's why we've been voted in as the largest party – by one seat in terms of seats, but by a very, very substantial vote in terms of the popular vote and we've got to fulfil that obligation and to approach people in that manner.

JACK MCCONNELL, Leader, Scottish Labour
Five days ago all of the pundits were writing us off and Labour has achieved the most significant turnaround in the final week of an election campaign in Scotland in living memory.

Wednesday 9 May 2007
STV News
Scotland's 129 new MSPs were sworn in today at the Scottish Parliament, however they failed to elect a Presiding Officer and had to adjourn proceedings until Monday. Meanwhile, talks between the SNP and the Greens to set up an Executive are ongoing, but the Liberal Democrats are still refusing to negotiate.

One of the first acts of the new SNP administration was to change the title of the Scottish Executive to the Scottish Government.

Wednesday 9 May 2007 (cont)
STV News
Glasgow's Commonwealth Games Bid team have made their final pitch to host the competition in 2014. During a ceremony in London earlier, they submitted their final plans for the Games with a display of traditional Scottish song and dance to convince the judges of their merits. Our reporter Debi Edward was there and joins us now from London, Debi, how did it go?

DEBI EDWARD, *STV* News
I think the judges couldn't fail to be impressed with the bid team and a rousing rendition of 'Scotland the Brave.' As for the bid document itself, well I haven't quite had time to digest all of its 600 pages but it does give a comprehensive breakdown of the venues and costs of the Games. The team claim to have the £338 million bill covered and 90 per cent of the infrastructure already in place or due for completion within 3–4 years. This all made for a confident presentation this lunchtime.

Monday 14 May 2007
STV News
The days continue to pass, there are still few leads, but the McCann family's belief that their daughter, Madeleine, is safe and well is unwavering. Her father Gerry McCann said that until the family

saw 'concrete evidence to the contrary' they continued to be convinced she is safe. His wife Kate, clinging to hope, said she could not even consider leaving Portugal without her daughter.

Madeleine McCann disappeared on holiday with her family in Portugal on the evening of 3 May 2007. The story circulated on the 4 May, but because of the Scottish Election result and the verdict in the first Peter Tobin trial, there was no space to carry it. At the time that didn't seem significant. The story has never gone away as her parents continue to hope that she will be found.

ALEX SALMOND BECOMES FIRST MINISTER

Wednesday 16 May 2007

STV News

Scotland has a new First Minister and, for the first time, he is a Nationalist. The SNP leader Alex Salmond was elected after winning a vote of all MSPs. He beat the Labour leader Jack McConnell by the narrowest of margins. But with the Conservatives and the Lib Dems abstaining, it was enough for history to be made.

Live now to our Political Editor Bernard Ponsonby at the Scottish Parliament. Bernard, a day of enormous historical significance for the SNP?

BERNARD PONSONBY: Yes John. After so many false dawns they are finally in Government. Independence is closer but only really in a theoretical sense. Why? Because tomorrow the cold chill of realpolitik will hit Alex Salmond. He has no majority in this place. No majority on the bureau that decides the business and no majority on the committees. The next four years will be a long slog, but an exciting one nevertheless.

JM: Politicians from all parties have also been paying tribute to the outgoing First Minister, Jack McConnell. Today he said it had been a privilege and an honour to lead Scotland for the last five-and-a-half years and he hoped he had left the country in a better state than when he had come to power.

MICHAEL CROW, Political Correspondent:
He defined Devolution by tackling hitherto taboos – the smoking ban, sectarianism, Labour's hold on local government. The legacy is one of steadying Devolution.

GORDON BROWN BECOMES PRIME MINISTER

Wednesday 27 June 2007

STV News – live from Westminster

Good Evening. It has been a day of ceremony, a day of history here at Westminster – the day a Scot once again became the Prime Minister of the United Kingdom... The 27th of June 2007, a date Gordon Brown is unlikely to forget. As power was handed from Tony Blair to Number Ten's new incumbent, it marked the realisation of a life long dream for the boy from Kirkcaldy.

TONY BLAIR, Prime Minister – in the House of Commons:

I wish everyone, friend or foe, well. And that is that. The end.

GORDON BROWN, Prime Minister – outside 10 Downing Street:
I have just accepted the invitation from Her Majesty the Queen to form a Government… I grew up in the town that I now represent in Parliament. I went to the local school. I wouldn't be standing here without the opportunities that I received there. And I want the best of chances for everyone. That is my mission.

JM: It's important to Scotland obviously that the relationship between the First Minister and the new Prime Minister is workable. Do you think you can achieve that?

ALEX SALMOND, First Minister:
I'm quite certain I'll get on with Gordon Brown a lot better than I could get on with Tony Blair. Indeed, I'm certain I'll get on with Gordon Brown a lot better than Gordon Brown got on with Tony Blair. So I'm looking at this very constructively and I want to work as best we can for the people of Scotland, as well as having legitimate disagreements about the constitutional future of our country.

JM: So Gordon Brown is now the Prime Minister of the United Kingdom. The Blair era is over. The Brown era has begun. From Westminster, from all of us, goodnight.

Our programme from Westminster was a challenging one. I was standing beneath a pergola to protect me from the rain that had been pouring all afternoon. Minutes before going on-air, the cameraman asked me to take a few paces back to catch more of the light. At that instant a gust of wind blew beneath the pergola, lifting up the roof and a pool of water that had gathered there. I was soaked and had no idea where it had come from. I thought someone had thrown something onto me. The only choice was to run the few hundred yards from our position on College Green back to the media centre at Millbank. An alert member of staff there had seen what happened and came running out with towels. The quickest of dry downs and then ready to go on-air. What more could go wrong? I had pre-recorded our opening titles. As soon as they started playing all contact with the studio was lost (including mobile phones). I knew the titles were running and I tried to judge when I should start speaking. It wasn't entirely clean, but it could have been much worse. Bernard Ponsonby was at Downing Street and comms with him went down during our two-way. Bernard's input was a significant part of the programme, so he had to make his way quickly from Downing Street to our broadcast position on College Green. It is an abiding memory of Bernard running towards me with, in his own words, 'my three arses bouncing off the pavement.'

Tony Blair's premiership will be remembered as one that started with energy and hope in 1997, but was overtaken by spin and will be forever tainted by the Iraq War. How a man of Tony Blair's apparent political surefootedness could have got it so wrong will always be a mystery. We went to war in the pretext of Iraq having weapons of mass destruction ready to strike against us. They didn't and few people believed they did.

Saturday 30 June 2007

DIARY: **Two Islamist terrorists drove a jeep loaded with gas canisters into the entrance of Glasgow Airport. They had based themselves in a house in Houston in Renfrewshire, as they prepared to explode two car bombs in London. When that plot failed and they knew the police were onto them, they tried to carry out a terror attack at Glasgow Airport. That failed also through a combination of their incompetence and the heroics of police and public at the scene.**

I had gone on holiday that day and the Glasgow Airport attack must rank as the biggest story I missed.

BILLY CONNOLLY
Thursday 2 August 2007
STV News

Billy Connolly says the silent majority in Scotland should stand up to the minority of bigots who give the country a bad name. He has been named as patron of the Celtic Foundation, which has tackling sectarianism as one of its principle aims. Speaking to *Scotland Today*, the Scottish comic legend was frank in his condemnation.

BILLY CONNOLLY: I think the only way to prevent bigotry is by example – by children looking at you at a game, by looking at you standing up for yourself and saying how much you dislike this thing... It's not good saying something when the news is on. A sort of 'That'll be right' attitude when someone says something about Israel, about Protestants... It's a sharp intake of breath when someone says something, that's where it all begins. It starts at home. And then they start hanging out with people who feel the same way. I am not a bigot, I don't spend time with them. I know I can recognise them a mile away, the Celtic supporter with their weird tattoos. Guys approach me with them. I think it's getting better.

Billy Connolly was a comedy hero of mine and as we waited to do the interview he proved why. He didn't work a routine, he was just a naturally funny, funny man.

JACK MCCONNELL RESIGNS AS SCOTTISH LABOUR LEADER
Wednesday 15 August 2007
STV News

The former First Minister Jack McConnell has resigned as leader of the Scottish Labour party. He had been under pressure to quit his job after losing power in the Holyrood elections back in May. He will remain an MSP, but will also carry out education work in Africa. Tonight Wendy Alexander has emerged as the overwhelming favourite to take over as leader.

JACK MCCONNELL: I was in no doubt when I took over that Devolution was in trouble and I had to steady the ship. That was very much my view at the time. And I think we proved over the last four years that once you've steadied the ship and you've set a course, it is possible to make progress, and that happened in a whole range of areas.

ALEX SALMOND, First Minister:

I think he once said – you would judge every First Minister by whether he left Scotland a better place than he found it – I think judged on that criteria leaves a substantial contribution to Scottish public life and I wish him well.

NICOL STEPHEN, Leader, Scottish Liberal Democrats
He was always prepared to set aside narrow party dogma to work in coalition. Being First Minister when there are two parties in power is never easy.

WENDY ALEXANDER BECOMES NEW LEADER OF SCOTTISH LABOUR

Tuesday 21 August 2007

STV News
Wendy Alexander is the new Leader of the Scottish Labour Party. She was the sole candidate for the position when nominations closed today and she will be formally installed on the 14 September.

WENDY ALEXANDER, Scottish Labour Leader:
I think what happened today is that Labour signalled it's ready to move on. We need to reform the party, we need to review our policies and we need to reconnect with voters and that's what we're all united in doing... I think what Scotland is looking for from its politicians is change, there's no doubt about that. But I think the change they're really looking for is social and economic change. It is about schools and hospitals much more than they're

looking for constitutional change and so the real question is, is Scotland interested in the people's priorities or in Alex Salmond's priorities? And that's the debate that we're going to take to him on behalf of the people.

Monday 8 October 2007

STV News
The Prime Minister has been defending his handling of the on/off election debacle. Gordon Brown did admit that he had considered calling a snap election, but denied he'd been put off by a Tory surge in the opinion polls.

There was intense speculation, fuelled by Downing Street, that Gordon Brown would call a quick election soon after becoming Prime Minister to take advantage of favourable polls. His reputation was damaged when he decided not to, being accused of being a bottler and a ditherer.

Tuesday 23 October 2007

DIARY: **Lucky enough to get a ticket for tonight's Rangers v Barcelona clash in the Champions League. It was a defensive siege for most of the game, but Rangers held out for a 0–0 draw in an enthralling game. The young Argentinian Messi is superb.**

Reporters at Ibrox were served with scotch pies and bovrils at half-time. It was amusing to watch the Spanish journalists studying the pies in wonder, despite the reassurances from their Scottish counterparts. At the end of the game, almost to a man, they had nibbled away at the crust of the pie, but the meat was left untouched.

Wednesday 31 October 2007

DIARY: **The Chief Inspector of Prisons**

made yet another report from yet another prison highlighting overcrowding. We could have taken any report from any month over the past ten years and done the same thing. It's dull and repetitive and, frankly, most people couldn't care less.

Friday 9 November 2007

STV News

Good evening from Glasgow – tonight the heart of the Commonwealth. Over a quarter of the world's population – that's almost two billion people – have chosen this city to host the 2014 Games.

DEBI EDWARD in Sri Lanka: Yes in seven years time it's hoped the result which was dramatically delivered here in Sri Lanka will transform Scotland's biggest city, its people and its health.

JM: So this is where the hard work begins. Glasgow has got seven years to get ready for 2014. A great deal of planning is already in place to make sure we have world class facilities capable of hosting top flight events.

Wednesday 14 November 2007

STV News

For 16 years, the family of Scottish schoolgirl Vicky Hamilton have endured the agony of not knowing where she was. Tonight that long wait is over. Her remains have been found in the garden of a house in Kent by police investigating the disappearance of another teenager. The house was previously occupied by Peter Tobin.

2008

Wednesday 9 January 2008

STV News

Kenny Richey spent 20 years on death row, but tonight he is only moments away from a new life at home in Scotland. The 43-year-old was freed from prison in Ohio on Monday. On leaving jail he thanked all those supporters 'who believed in his innocence'. Tonight he will have chance to thank them in person and will be coming through the terminal at Edinburgh airport shortly.

DIARY: **Successful coverage of the return of the 'Death Row Scot' Kenny Richey to Scotland, live on the programme. Our reporter David Cowan was in the airport and Bernard Ponsonby was outside, so we got two bites at him. It was a very fluid programme, but we handled it well.**

Kenneth Richey, who had been raised in Scotland, had been sentenced to death 21 years previously for setting fire to an apartment in which a 2-year-old girl died. He consistently denied guilt.

DIARY CONT: **The First Minister, Alex Salmond, was touring the building. When he came into the studio where I was waiting, we had a brief conversation about Hearts – his team. He seems dry, relaxed and assured in his role.**

Saturday 15 March 2008

DIARY: **Down to London for the ITN News Awards which are not as prestigious as the RTS (*Royal Television Society*) Awards. Quite a squad of us. The usual routine with these award** ceremonies is that your seating indicates how you've done. We never anticipate much at the ITV awards because we're not formally part of ITV. Anyway, my seat was A1 with the others beside me. I assumed we must have done well. We hadn't. Only won 'Image of the Year' for the burning Cherokee at Glasgow Airport and that was actually taken by a viewer.

Wednesday 23 April 2008

DIARY: Billboards featuring the news team are now on various sites around Glasgow promoting the programme. For today's *Real MacKay* blog – and indeed it ran as an '… and finally' in the programme – I got Sean (*Sean Batty – weatherman*) to stand with me as the poster was pasted up on Shieldhall Road, then sped through it. Worked quite well, but required us to stand in the rain for about 15 minutes. Soaked!

RANGERS IN THE UEFA CUP FINAL 2008

Wednesday 7 May 2008

STV News

George Burley (*Scotland Manager*) has weighed into the Rangers SPL (*Scottish Premier League*) fixture row – saying it's 'ridiculous' a club has been told to play seven games in 18 days. Burley says the Ibrox club have been treated unfairly and are being punished for being successful.

DIARY: A great deal being made of the fixture congestion Rangers are facing and the SPL's unwillingness to help a Scottish team in Europe.

That a Scottish team competing in a European Final was not given the time to prepare properly was yet another indictment of the self-interest that has long plagued the bigger picture in Scottish football.

Wednesday 14 May 2008

STV News from Manchester

Good evening from Manchester on a night when a team from Glasgow are now on the brink of becoming European legends. Rangers play Zenit St Petersburg in the UEFA Cup Final. There will be a worldwide audience of half a billion people and STV is the only place to watch all the action, live from seven O'Clock. We have reporters with the hundred thousand fans in Manchester, with the fans as they travelled down and tens of thousands of those back home in Glasgow at Ibrox.

(*aerial shot*) Outside the stadium we can see some dramatic images from Manchester City centre. They were saying earlier that the sun was out, the sky was blue and the earth was blue, too.

STV News at 10.30pm live from Manchester

Ranger's UEFA cup dream has come to an end. In an enthralling cup final in Manchester, the Ibrox side lost 2–1.

DIARY: A big day and one that ended in predictable disappointment.

Until mid-afternoon I was focused on the fanzone at Albert Square, presenting the morning and lunchtime bulletins from a bus there. I attempted to go in amongst the crowd to do my blog around 10.00am, but was mobbed and pulled almost to the ground and had beer sprayed on me, which made it pointless. Even at that time some people were hammered and I sensed that the exuberance could spill over into trouble. In fairness, there were a lot of people just having a good time, but the usual scum let them down. The state of some fans in the streets was appalling. I was embarrassed. Mind you, at that stage the local Mancunians I spoke to seemed to be enjoying the atmosphere.

I went to the City of Manchester stadium for late afternoon, passing so many pissed fans on the way. Our programme at 6.00pm mostly went well. Everyone seemed pleased and it felt like a good programme, all anchored from trackside.

As for the game, Rangers played their usual ultra-defensive style, although came out a bit more in the second half. After the hour mark I really began to think they might nick something, but the Russians scored around 72 mins and you couldn't see Rangers coming back. Arguably, Walter Smith was slow to respond, but the Russians scored again with almost the last kick of the ball. Disappointing, but Rangers didn't deserve to win. I waited for the presentation of the trophy just about ten rows behind me and headed off to do the late bulletin outside the stadium. Credit to the fans inside the stadium who applauded Zenit as they took the trophy. The late bulletin was really very good, but already reports of trouble after a big screen failed at the Piccadilly fanzone. Got a lift back from cameraman Michael Hunter and others and the flotsam on the streets was a grim sight.

Thursday 15 May 2008

STV News

It started in high spirits, an invasion of Scottish football fans partying in the sun, excited by a UEFA Cup final. But when a big screen failed, leaving thousands of fans unable to watch the game, the night turned into one of running battles and violence. Gordon Brown today said the minority of Rangers fans involved in the chaos in Manchester were a 'disgrace'

DIARY: The usual excuses will be trotted out about the failure of the screens and police overreaction. The fact is that, unfortunately, Scotland has a significant population of idiots who cannot control themselves with alcohol. There was the usual bottle throwing of course, which beggars belief. Who are they trying to hurt?

When we had travelled down to Manchester we saw banners stretched out on motorway footbridges and flyovers as far down as Liverpool wishing Rangers all the best. On the way home we saw only two as we came into Glasgow. One said, 'Welcome home losers.' It was quite funny.

STV News

The man who many said put the Celtic back into Celtic, Tommy Burns, has died from cancer at the age of 51. The former Parkhead player and manager was loved and respected by fans across Glasgow's often bitter footballing divide. Hundreds of them have been paying tribute to him at Celtic Park since early this morning.

RESIGNATION OF WENDY ALEXANDER AS SCOTTISH LABOUR LEADER

Thursday 26 June 2008

STV News

It has been another traumatic day for the Scottish Labour Leader Wendy Alexander. The Scottish Parliament's Standards Committee has voted to suspend her from Parliament for a day for failing to register donations to her leadership campaign. Tonight she insists she will remain as Labour Leader as she suffers the potential humiliation of being the first party chief to be banned from Parliament.

Wendy Alexander resigned as leader of Scottish Labour two days later. She maintained throughout that she had followed parliamentary advice on registering donations.

Monday 15 September 2008

STV News

Share prices at two of Scotland's largest banks, Bank of Scotland (*HBOS*) and The Royal Bank of Scotland (*RBS*), have fallen sharply in response to news that America's fourth largest investment bank, Lehman Brothers, has filed for bankruptcy. *HBOS* saw its share price plummet by 30 per cent while RBS saw a drop of more than 12 per cent.

Tuesday 30 September 2008

DIARY: **Still concerns about the financial meltdown of the markets and threats of bank collapses. For most people, though, I think it is a bit removed. Maybe when the costs of loans increase, or if the economy begins** to collapse and jobs are hit, then people will feel affected, but not yet.

LIVE BROADCAST FROM INSIDE BARLINNIE PRISON

Wednesday 12 November 2008

STV News live from Barlinnie Prison

Good evening from behind the bars of E-hall in Glasgow's Barlinnie prison. Within these century old walls are 1,664 men. Among them fraudsters, drink drivers, gangsters, murderers, child abusers and rapists.

Scotland's biggest jail, currently at 40 per cent over capacity is bursting at the seams with criminals. Rough justice – or just desserts – is what we're looking at tonight, as our reporters are granted unprecedented access to all areas. Over the next half hour – how the prison copes with such numbers. The scourge of drugs. The habitual criminal who continually reoffends. We'll also hear the victims of the inmates and how their lives have been ruined.

JM: The highs and lows of drug dealing and drug abuse are what brings large numbers here. The habits don't end at the jail cell door. Barlinnie is the largest single supplier of methadone in Europe. A lot of hard work goes into rehabilitating addicts before release, but vital efforts are hampered by the smuggling of a steady flow of drugs into the prison.

DIARY: **As we went on-air I was only getting white noise through my ear piece, but I had to keep it in my ear or it would have been seen. I relied on a** visual cue and that went smoothly. The prisoners started shouting and hammering doors when I made reference to 'murderers and rapists' being among them – which is true, although there aren't many there. That noise was maintained for much of the programme.

It all seemed to pass very quickly. I could tell it had gone well. The prison guys were pleased as well, they thought it had been fair.

I was very taken by how comparatively relaxed the regime seemed to be, with prisoners and guards and us mingling. That doesn't change the fact that there are bad bastards in there. However, clearly there are people in there who shouldn't be and nothing is gained by society or them by their incarceration.

Tuesday 2 December 2008

STV News – live from Bathgate

Good evening from Bathgate in West Lothian, the town where convicted killer Peter Tobin lived. The town where Vicky Hamilton died. 17 years it took to bring Tobin to justice, a 17-year long nightmare for Vicky's family. But at the High Court in Dundee finally justice, closure. And a life sentence for the Butcher of Bathgate.

2009

Wednesday 7 January 2009

STV News

The first seven days of 2009 have been dominated by the cash crisis across the globe, the effects on the UK economy and the very real impact on Scots facing a new year on the dole. Tonight the car industry here is the latest to be hit by the worldwide economic tsunami. Figures from the Scottish Motor Trade Association show that car sales in Scotland fell by 15 per cent last year. There are now calls for the Treasury to step in and ensure banks release more finance to consumers.

Monday 19 January 2009

STV News

The Prime Minister today said he was angry with the Royal Bank of Scotland as it announced it faced the biggest loss in British corporate history. Gordon Brown spoke out as the Government announced its second multi-billion pound bail out of Britain's banks. He said the Edinburgh-based bank had taken irresponsible risks with people's money.

Thursday 26 February 2009

STV News

As report cards go, it's the worst possible result. RBS – once the world's fifth largest bank has posted the worst loss in UK financial history – £24 billion. The dire news comes as it emerged that the bank's former Chief Executive Sir Fred Goodwin, widely blamed for the bank's demise, is receiving a £650,000 a year pension.

And there are reports tonight that Sir Fred has rejected calls to give up that pension.

(*STV News cont*)

He boasted about how well he got on with the boy, but behind the facade was a cold and calculating man who killed his girlfriend's son. Robert Cunningham dabbled with heroin and smoked cannabis every day. One afternoon last March, he lost his temper with Brandon Muir and stamped on the toddler hard enough to rupture the child's bowel. Today at the High Court in Glasgow a jury took just an hour and a half to convict him of killing him.

DIARY: **An unremittingly grim case. His mother's scumbag 'lover' hit the child so hard that his intestines burst and then they didn't get him help. The animal got off with culpable homicide because the child might have survived if he had received emergency treatment, which the bastard didn't get for him. Once again, the law is seen to be an ass. I cut my interview with the social workers. They were saying bureaucracy, lack of manpower and public support make their job very difficult.**

Tuesday 10 March 2009

DIARY: **A newsroom meeting this evening to discuss the new relaunch on 23 March. The bombshell dropped was that the name 'Scotland Today' is being ditched – as is 'North Tonight' – and we're all now 'STV News'.**

Wednesday 11 March 2009

STV News

Falling house prices, rising repossessions – the Scottish property market is in the grip of decline. The situation is blamed on a shortage of available credit with under-fire banks refusing to lend. Today, light at the end of the tunnel. Edinburgh-based RBS announced a massive cash injection in a move it's hoped will kick-start Scotland's property market.

Tuesday 24 March 2009

DIARY: **The new set seems to have been well received, with people liking the freshness and new colours. Still some doubt over the loss of the title 'Scotland Today', but that should pass.**

Thursday 2 April 2009

STV News – Live from Aberdeen Harbour with Andrea Brymer

Good evening from the harbour at Aberdeen. Tonight Scotland mourns 16 oil workers lost to the North Sea. 16 men who were just doing their job. 16 men who were just miles from home. In the hours since the tragedy happened, the search for the men and the reasons for the tragedy go on. On *STV News at Six* tonight, the very latest on our country's worst offshore disaster since Piper Alpha.

(*David Marsland script*) Officially, this is still a search and rescue mission… but it was long ago conceded that there is no hope of the eight men still missing being found alive… some wreckage has already been recovered. It's being examined for clues as to what caused a helicopter flying in perfect conditions to suddenly crash, apparently without warning.

The cause of the accident was the failure of a gearbox.

Monday 25 May 2009

Sir Alex Ferguson Documentary

In 48 hours Sir Alex Ferguson is poised to become the greatest ever British manager. Victory in the Champions League Final in Rome will propel him to a realm never achieved before. Greater than Busby. Greater than Paisley. Greater than Clough. Greater, even, than Stein.

SIR ALEX FERGUSON (*speaking in 1993 on taking his Manchester United team on a tour of Govan*):

I took them down to my wee bakers in Shaw Street and I got ten dozen tattie scones, six dozen scones, cakes, biscuits, the lot. And the players are going off their heads waiting for me. And, of course, all the punters are congregating around the bus. The window opens about the third storey up. 'Haw Alex, come on up for a cup of tea.' I says, 'I can't, I've got the team.' She says, 'Bring them up!' (*laughs*).

DIARY: My Sir Alex Ferguson documentary went out this evening and I got a few complimentary texts. I was pleased with it, but it could have done with being longer and breathing a bit more.

The documentary was to mark Sir Alex's attempt to win the Champions League for a third time with Manchester United. They lost 2–0 to Barcelona.

Thursday 20 August 2009

The Lockerbie Bomber Abdelbaset al-Megrahi – Britain's biggest mass killer – was freed on compassionate grounds because he was suffering from terminal cancer.

KENNY MACASKILL, Scottish Justice Secretary:

Mr al-Megrahi did not show his victims any comfort or compassion. No compassion was shown by him to them. But that alone is not a reason for us to deny compassion to him and his family in his final days. Our justice system demands that judgement be imposed, but compassion be available. For these reasons and these reasons alone, it is my decision that Mr Abdelbaset Ali Mohmed al-Megrahi, convicted in 2001 for the Lockerbie bombing, now terminally ill with prostate cancer, be released on compassionate grounds and be allowed to return to Libya to die.

I was on holiday at the time of Megrahi's release and had no involvement in the story.

Wednesday 16 December 2009

STV News

He abducted, drugged and murdered three young women, showing not a shred of remorse for his victims or their families. But Peter Tobin has finally been revealed for what he is, a sexually motivated serial killer. A jury found him guilty of murdering 18-year-old Dinah McNicol in 1991. He's already serving life sentences for taking the lives of Vicky Hamilton and Angelika Kluk. Tonight the police have issued photographs of jewellery they believe could be trophies from other victims.

DAVID COWAN, Chief Reporter, STV News

Every night during Peter Tobin's trial for the murder of Angelika Kluk, our cameras were able to film him being escorted to a prison van parked outside the High Court in Edinburgh. The vans were too big to fit into the garage at the back of the building, and we stockpiled footage of the daily ritual.

Tobin was clearly concerned about his image. With one eye on the TV crews, he would chat amiably to his guards about what was for tea in the jail that night, looking like the harmless old victim of a terrible misunderstanding.

The mask dropped with an almighty clang after he was convicted. As he was frogmarched away to start his first life sentence, Tobin kicked a crouching photographer in the throat. For the first time we saw Mr Hyde, his face contorted with rage.

I looked into Tobin's background for STV's coverage at the end of the trial. He was a convicted sex offender on the run from the police, working under a false name at a Glasgow church, when he subjected Angelika to a hideous death. One church volunteer said to me with complete sincerity, 'How often do you meet evil? I don't know. But I know I met it the night I met Peter Tobin.'

In the months that followed, the true extent of that evil emerged. Two more victims, murdered years before, buried in a back garden in the south of England.

Reporting on Tobin was a challenge. There was pressure to break new lines, not to miss anything, to beat the competition, which in STV's case is mainly BBC Scotland. The newspapers were all over the story.

It was impossible not to become involved emotionally. I got to know the families of the two girls later discovered in England and realised the unique hell suffered by the relatives of missing people. After years of tortuous uncertainty, it was almost a relief when they were told the bodies had been found, because at last they knew where they were, at last they had them back.

Some weeks after the Angelika Kluk verdict, Tobin was brought back to court to face the music for going on the run. Given his life sentence, it was academic, but I went along for the sake of completeness and a chance conversation opened up a new chapter.

I was told the police were going to search Tobin's former home in Bathgate, having realised he was living there in 1991, when a teenager called Vicky Hamilton went missing in the town. The police confirmed their plans and we broke the story that night. Their search uncovered a knife hidden in the attic, bearing traces of Vicky's DNA. Tobin was charged with abduction.

Soon afterwards, another police force started searching another house, 400 miles away in Kent. Tobin had moved to Margate from Bathgate a few weeks after Vicky went missing. The police were looking for Dinah McNicol, an 18-year-old who'd vanished later that summer as she made her way home from a music festival. They found a body in the back garden.

I phoned a contact. I told them I didn't expect them to say whether it was Vicky, but would it be a waste of stv's money if I flew down south? I was told it wouldn't be.

Later that day, outside 50 Irvine Drive, I saw two big guys who looked like forwards from the Scotland 1st xv. They were Lothian and Borders Police. We didn't talk at the time but Detective Chief Inspector Keith Anderson later told me they were astonished Vicky was there. They had evidence suggesting a link to Dinah, but not Vicky.

I struggled to find words for my report that night. It was incredible and horrible. Vicky had disappeared in West Lothian years before, but she was here. A Scottish schoolgirl whose face we all knew, buried in a rundown council estate in a fading seaside town at the other end of Britain.

The police continued searching for Dinah. I heard her father on the radio and realised he had a Scottish accent. Ian McNicol told me off for addressing him as Mr McNicol. He was an old jazz musician from Glasgow whose travels had led to retirement in a sleepy village in the Essex countryside.

I went to see him and we were halfway through the interview when the doorbell rang. A young reporter from the local itv station told us the

police had found more human remains. Ian agreed to continue. In a gesture I'll never forget, he raised his hand with his fingers crossed and said, 'If that's what they have said, please be Dinah… and get us out of this… misery.'

It was snowing when Vicky went missing in Bathgate, and it was snowing 16 years later when her family arrived at the High Court in Dundee to watch an unperturbed Tobin receive his second life sentence. I'd interviewed Lindsay and Lee Brown, Vicky's younger brother and sister the night before, and watched as Lindsay read out a gut-wrenching statement to Britain's media.

We had a second interview to ourselves. Detective Superintendent Davy Swindle had led the investigation into Angelika Kluk's carefully concealed murder, and had realised it was unlikely to be the first time Tobin had killed. He launched Operation Anagram, a nationwide scoping exercise which tried to unearth every scrap of information about Tobin's entire life. A team led by Detective Sergeant Graham MacKellar linked Tobin to Bathgate, which led in turn to Margate.

Tobin was tried for Dinah McNicol's murder at Chelmsford Crown Court. In a preliminary hearing I had to stand up in the press box and dissuade the English judge from banning us from reporting the proceedings. They were worried the coverage might muddy the waters if Tobin appealed against the verdict from Dundee. I was baffled and told the judge there was unlikely to be anything he could appeal about. From the dock, Tobin fixed me with a baleful glare. I looked away first.

Anagram led to more searches of properties associated with Tobin. He'd lived in Brighton when an 18-year-old girl called Louise Kay disappeared just along the coast. We spoke to Louise's sister and learned of another family who'd been through years of grief and pain. The police were convinced Tobin had murdered Louise, but nothing was found.

The Chelmsford trial was the last time Tobin was seen in public. Locked up forever in HMP Edinburgh, far away from the cameras, he'll still be playing the part of a streetwise old rascal, and not the monster and pervert that he is. The only one he's fooling is himself.

2010

Monday 1 February 2010
STV News
Sir Alex Ferguson enjoyed a roll and sausage today as he returned to his roots in Govan. The Manchester United manager, fresh from a victory over title rivals Arsenal, was back home to lend support to local charities and tonight will celebrate the centenary of his old school.

DIARY: **Sir Alex Ferguson was touring some projects in Govan and I was sent to the first one – a drug rehabilitation centre of which he's the patron. Got quite a lot of colour as he spoke to people in the place and I got as close as I was going to get to a one-to-one. Asked him about Govan, but also what he would say to tennis player Andy Murray, who lost in the final of the Australian Open yesterday. I've always found him reasonably friendly and approachable, although I'm never harrying him with football questions.**

Friday 12 February 2010
STV News
David Cameron has asked the Scots to back him to become Prime Minister during his latest trip north of the border. The Conservative leader insists it is a straight choice between him and Gordon Brown. He told the Scottish Conservative conference in Perth that in a tight election, Scottish votes cannot be written off.

DIARY: **Went to the Journalists' Charity lunch at the Thistle Hotel today, where the main speaker was the Conservative** leader David Cameron. He could possibly be Prime Minister in a little over two months. I was very close to him to get a good impression. And he is impressive – very fast on his feet, very comfortable, very slick. His main political point was essentially that whoever comes to power will have 'no money' because of the financial crisis of the last 18 months, and also that he wanted to work closely with the Scottish Parliament. He maybe didn't have quite the air of authority that Tony Blair had, but that may come. With Cameron the question is always; is there substance behind the gloss?

Thursday 25 March 2010

STV News

An alliance of three newspaper groups has been named as the preferred bidder to produce publicly-funded Scottish news programmes on STV. The *Scottish News Consortium* says it's planning, 'the biggest shake-up of news in Scotland for decades.' The newspapers defeated a rival bid from three broadcasters, including STV itself.

The Labour Government had initiated a process to make public money available for the funding of news on Channel 3.

DIARY: We've lost out on the public funding. An absolutely gobsmacking decision that can only be explained as being political, with members of the selection panel in thrall to the newspapers. How can you award a TV news pilot to a consortium that could not even provide a video in its bid? Inexplicable.

It makes for a very uncertain future.

This consortium must ensure contracts are signed before the Election is called (as we would have been obliged to do). They must decide who of the STV News staff they want to keep. After a year they can change conditions and they have a ruthless reputation for doing that. Everyone in the newsroom shattered. Reporting Scotland headline tonight was me with my opening line, 'I'm John MacKay. This is the STV News at Six... but for how much longer?' Sore one.

Thursday 15 April 2010

STV News

A risk not worth taking. All flights in and out of the UK are grounded until seven o' clock tomorrow morning at the earliest, as a gigantic ash cloud engulfs the British Isles. That ash from an erupting volcano in Iceland, carries a deadly safety risk for every passenger jet. With millions now stranded, we're live at Glasgow Airport with advice for worried travellers, and we get the latest from the scene of the eruption in Iceland.

DIARY: The prevailing winds are pushing this cloud across northern Europe at about 20,000 feet and the silicon particles in it can seriously damage jet engines, so flights have been grounded. Never heard the likes before.

GENERAL ELECTION 2010
Thursday 15 April 2010 (cont)

STV News

Another milestone in television and political history tonight as the leaders of the three main UK parties go head-to-head in the first ever Prime

Ministerial debate. But as Gordon Brown, David Cameron and Nick Clegg prepare to battle it out on this channel, Alex Salmond, who's been excluded from the televised event, says none of it will apply to Scotland.

DIARY: The SNP have rightly made a fuss about not being involved and up to half the issues discussed were irrelevant to Scottish viewers because they come under the power of the Scottish Parliament.

Clegg did well, Gordon Brown better than expected and David Cameron not so well. Clegg was personable and did simple things like speaking directly to camera. I don't know who advises politicians, but they get it wrong so often.

Tuesday 20 April 2010

Scotland Debates

Good evening. Welcome to *Scotland Debates* live from the National Piping Centre in Glasgow and broadcasting to the whole of Scotland. Everything you hear tonight will have a direct relevance to Scotland. Over the next hour, four of Scotland's leading Westminster politicians will be facing questions from an audience of voters.

(*Opening statements*)

JIM MURPHY, Labour:
I know that people are angry as we go into this election campaign. I think there has been the perfect storm of the recession, there's been the expenses scandal, there's been the bankers taking enormous immoral bonuses, and I think all of that has come together and created this perfect

storm that has scunnered so many people across Scotland.

ANGUS ROBERTSON, SNP:
We've got huge economic problems that we have to deal with, we've got a Westminster system which is broken – there's a break in trust between the public and politicians – and we have to try and fix that because I fear an ever-growing number of people are totally scunnered.

ALISTAIR CARMICHAEL, Liberal Democrat:
I've been a political activist man and boy since I was 14, that's 30 years of political activism, and I have to say I have never known an election which I found as genuinely exciting and inspiring as I find this one.

DAVID MUNDELL, Conservative:
This is one of those once in a generation elections where there is a real chance to change the Government. I think if we're honest the last couple of General Elections, the outcome was a foregone conclusion. This time your vote... really will count.

The dominant issue was the economy and measures to tackle Britain's budget deficit. The other issues the audience focused on were the ongoing wars in Iraq and Afghanistan and the timetable for withdrawal, restoring public trust after the expenses scandals and the possibility of a hung parliament.

Tuesday 4 May 2010

DIARY: Had a 20 minute conversation with the First Minister Alex Salmond this evening. He was in the newsroom to do a down-the-line interview with Channel 4 and afterwards started talking and seemed in no great hurry. At one point he referred to his absence from the leaders' debates as 'fucking disgraceful', which amused me. First Ministers are human.

Thursday 6 May 2010

DIARY: Election Day in one of the most interesting elections for years. The exit polls indicate a hung Parliament, which is pretty much what has been predicted by previous polls.

Travelled down to London to meet Andrea Brymer for election programmes.

Friday 7 May 2010

STV News from Westminster with Andrea Brymer

Good evening. It's 7 May 2010. A day that will go down in history as one of the most dramatic days in modern British politics. The people of the United Kingdom have exercised their democratic right and the result is a constitutional conundrum.

Tonight, we don't know for sure who will lead our country in this most difficult of times. Throughout the day, the party leaders have stated their positions in public. Behind the scenes here at Westminster, the activity may be even more frenetic as the parties fight for power.

This is the national picture. The Conservatives have 306 seats – short of that magic number of 326. Labour have 258. The Liberal Democrats are on 57 and others 28.

And this is how the picture looks in Scotland.

The seats remain the same as the last Election, but Labour increased their percentage share for the first time since 1997. In terms of seats, the Conservatives continue to hold just one in Scotland, Labour have 41, the Liberal Democrats are still on 11 and the SNP held their six, far short of the 20 they had predicted.

DIARY: A long, eventful and uncertain day. I wrote most of the intros. Apart from that – and keeping across the day's developments – it wasn't especially stressful. Neither was there any real sense of atmosphere around Parliament, apart from College Green with all the media platforms.

Monday 10 May 2010

DIARY: Back down to London this morning in what proved to be an eventful day. Met Clair (*Clair Stevens – producer*) and we spent much of the day getting a feel for what was happening – which in terms of what could be seen – wasn't much. We walked between Whitehall and Westminster, but it was just busy with tourists. Only really on College Green was there any real buzz and that's because it was the media base with TV platforms everywhere.

STV News from Westminster – never transmitted

Good evening from Westminster which today has seen the most dramatic events since the resignation of Margaret Thatcher. In the last hour the Prime Minister Gordon Brown has said he will resign as leader of the Labour Party. The move is designed to encourage Liberal Democrats to form a coalition with Labour. It follows a day when it seemed that talks between the Lib Dems and the majority Conservative party had been progressing well.

DIARY CONT: Drama at 5.00pm when, without any sign of an agreement between the Tories and Lib Dems, Gordon Brown – who's still Prime Minister – appeared on the steps of Downing Street to say that he would stay on to help facilitate a Labour–Lib Dem coalition, then step down later in the year. That's put the cat among the pigeons, and things might take an unexpected turn.

I was standing in position ready to go when at 5.55pm we were told ITN were taking the full hour. Disappointing. We had a cracking programme ready to go, even with the late drama.

Tuesday 11 May 2010

STV News

Tonight Britain stands on the brink of a new Government. A deal seems imminent between the Conservatives and the Liberal Democrats that will put David Cameron into Downing Street. Late overtures from Labour came to nothing and tonight Gordon Brown is preparing to resign as Prime Minister.

DIARY: It looks like the Conservative–Lib Dem coalition is going ahead. Despite yesterday's attempt by Labour to woo them, it frittered out quickly.

Tonight Gordon Brown resigned as Prime Minister in a statement outside Number Ten. He then left with his wife and two sons, an image that shows a human side to the man, but which to his credit he didn't try to exploit.

He was an impressive Chancellor at first, but he and Blair threw away what they could have achieved when first elected. Blair over Iraq and Brown because of his belief that he had some sort of right to become Prime Minister. I think history will reflect on him as a thwarted man who did much to undermine Tony Blair and who came to power when it was too late for him.

Wednesday 12 May 2010

STV News

It's been a day when political enemies became allies to form a new government. A handshake at the door of Number Ten showing the unity of the coalition at the very top of British politics. Prime Minister David Cameron and his deputy Nick Clegg promised a government built on freedom, fairness and responsibility.

DIARY: Strange to see today's news conference with Cameron and Clegg standing side by side. They came across well, but I can see these images coming back to haunt Clegg. Maybe I'm wrong and the 'new politics', as they've called it, might work. They seem to have made a good start, but a lot of commentators give it 18 months maximum.

The Conservative–Liberal Democrat Coalition lasted the full five years of the UK Parliament, but the Liberal Democrats suffered heavily in subsequent local elections and were reduced to a rump party in the 2015 General Election, from 57 seats to only 8.

Tuesday 8 June 2010

STV News

Plans to use public money to subsidise regional news, including this programme on STV, have been scrapped by the coalition Government. The Culture Secretary Jeremy Hunt today axed a series of pilots set up by the previous Labour government.

DIARY: **The Independently Funded News Consortia (IFNC) that has been hanging over us at work since that perverse decision in March has definitely been binned.**

Tuesday 8 June (cont)

STV News

A woman has been jailed for three years for dipping a baby's dummy in methadone to stop him crying. The ten-week-old boy almost died after the incident in Edinburgh. Another woman has been jailed for ten months for failing to tell medics what had happened.

DIARY: **A junkie mum jailed for dipping her 10-week-old son's dummy in methadone was a real 'pride in Scotland' moment.**

POPE BENEDICT'S VISIT TO SCOTLAND

Thursday 16 September 2010

STV News – live from Bellahouston Park with Andrea Brymer

Hello and welcome to this special edition of the STV News – broadcast across the nation – as Pope Benedict the 16th celebrates mass with the faithful here in Bellahouston Park on the southside of Glasgow. 28 years ago his charismatic predecessor John Paul the Second made history with the first ever Papal visit to Scotland. 300,000 came here from far and wide. Now, as his successor follows

in his footsteps on Scottish soil, the crowds may be smaller, but the welcome is every bit as enthusiastic. The 83-year-old Pontiff undertakes this journey, however, against a radically different backdrop from the historic and joyous visit in '82. Dissent, controversy and falling congregations cast their shadow. But this first state visit to the UK remains, as First Minister Alex Salmond says, 'an important and inspiring day for Scotland as the world watches.'

This was one of the first occasions that I and several of my colleagues used Twitter to report what was happening. It was basic observations about the crowds arriving and such, but it was about the first time we did it seriously. I also noted at the time that I was 'taken with Twitter which, amid the dross and nonsense, can be extremely informative'.

Monday 20 September 2010

STV News

A maximum break. It's what all snooker fans want to see. And yet in Glasgow today, the paying audience were nearly denied it because a top snooker player – Ronnie O'Sullivan – didn't think it was worth the £4000 he would have won. All this on the day that world snooker chiefs launched an integrity unit to stamp out match fixing, and urged players to go back to playing for the love of the game.

DIARY: **That's what's wrong with so much sport – money not glory.**

Tuesday 28 September 2010

STV News

The new Labour leader, Ed Miliband,

says he will drive David Cameron from office after one term. In his first leader's speech at the party conference, Mr Miliband said he represented a new generation which would change Labour and the country. He accepted that Labour had made mistakes in power, and must address voters from a position of humility.

DIARY: **Producing and presenting today. An obvious lead was the first speech to the Labour conference by the new leader, Ed Miliband. I think Labour have made a big mistake. This guy will not appeal to the electorate.**

THE BIG FREEZE
Monday 6 December 2010
STV News

Chaos has continued across Scotland today with renewed falls of snow and – now – icy temperatures. Many drivers have spent hours trapped in their cars as the roads seized up in gridlock. Journeys that would normally take no more than 20 minutes have become a four hour endurance. Airports have been closed again and passengers left stranded.

Tuesday 7 December 2010
STV News Special – live outside on the STV balcony in –14C with weatherman Sean Batty

Scotland in the winter. A picturesque winterscape from the air. On the ground some have described it as a winter apocalypse.

Weather fronts from Siberia and the Arctic have dumped inches of snow and sank temperatures to near record lows.

Communities have been isolated. Schools have been closed.

And the country ground to a halt. Hundreds trapped in their cars for ten hours and more.

Children forced to sleep in their schools, cut off from their families.

In this *STV News Special* we will be reporting from the north, south, east and west, hearing your stories and asking how could the country be so crippled by the weather.

Good evening. Scotland is back in the grip of the Big Freeze, shivering in record breaking cold weather. The central belt is going through the perfect storm. Just yesterday, three hours of heavy snowfall – right in the middle of rush hour resulting in quite horrendous problems for thousands of drivers.

The real drama happened overnight. Hundreds of drivers were stranded in their cars – in Lanarkshire, Stirlingshire and West Lothian, stuck in the middle of motorway misery – many having taken hours to move less than a mile.

That's it from your news team at STV on this bitterly cold December night. A night that follows a day of turmoil for thousands of people in a long week of disruption, gridlock and standstill. In the warmth of your home this evening, you could perhaps be forgiven for dreaming of a Christmas that's not quite so white. Goodnight, keep warm and stay safe.

Tuesday 17 December 2010

STV News

Two young women waiting to cross a road in Glasgow city centre have been killed after a four by four lost control and mounted the pavement. Another man was hit just seconds before. Other motorists stopped to help the injured, as emergency services rushed to the scene.

I was tweeted pictures from the scene, nothing graphic, but enough to alert me to the fact that this was a serious incident. We would never use Twitter as a confirmed source, but it did get us onto the story far more quickly than we might have otherwise. That is where Twitter has become so useful.

TOMMY SHERIDAN'S CONVICTION

Thursday 23 December 2010

STV News – Live from the High Court in Glasgow with Bernard Ponsonby

Good evening from inside the High Court in Glasgow where, for the last three months, Tommy Sheridan has been defending himself against charges of perjury. But tonight he has lost and been found guilty of lying. The former Socialist MSP now faces up to six years behind bars. In this special edition of the STV news at Six O' – the first time a news programme has been fully broadcast from inside a court in Scotland – we bring you the full story of the firebrand's fall.

DIARY: **It brings to an end a soap opera that's been going on for more than four years now. I always liked Tommy Sheridan's presence in Scottish politics.**

He was a very charismatic figure. If we start trying people for perjury in every trial then the courts will be chock full. But we won't. This is one of the few. This particular trial has lasted three months and it kept us going at quiet periods. We got an indication that he was going to be convicted when the jury returned to ask whether part of one charge could be deleted. We did the entire programme from inside the High Court – a broadcast first.

Tommy Sheridan was released from jail in 2012 and returned to the political stage with a speaking tour during the Independence Referendum.

2011

Friday 7 January 2011

DIARY: Filmed two more blogs this morning. Twitter keeps me busy too. You have to limit the time you're on it because people will keep coming at you if they know you're online.

As part of my embracing social media I had begun filming The Real MacKay *daily video blogs. Initially they were to provide an insight behind the scenes in the STV newsroom, but they soon took on a life of their own and covered the most ridiculous of subjects – getting colleagues to play the air-trombone, confirmation that I don't dye my hair. They were fun to do and built up quite a cult following (which means the people who liked them really liked them, but most people were unaware). They petered out because of time constraints when I began to present* Scotland Tonight.

Tuesday 1 February 2011

DIARY: Group of school kids touring at lunchtime and they came into the studio. I gave them a quick talk – no point in making it too long – and then asked them if they had any questions. Wee girl at the front throws her hand up enthusiastically. 'Yes,' says I. 'Who are you?' she asks.

Thursday 3 March 2011

STV News

A top level summit will be held to review the ugly scenes at last night's Old Firm game. Neil Lennon and Ally McCoist squared up at the final whistle of a Scottish Cup tie which saw three red cards, 13 bookings and 34 arrests inside the ground. The actions were condemned by the First Minister as repugnant. The SFA Chief Executive said he was saddened and deeply embarrassed.

DIARY: All about last night's explosive Old Firm game and the usual uproar. First Minister calling it a disgrace and there's a summit to discuss the problem. All old hat as far as I'm concerned. However, my inclination to leave it as something that occasionally happens at Old Firm games is tempered by reports of the domestic chaos that ensues and first-hand acounts I've heard of A&E being a battleground.

Monday 18 April 2011

DIARY: The big issue for us on an otherwise quiet day was the continued news blackout on three bombs (one at least was viable) sent to Celtic's QC Paul McBride, manager Neil Lennon and a Celtic supporting former MSP Trish Godman. Howard (*Howard Simpson – News Editor*) was called to a police briefing along with all the other Scottish editors. The police seem to be very touchy about this and fear copycats.

Tuesday 3 May 2011

STV News

The SNP are on course for a landslide victory in Thursday's Scottish election. An exclusive poll for STV News shows a surge in support for the Nationalists – with a major slump in backing for Scottish Labour. It comes as all four main party leaders prepare for tonight's crucial final televised debate on this channel.

SCOTTISH PARLIAMENT
ELECTION 2011

Thursday 5 May 2011

STV News

Good evening. The long Scottish election campaign is over. The TV debates are done and dusted, the pledges and promises published. Now the battle of the ballot boxes has begun. Polling stations opened at seven this morning and close in just four hours time. The final 24 hours saw party leaders criss-cross the country fighting for every vote. Activists in towns and cities across the nation are now focusing on getting their supporters to the polls.

DIARY: **It's been a remarkable turnaround because polls over the last 12 months have suggested a Labour win. I think, though, that the SNP leadership team – Salmond, Sturgeon and Swinney – have impressed people.**

Friday 6 May 2011

STV News – Live from Holyrood with Andrea Brymer

Good evening live from Holyrood – the heart of Scottish democracy. The people of Scotland have voted for a once-in-a-generation transformation to Scottish politics. Tonight Alex Salmond is returned as First Minister and the SNP has a majority of seats. And this parliament will deliver a referendum on Independence. Labour has seen its traditional power base in the central belt destroyed. The party leader Iain Gray will resign in the Autumn. Many of its big names have lost their seats. The Liberal Democrats' vote collapsed. The

Conservatives are not the king-makers they hoped to be, and none of the small parties, including the Greens, could break through.

Tonight, with the last of the votes counted, this is the shape of the new Scottish Parliament. The SNP hit 69 seats. Labour on 37. The Conservatives have 15. The Lib Dems have five and the Greens have two. The one Independent is Margo MacDonald.

ALEX SALMOND, First Minister:
We're not fixed on the past in all its bright colour. Our eyes are on the future and the dreams that can be realised. I'll govern for all of the ambitions of Scotland and all the people who imagine that we can live in a better land. This party, the Scottish party, the National Party carries your hope. And we shall carry it carefully and make the nation proud.

JM: We're joined now by the Deputy Leader of the SNP, Nicola Sturgeon. Congratulations on a momentous vote. You couldn't possibly in your wildest dreams have seen that coming.

NICOLA STURGEON, Deputy First Minister:
I think it's fair to say it was beyond our expectations. We had been quietly confident over the past few days of winning the Election... I remember the days, as I'm sure do many of your viewers, when people said we'd never have a Scottish Parliament or we'd never have an SNP Government. Now these same people say we'll never have Independence. It's right that the issue of Independence is decided in a referendum. When that

referendum comes the SNP will campaign vigorously for a Yes vote and I'm confident that we will win the day on that.

IAIN GRAY, Scottish Labour Leader: We have to address some fundamental questions about the structures and organisation of the Labour Party in Scotland, what went wrong and where we go from here. I want to start that process off, but in the Autumn I will stand down and it will be for the Labour Party to decide how we go forward from there.

VOX POPS: Labour must be reeling in shock.

I'm not surprised. Not with what's been happening currently and everybody being out of jobs.

They've really got us into the mess that we're in.

Anything you ask them to do or whatever, not interested.

They're just not for the people now, they're out for themselves.

If you put a monkey in a Labour suit they would get in here and that used to be the case, but unfortunately it's come back to bite them.

JM: The people of Scotland have delivered a Parliament which overwhelmed all expectations. Our political editor Bernard Ponsonby joins us now. Bernard, put this result into context for us?

BERNARD PONSONBY, STV Political Editor:
The word historical is the most over used word on election night, but last night it was absolutely apt. Historical because it is the first time any party has won a majority under a voting system almost designed to prevent it. Historical because there is a majority for an Independence referendum and that turns the nature of the constitutional debate on its head. Historical because the SNP victory came in the north, the south, the east and the west and they can legitimately claim, tonight, to be a national party representing all communities and classes.

JM – Your overall assessment?

BERNARD PONSONBY: The political map of Scotland has been redrawn but more than that, the mould of Scottish politics has been recast and it suggests that the SNP are a natural party of Government. Labour's dominance is at an end and for them, some far reaching soul searching as generational loyalty seems to be a thing of the past. With this victory comes a new chapter in Scotland's evolution. The campaign for Independence starts right here.

DIARY: No one saw this coming, no one. It means there will be a referendum on Independence within the five year term of this Parliament. Labour have lost their power base in the Central Belt with some of their senior people losing their seats. The Lib Dems have been crushed – a direct consequence of their involvement in the Coalition at Westminster.

The polls had predicted an SNP win, but nothing on this scale. This is a sea change – a once-in-a-generation transformation.

I don't believe it means Scotland is marching towards Independence, rather they recognised that the SNP have governed well this past four years and that Labour are a complacent shambles. Still, you never know what the debate might bring.

Into work where I wrote most of the scripts for the evening special before 10.00am. It was that clear. I headed through to Edinburgh with Bernard who'd been up all night. The programme with Andrea went very smoothly – perfect they said in Glasgow. Train back to Glasgow. Went to the India Quay where some were gathered and enjoyed a relaxing few hours there.

Monday 9 May 2011

STV News

The resignation of Annabel Goldie as leader of the Scottish Conservatives came on the day new MSPs started to arrive at Parliament to familiarise themselves with their new home for the next five years. It begins a new political era with SNP holding power with a majority government...

Friday 20 May 2011

DIARY: Last time broadcasting to the east of the country tonight. In my pay off I made a goodbye of sorts, telling them it had been my pleasure over the years, but they had a new programme to look forward to.

STV split the Central news operation into two, one covering Glasgow and the West, the other Edinburgh and the East.

Thursday 23 June 2011

STV News

The First Minister Alex Salmond is backing calls for a public inquiry into Edinburgh's trams, as council officials published a long awaited report into the troubled project. The report recommends the councillors press ahead with a tram line from the city centre to the airport, at a cost of more than £770 million. As STV News revealed last night, officials say that cancelling the project would cost up to £740 million.

Tuesday 16 August 2011

STV News

Hollywood stars Brad Pitt and Angelina Jolie arrived in Glasgow today, but it wasn't by private jet or helicopter – instead the couple chartered a train. The arrival of the actors and their family prompted great excitement amongst commuters and their fans, many of whom are on a mission to meet Brad while he's here filming his latest movie.

DIARY: Big excitement with Hollywood star Brad Pitt in Glasgow to film his movie *World War Z* – Glasgow is playing Philadelphia. He arrived in a specially chartered train, but hid from his fans. An arse thing to do.

Monday 5 September 2011

DIARY: A 13-year-old dies after a weekend incident. 16-year-old in custody. Two wasted lives right there.

A new STV current affairs programme was first mooted in the late summer of 2011. Scotland was crying out for it, especially in the wake of the Scottish Election and the anticipated referendum to come. The BBC's *Newsnight Scotland* was a compromise right from its inception and never recovered from that, being widely dismissed as 'Newsnicht'.

The former Sky News correspondent Rona Dougall was the surprise choice as my co-presenter over other, more obvious, candidates after an impressive audition. The intimate set, with its black and red sofas and colour scheme of burnt orange, reassured me that the programme would be a success. With a small, enthusiastic production team behind us we went on-air on the 24 October 2011 and it was a success from the very beginning, critically, anecdotally and in the size of our audience.

HOWARD SIMPSON, Editor, STV News and *Scotland Tonight*

I always thought that Scotland had waited too long for a programme about current affairs that wasn't either too anoraky, too insular or too aggressive. The brief for *Scotland Tonight* was for a programme that felt at ease with politics, but also took other walks of public life just as seriously. Sports, cinema, art, business and most importantly world affairs. I think that as long as programmes in Scotland feel they have to be 'just Scottish' first and foremost then we are not being ambitious enough. We just have to think in terms of what the most interesting stories are from the day, no matter where they are. On any given *Scotland Tonight* we could be doing the Greek financial crisis, the business problems at Rangers and an examination of the Scottish film industry. This eclectic mix keeps the audience fresh. They know they are not just going to get a strict diet from Holyrood.

The feel of the show is as important as the subject matter. We are on at 10.30pm at night, so the audience need to want to watch the programme as opposed to the news, which can become habitual. We picked presenters who relate to the viewers, not agitators, perpetually probing and interrupting. We want to keep the programme as modern as possible – social media is at its core, being able to hold a conversation with our viewers. We also endeavour to get as many fresh voices on as possible, and new ways to report on the stories that matter. *Scotland Tonight* has changed the way current affairs is broadcast in Scotland. Our competitors have adopted our style, but *Scotland Tonight* remains the pre-eminent show.

Monday 24 October 2011

Scotland Tonight

This is *Scotland Tonight*. The US Billionaire Donald Trump divides opinion. A would-be President. One of the richest men in the world. Trump Tower in New York City tells you that this is a man who doesn't do 'small'. And yet it's to Scotland he came with a big idea – the greatest golf course in the world. But it's been plagued by endless planning rows and protests, yet it's him who is objecting now. He doesn't like plans for an offshore wind farm near his luxury resort.

The first programme came close to falling around us. Our opening item was a set piece interview with Donald Trump, who was in a wrangle with the Scottish

Government over a luxury golf resort he was building in the North East. A satellite link would be prohibitively expensive, so with the sort of imagination that has characterised the programme, we arranged for a US crew to film him as he answered my questions which he was hearing down a regular phone line through an ear piece. Meanwhile, my side of the interview was recorded in the studio. We would get the American footage sent back and marry the two together. The interview went well and he was as colourful and controversial as we'd expected. The American crew duly sent the material to us, but inevitably it got lost somewhere in the ether. With little more than an hour to go, it looked like we had no programme on our launch night. Fortunately, we tracked it down and it was edited together at the last moment. The success of *Scotland Tonight* might have been very different if we'd got off to a bad start.

Tuesday 25 October 2011

DIARY: *Scotland Tonight* got great ratings for last night, a 10 per cent share peaking at 13 per cent. That's about double what we were expecting. The feedback continues to be good. Rona's debut tonight and I stayed on to give her some support. It went well.

The feedback included my Faither's view that, 'It's no' bad. You're fair losing your hair.' This was prompted by a favoured shot of the programmes's directors which showed the back of my head and emphasised my expanding bald patch. I call it the 'bastard shot'.

Tuesday 29 November 2011

STV News

Hundreds of thousands of cleaners, teachers, nurses and civil servants took to the streets today, angered by cuts to their pensions. Schools, hospitals, transport and the courts were all affected in this national walk out involving millions across the UK. A defiant David Cameron described the strike as a damp squib. Our Chief Reporter David Cowan followed the biggest mass action in a generation.

JM: The strike caused division amongst politicians north and south of the border. In Scotland the SNP crossed picket lines at the Parliament while Labour boycotted a debate on the pension reforms. At Westminster Ed Miliband was branded irresponsible, left wing and weak by the Prime Minister who was in turn accused by the Labour leader of revelling in the strike action.

Wednesday 30 November 2011

DIARY: The champion Scottish cyclist Graeme Obree was the Scotland Tonight guest in a discussion about suicide – he's attempted it twice himself. He talked about the state of mind that takes you to 'kicking away the chair'. One of the most powerful interviews I've ever done and that was down to his candour and the experience he'd endured. Scotland has a high level of suicide and it is deeply disturbing that people can be that desperate and yet those closest to them don't know. It's one of those times when the team sit down afterwards and know they've done a good job. I'm enjoying this programme.

GRAEME OBREE, Former World Cycling Champion:

I feel obliged because people like Gary Speed (*the Welsh football manager who committed suicide*) are not here to say how much I wish I hadn't done that. I was the guy who kicked the chair away with two kids and a wife who I dearly loved. People in the family of those who've committed suicide, they struggle to understand the reasons and there's a lot of resentment, there's a lot of anger, there's a lot of feeling that the person didn't love them enough. There's all these resentment and feelings left over. I feel they need to hear it from somebody who's actually done that and survived and lived to tell it.

JM: That phrase you used there, you kicked the chair away. What took you to that position? What was your mindset?

GO: One was a feeling of isolation. I felt, even in company, I felt there was a bell jar around me, I wasn't part of the world, I was observing it, I was no part of this world whatsoever, wasn't connected.

JM: Even with a wife and two children?

GO: Even with that I felt totally disconnected and purposeless. You could have given me a million pounds and I'd have gone, that's great, but pointless. People, can't understand that. Can I give you an analogy, just to nail it for people, ordinary people who just can't understand this? Supposing you went to a party and you really, really didn't want to be at that party, you thought, oh I really want to go home now, I'm tired, I really hate this company, but you keep it happy, smiley and chatty, you're clock watching, you're thinking it's going to be over soon. Imagine you woke up and every day was like that and it takes ten times the energy to deal with each person, just happy, smiley. And life went on like that. And you ultimately go, I want to go to sleep now, but there is no sleep. So it seems like the only option is actually just not to be here anymore. And also that state of mind is proper mentally ill and it changes your perspective of reality. I actually believed that I was a terrible person, my kids would be so much better off if I wasn't here, I'm a terrible person. And it wasn't that I didn't love them... the main thing I want to say is that if somebody has left you through suicide, it's not because they didn't love you.

HURRICANE BAWBAG

Thursday 8 December 2011

STV News

Don't drive. Keep the kids at home. Stay off the streets. The stark warnings across the country tonight as the nation is put on red alert. Throughout the day storms battered roads, railways, hospitals and schools with gusts reaching 85 miles an hour. Thousands were forced to take the day off or headed home early. A picture of widespread damage is emerging. So far – fortunately – there have been no fatalities.

DIARY: **Weather red alert with winds of up to 85mph hitting urban areas.**

165mph on top of the Cairngorms, close to the 175mph record. It was certainly bad, but perhaps not to the extent that had been feared. It has very quickly become known as Hurricane Bawbag – a term which was trending worldwide on Twitter. Some disruption and damage.

2012

Monday 9 January 2012
Scotland Tonight

A referendum on Scottish Independence is coming. But as yet it's unclear when it will happen and what, and how many, questions will be asked. Claiming that uncertainty is damaging the economy, the UK Government is now ramping up the pressure on the SNP administration to hold an early poll with a clear cut Yes or No option for voters.

DIARY: **Constitutionally any referendum has to be approved by Westminster – most see this as a technicality. The point is that the debate has started for real and the unionists are taking the fight to the SNP, who have been making the running until now.** *Scotland Tonight* **was lively with four parties represented. It was a problem at times to keep order.**

Tuesday 10 January 2012
Scotland Tonight

Autumn 2014. That's the date the SNP Government wants to hold a referendum on Scottish Independence. Tonight's disclosure from Alex Salmond came just after Scottish Secretary Michael Moore had told MPs that, as things stand, a Holyrood organised vote would be unlawful. UK ministers have indicated they're prepared to devolve authority, but only if certain conditions are met.

DIARY: **The Scottish Independence issue kicked off big style today. The Scottish Secretary Michael Moore stood up in the Commons and confirmed** what had been revealed yesterday, ie that the Scottish Parliament has no legal right to hold such a referendum. Westminster will hand over that power, but with conditions attached. That much was expected, but then First Minister Alex Salmond – live on our news at 6.00pm – announced that the referendum will be in the Autumn of 2014. Up until now he's only ever said it would be in the second half of the Parliament. So Holyrood and Westminster squaring up to each other. At first look it is a political masterstroke by Salmond, regaining the initiative straight away, but it is also a bit disrespectful to the Scottish people. Why wait when he clearly knew all along? Of course 2014 is the 700th anniversary of Bannockburn and the year of the Commonwealth Games. National fervour will be high. It's the nature of politics I suppose.

Monday 16 January 2012
Scotland Tonight
Yes or No to full blown Independence. That's the simple choice the Westminster Government wants voters to have in the referendum on our constitutional future. But a string of recent surveys has shown that a third option is the one which most Scots want. Under Devo Max, our MSPs at Holyrood would get far greater powers, but Scotland would remain in the UK. Tonight a YouGov poll showed 39 per cent of the public backing for a separate Scottish state, with 61 against. But, when the option of greater powers within the UK was offered, 58 per cent backed 'devo max' with 42 against.

DIARY: A good *Scotland Tonight*. First discussion on 'What is Devo Max?' and the answer is 'no one really knows,' although polls show it to be the favoured option to the status quo or full Independence. Second chat was about the risks of social media for people in the public eye as another MP resigns over something inappropriate (*Tom Harris Labour MP, over a spoof video of Alex Salmond as Hitler in Downfall. I think it's a nonsense he had to resign*). That worked well. Best of the lot was an enthusiastic professor from Glasgow University talking about the use of apostrophes (*Waterstone's dropping it from their name*). His name was Jeremy Smith and he was excellent. The entire crew adored him. Good programme.

Tuesday 17 January 2012
Scotland Tonight
Ed Miliband is leading Labour to electoral disaster. The stark assessment today from the boss of Unite, the UK's biggest union and Labour's biggest donor. Len McLuskey made the comments following the party's decision to accept Coalition cuts and a public sector pay freeze. Mr Miliband dismissed the attack, insisting his position was both 'right' and 'responsible'. But today's public battle has fuelled speculation that his days as Labour leader are numbered.

DIARY: During an interview with one contributor in London a monitor on the screen behind him flashed up images of a vivid sex scene with bouncing breasts prominent. Nothing I could say because he knew nothing of it and it would have thrown him. It was only brief, but I'm sure we haven't heard the last of it.

Thursday 19 January 2012

DIARY: The bouncing boobs on *Scotland Tonight* made the front page of *The Sun* as an 'exclusive' today – exclusive 36 hours after it appeared on live TV. *Daily Record* lifted it, on *Daily Mail* website, page three of the *London Evening Standard* and has even been picked up by foreign media outlets – Russia, Belgium, Vietnam. It's all good publicity, but ridiculous given that it was a 2 second flash. Some people get very excited about such froth.

RANGERS GO INTO ADMINISTRATION

Monday 13 February 2012

STV News

Rangers Football Club have applied to go into administration. The SPL Champions lodged notice at the Court of Session this lunchtime. And tonight the Ibrox club stated the tax bill they owe could be substantially more than the £50 million that has been widely reported. That is, of course, £50 million pounds the club cannot pay. Within ten days, administrators will move in to run Rangers who will be deducted 10 league points.

DIARY: **All went crazy this afternoon when it was announced that Rangers had applied to go into administration. We'd just come to the end of the *Scotland Tonight* production meeting and had a detailed discussion on what we were going to do, but that all had to get ripped up. Filled the news and tonight's programme. Gloomy day for Rangers.**

MIKE FARRELL, STV online sports reporter:

'Oh aye, they filed something this afternoon.' I nearly fell out my chair and dropped the phone when the clerk at the Court of Session confirmed what we'd been expecting for weeks – Rangers Football Club were going into administration. That call on the afternoon of 13 February 2012 was the culmination of a fortnight of daily 'check calls' with the petitions department.

After putting the receiver down, I stood up and shouted something to the newsroom about Rangers going into administration, despite barely believing what I'd been told. The place went haywire and I recollect spending the rest of the day writing and checking out other lines, often with senior members of the news team looking over my shoulder.

It soon transpired that Craig Whyte had not just taken us by surprise by signalling his intention to appoint Duff and Phelps – he hadn't told any of his staff. He managed to beat officers of HM Revenue and Customs to the doors of Parliament House by a matter of hours. The tax authority was seeking to declare The Rangers Football Club PLC insolvent. It turned out that Rangers hadn't paid millions in national insurance and PAYE in Whyte's nine months in charge.

But, as ever is the case with this story, it was not as straightforward as laying the blame at the door of one party – in this instance an asset stripper who convinced many he was a 'Motherwell-born billionaire' despite having no discernible wealth. The meltdown had its beginnings in the two decades Sir David Murray ran the club using a seemingly limitless credit-line with Scottish banks and a ruse to avoid paying tax on the inflated salaries of players and directors (*the Big Tax Case*).

As a journalist, it has emphasised to me the importance of the written word. Talk around finances, plans and ambitions – especially in football – is cheap. This was demonstrated through the Murray years, where mega casinos and getting Ronaldo to switch the Galacticos for Govan were reported as stories.

What has often mattered in covering this has been the 'paper trail'. It has not been what 'off the record steer' a PR man has given me – it was what was put down in black and white. It has involved seemingly endless hours trawling through company documents, poring over court cases and attempting to map out an increasingly complex cast of players.

It's often been through doing this that some of the most remarkable lines in the saga – including Craig Whyte's dealings with newco frontman Charles Green – have been found. But it has also involved a lot of 'old fashioned' journalism, such as door-stepping those involved.

Tuesday 14 February 2012

STV News

Rangers Football Club are tonight in administration. And question marks over the Club's fixture with Kilmarnock on Saturday as Strathclyde Police threatened not to commit resources to the match unless they received guarantees about payment from the administrator.

DIARY: **Basically, it gives them time to try to reach a deal with creditors. If they fail to do so, it means the club goes bust. Given the main credit seems to be the Tax Office and they have been playing hard ball, there could be every chance of this happening. It's that serious. A black, black day for the club, probably the worst ever after the Ibrox Disaster. Rangers going bust is unimaginable.**

Also last night I made a reference to 'the situation we're in now' and, of course, rather than being seen as the generic reference it was, plenty have been claiming it showed my loyalties. There really is no point in arguing.

DEATH OF LOCKERBIE BOMBER

Sunday 20 May 2012

STV News

The Lockerbie Bomber, Abdelbaset al-Megrahi has died in Libya. His family said that he passed away around 11.00am this morning UK time. Megrahi was convicted of the worst ever terrorist atrocity on UK soil. 270 people died when Pan Am Flight 103 was blown out of the skies over Lockerbie in 1988. Nearly three years ago, he was controversially released from a Scottish jail on compassionate grounds because he had terminal cancer.

DIARY: The obituary, pre-prepared since his release, has been sitting at the bottom of our running order for years now. Had always planned for a big programme, but in the end just did a bulletin that I presented.

I always thought the release of the Lockerbie Bomber was a misstep by the SNP administration. I suspect that they were unconvinced of Megrahi's guilt and didn't want him dying in a Scottish jail if that was later proved.

IMRAN KHAN INTERVIEW
20 May 2012 (cont)

DIARY: Interviewed Imran Khan this evening at the Marriott Hotel. Surprised by lack of security, given the record of political assassinations in Pakistan. He was a bit cold at first, ignoring my preambles, but warmed up as the interview progressed. Interesting on Western misconceptions about Pakistan.

He was in Scotland to raise funds and encourage the Scottish Pakistani community to get involved in the country's election.

Monday 21 May 2012
Scotland Tonight

IMRAN KHAN: Pakistan is stuck in this war on terror. We had nothing to do with it. We ended up becoming a frontline state and that has devastated the country. 40,000 people have died the economy has lost about 70 billion dollars, about 3 million people internally displaced because of this war, and there's no end to it... If I was an American, I would be very concerned about the impact of drone attacks. Number one – it violates all humanitarian laws. Here's America and the US, telling the world about human rights. No humanitarian law allows suspects to be eliminated, their relatives, their friends – anyone in the neighbourhood could be eliminated through these bombs, through drones. So that in itself creates a lot of hatred against the US – it creates anti-Americanism.

Friday 25 May 2012
STV News

It is the campaign determined to capture the hearts and minds of the Scottish people. The battle for an Independent Scotland is underway. Alex Salmond set the party a target of enlisting the support of a million Scots for a declaration of Scottish Independence. The nationalists say their campaign will be the biggest community effort in Scottish history.

THE OLYMPIC TORCH

I was chosen to be an Olympic Torchbearer, presumably because of my TV profile. I did feel rather unworthy in comparison to many of the other torchbearers, but it was a great honour and if you're asked to carry the Olympic Flame you're not going to say no.

Friday 8 June 2012
STV News

The Olympic Torch has arrived in Scotland to an enormous welcome. Huge crowds have greeted the flame as it begins a tour around the country. It arrived in Glasgow this evening, where thousands are at a party organised to celebrate the occasion.

DIARY: The meeting point for the first Torchbearers was an hotel in Stranraer for processing and briefings. When we left the hotel just before 6.00am the crowds on the street were astonishing – later estimated at 2–3,000. An incredible turnout and replicated at all the stops north to Glasgow. A real sense of community engagement with children, especially, prominent. I'm not sure I've seen anything like it.

It's all very choreographed and the exchange or 'kiss' of the flame was all pretty much done by the supervising runners. Then off on my run. I made a point of proffering the torch and flame to the onlookers because that was what was important. I took it to the edge of the town, so the crowds thinned out considerably. Had to say something to camera as soon as I finished. I thought in advance what would be appropriate and I think I pitched it right, emphasising the pride and privilege I felt. The torch convoy was already off to the next stop – the flame having been transferred from my torch to a lantern. When I came back into work, one of the cameramen had collected my torch for me and left it on my desk. In my absence loads of colleagues took the opportunity to have their photos taken with it – not all of them as respectful as they might have done – baseball and golf poses for example! Many more from the building came to me asking if they could pose with it too. Genuinely amazed by the reaction to it – shows what it means.

Later to George Square for a big event. Again astonishing crowds. We were doing a live on top of a bus. Leaving the Square, I was stopped by scores of people wanting their photo taken with the Torch. Amazing day.

RANGERS GO INTO LIQUIDATION
Tuesday 12 June 2012

DIARY: Rangers are going into liquidation. The tax authorities, HMRC, have rejected a debt deal with the new owner Charles Green because they don't believe it's in the best interests of the tax payer. So now that's it. Interesting question is whether the SPL clubs will allow them to stay in the SPL or will they have to drop down the leagues? Many clubs' supporters believe Rangers should be forced down, but the club owners realise the financial implications of that. They'll vote by the end of the month. It's sad that a Scottish institution should be brought to its knees like this. And the HMRC have not performed well. If this is their policy, why wait until now to say it? A reference on a website isn't enough. They should have stated their position publicly at the outset.

(*Scotland Tonight* Special)

This was the day of reckoning. The day the old Rangers died and the new Rangers was born, fighting to stay alive.

(*Shareholder vox pops*)

'It's like being at a funeral with no coffin there.'

'Quite emotional. (*voice breaking*) Disappointing.'

'I'm sick. I haven't slept for three months.'

'Words fail me. It's shattering.'

ARCHIE MACPHERSON, football commentator: This is almost historically overwhelming. This is a turning point in the Scottish game as a whole, not just for Rangers.'

JM: In football terms, this would be a classic. It's got all the ingredients; dramatic high stakes, passion, players who are loved and loathed, a match that ebbs and flows and now seems to be going into extra time. Rangers are fighting for their very existence. After more than one hundred years they have a new name – THE Rangers Football Club. And it has a new chief executive, Charles Green. Its most successful manager Walter Smith has also dramatically emerged to front a bid to buy the club from Green. But either way, it'll be a new Rangers, a newco. For many fans it'll never be the same.

JM: For 140 years Rangers entertained and allowed a vast diaspora of followers to dream. They are more than just a club and always will be. Some of their traditions have alienated those who do not follow them. Not all the tears being shed are done in sorrow. This is a chapter in which a once great club has been brought to its knees. Other indignities lie ahead. But tonight those who might consider themselves Rangers men are refusing to lie down. The passion for the red, white and blue will transcend and endure what is, after all, a corporate kill off. Rangers will be reborn to fight another day. For the moment, though, purgatory is their state.

This was the closing section of a piece I recorded on Rangers history. Several Rangers fans said it expressed exactly how they felt. The irony was that it was based upon a script written by my Celtic-supporting colleague Bernard Ponsonby.

DOLLY PARTON INTERVIEW
Wednesday 20 June 2012

DIARY: **Interviewed Dolly Parton via satellite from Nashville. It was one of a series she was doing, one after the other. Have to admire her professionalism. It was something like 5.00am over there, but she was very warm, while sticking to the corporate line and the country gal shtick. Good one to do.**

STV News

And finally – The Dolly Parton song '9 to 5' has become a dance floor and karaoke favourite. It comes from the '80s movie of the same name about three women getting their own back on their chauvinist boss. Now the stage show is coming to Scotland in November. Dolly has written the music for it and spoke to STV News from Nashville about Scotland, her music and the show.

JM: Some of the girls were asking how would you deal with a '9 to 5' type boss?

DOLLY PARTON: (*laughs*) You just got to stand up for what you believe and who you are, and if it means you lose that job go find another one, but don't let anybody mistreat you.

JM: When we told people that we were going to be interviewing you here in Scotland, there was great enthusiasm, there was a great deal of love for Dolly Parton. Why should that be, do you think?

DP: Well I think people relate to me. I think they feel themselves in me because I'm just a country girl and, like I say, the folks that came over all those many years ago, brought all those wonderful stories and songs, and that feeling that I have is just in my DNA to write these kind of songs, and I think we're just the same people, and I think they feel me, I feel them and I really think we just feel like relatives, because we really are.

JM: Well Scotland will always love you, Dolly Parton. Thanks for joining us.

DP: Thank you. Appreciate you.

My pay off to the interview looks cheesy in print, but it worked well in the moment. She has that effect on you. When we were establishing the communications with Nashville I could see and hear her playing with my name, 'John MacKaaaay', probably because the pronunciation was so different from the name written before her. I thought maybe I was witnessing the beginning of a new Dolly composition. I wasn't, but I wait in hope.

Monday 25 June 2012

DIARY: Formal launch of the No campaign in the Independence referendum. It was a bit better than the Yes campaign's misfire launch.

STV News

We're better together, that was the message today as the campaign to save the union got underway. Former Chancellor Alistair Darling is leading the movement and said that the vote on Independence would be the most important decision Scots will make in 300 years. He warned that voting for Independence would be an irrevocable move.

ALISTAIR DARLING, Leader, Better Together:

Chairing this campaign is one of the most important things I have ever done in politics. The decision we make is the most important we will make in our lifetime. If you're going to separate, you're on your own. There's no way back from that. I think that the debate has only just started, because it was necessary to ensure that we constructed a sensible campaign of people united in their view that Scotland should remain within the United Kingdom.

Friday 13 July 2012

STV News

Rangers have been told they'll have to play in the SFL's Third Division this season. Members rejected calls for the crisis hit club to start in the First Division by a massive majority vote. Tonight the newco's Chief Executive says he accepts the decision.

DIARY: That is where most Rangers fans want them to go – take the punishment and start again. However, there is a lot of resentment around and most Rangers fans also believe that going into Division 3 will force other SPL clubs to go bust. Scottish football has long needed a rebalancing. That said, I wouldn't be surprised if there's some attempt to create a new league (SPL 2) to move Rangers up more quickly. This is not over yet.

Tuesday 14 August 2012

DIARY: On *Scotland Tonight* we took

head on criticisms on Twitter last night that we do not have enough women on our discussions. Three guests – Lesley Riddoch, Annabelle Goldie and Lorraine Davidson to discuss it at some length. Quotas for women etc.

The issue of more female guests is a consistent one and not just for Scotland Tonight. *At every production meeting we select the subjects we will discuss and then the best panel to deliver that, always mindful of gender balance. It becomes much more difficult when the production team start contacting potential guests. It is not for want of effort on their part. Our experience is that women are less likely to be able to come into the studio for a live discussion – or even a pre-recorded one – on a few hours notice. The explanation most commonly given is child care issues. Often organisations will put up somebody to speak for them and more often than not these organisations will put up a male speaker. We are very aware when a panel is all male, but sometimes what are the alternatives? Drop the subject? That makes no sense. Have on a token guest who is not informed on the matter at hand? How does that serve the viewer?*

ANDY MURRAY WINS US MASTERS
Tuesday 11 September 2012
STV News

Many doubted whether he would ever do it. Last night Andy Murray proved them wrong and – at his fifth attempt – won his first Grand Slam trophy. He beat the World Number 2, Novak Djokovic, at the US Open in New York. It's another historic achievement to add to Britain's summer of sport.

DIARY: Andy Murray did it! As we have constantly been reminded, he's the first British male to win a major tennis honour in 76 years. He was two sets up, but lost the third and fourth set and I would have assumed at that point he would have lost. To his great credit, and it's where he's improved, he had the mental strength to come back and win the fifth. At STV we have archive of him as a 12-year-old. Everyone very pleased.

OLYMPIC HOMECOMING PARADE
Friday 14 September 2012
STV News at Six live from George Square

Good evening, live from Glasgow's George Square on a night where the true Olympic spirit lives on. Around me here, and along the victory parade tens of thousands have been cheering the remarkable sportsmen and women who have given us a summer to remember. This is their chance to say thank you to those who have supported them. This is also our chance to thank them for the legacy they leave – a legacy to build upon – as we look ahead to the Commonwealth Games in this city in just two years time.

JM: You're on the STV *News at Six* live. What's it been like for you today?

SIR CHRIS HOY, Six time Olympic Gold Medallist:
It's hard to express how I'm feeling, how the whole team are feeling just now. This is way beyond what we were expecting. Very emotional, overwhelming really. What a reception, not just here, but the

whole route from the start to the end was full. Amazing. Amazing… It's a strange feeling now. It's going to come to an end eventually, but these celebrations and these parades are just way beyond what you expect. And it's our chance to thank the public for their support. Incredible.

JM: And we can build on this for the Commonwealth Games in 2014?

CH: Absolutely. You see the energy and the enthusiasm, the positivity. And it's only two years to go now and everyone is going to be behind it. It's a great time to be a sports person or to be looking to get into sport.

DIARY: A great programme tonight on the welcome home to Scotland's Olympic and Paralympic athletes. I anchored it live from George Square where some 17,000 were packed in. It couldn't have gone better for us in terms of timing, just as we came on-air Sir Chris Hoy was still on the stage so I ad-libbed into that. We then got Sir Chris onto our platform along with Kathleen Grainger – gold medal rower – and Neil Fachie – gold/silver paralympic cyclist. By that point I was flying solo because I couldn't hear the gallery for the noise. I knew we had a report to go to, but I was concerned about losing the guests if I went into it, so I brought them on live which gave a sense of immediacy. I went with my gut on that and it seemed to work. I was impressed by the Olympians. Nice people, thrilled by the reaction. Sir Chris Hoy – our greatest Olympian – is a genuine guy. Also good to see what a boost the paralympians got.

Tuesday 25 September 2012

STV News

In what could prove to be one of the most important speeches by a Party leader since Devolution, Scottish Labour Leader Johann Lamont has warned that a whole range of benefits from free tuition fees, prescriptions, bus passes and free personal care may have to be axed as the age of austerity bites. She has asked a Party committee to provide policy options for her ahead of the next election when Labour could be ready to put some unpalatable choices before the voters.

Scotland Tonight

JM: The Scottish Labour leader is with us now. Johann Lamont, why did you make that speech?

JOHANN LAMONT, Scottish Labour Leader:
Increasingly I was conscious there was a gap between what we were being told in the chamber on a Thursday by the First Minister – everything is wonderful – and the people talking to me across the communities of Scotland. The woman who is the school secretary telling me how difficult it was in the school managing budgets; the care worker who told me she now goes in for a 15 minute visit to an elderly person, is told 'talk and go', nothing to do with personal support and care; the young teacher worried about whether they are going to actually have a permanent job; and I am concerned we are in a place now where with the SNP and the Scottish Government we

have this claim that everything is fine, but the reality on the ground is very different. We need to have a debate about it... I want the debate. I don't have all the answers, but I know there are some very hard questions we have to address.

JM: You cannot force the SNP to take part in this debate though, should this not have been a discussion your party had behind closed doors?

JL: Well, you could do that, but I have to say we lost badly in the last election just over a year ago and I think it would be unacceptable for people in this country to think that somehow we're going to go back off into a room, come out with solutions and present them to people. The first thing we have to do is recognise that there is a problem.

JM: But the SNP say it is affordable. They say they can pay for it.

JL: The reality is on the ground there are consequences to these policies. I am not saying that all of these policies are bad, but if at the same time the consequence, for example, of council tax freeze is a care worker is more stretched and more pressured in their work and the care they are delivering is less adequate then we have got a problem. I want to bring that out into the open.

JM: Johann Lamont, Thank you for joining us on *Scotland Tonight*.

DIARY: It's quite a stance for a Labour figure to take, but an honest one. My interview with her was not hounding – that's not my style – but firm. Praised

for it and I believe I was fair. I think Johann Lamont is a decent, honest woman, but as someone said, leaders lead, they don't open up for debate. They set the path.

Monday 1 October 2012

INTERVIEW WITH DEPUTY FIRST MINISTER NICOLA STURGEON
Scotland Tonight

JM: Johann Lamont was saying last week that we can't have universal free benefit, it is not affordable. Can it be afforded?

NS: It is afforded because the Scottish Government, within the constraints, with the resources that we have now, put forward balanced budgets. Politics is all about choices and we have made the choice to prioritise growth, but to protect household budgets.

JM: Can that continue with an ageing population and all that comes with it?

NS: What we have to remember is that many of these things are preventative spend as well. If we invest in helping older people stay in their own homes, to live independently for as long as possible, then we will reduce the expenditure in the long term on hospital admissions for example. So these things are all about preventing much costlier interventions. I think that was the mistake Johann Lamont made last week, as well as threatening many of the benefits lots of people in Scotland really really value. We are, notwithstanding these difficult economic times, a wealthy country, we have got massive natural resources, and it makes my blood boil that we have got so many kids living in poverty when we are an energy rich country. We can change that if we have the powers of Independence.

JM: Last week's First Ministers Questions was interesting with yourself, Johann Lamont and Ruth Davidson. A lot of people said that women would bring a different tone to Scottish politics. First Minster's Questions was described as a stairheid rammy.

NS: (*laughs*) I have to confess, you probably would say that.

JM: Why is that the case?

NS: Well, I am not sure you can expect the women who are in the Scottish Parliament now to single-handedly change the tone of our politics. We still have a very adversarial system, although I would say that although people see FMQs, a lot of what the Scottish Parliament does, our committee system for example, is not adversarial, it is consensus building and people across the political spectrum working together. I think I would like to see more women involved in politics. Scotland does a lot better than many other countries, but we can still do better. I would like to see lots of younger women get involved and that is why I am so encouraged by Women for Independence and what they bring to the debate.

JM: You were a younger woman who got involved.

NS: I still am!

JM: Of course you are, I beg your pardon. What sacrifices did you have to make in terms of who you were to compete with in this very male dominated environment?

NS: I think looking back on it, as a young woman I took myself far too seriously. Because I thought I had to be ultra serious in order to convince people that I was as good as male counterparts. One of the things I hope I have learned as I have got older is to take myself less seriously to concentrate on doing the best job I can do. But there are other things in life and I think it is always good to be reminded of that.

JM: And still young, Nicola Sturgeon. Thank you.

DIARY: **Always hugely impressive, but a warmer side coming through after being very stern for many years. Interview was fine, but only got as much out of it as she was prepared to give.**

KEVIN BRIDGES INTERVIEW
Saturday 10 November 2012
DIARY: **Interview with Kevin Bridges the comedian in Glasgow. I think he's superb. Just a funny, funny guy. A great half hour interview which ranged over many of things. It'll make a cracking piece for a *Scotland Tonight*. Relaxed chat with him as the cameras were set up. Really enjoyed the time with him.**

Scotland Tonight
JM: Kevin Bridges, thanks for joining us on *Scotland Tonight*.

KEVIN BRIDGES: It's a pleasure John, I've been a big fan for years.

JM: Really?

KB: Aye.

JM: It's been a great year for you. You're on tour of course, but nominated for two BAFTAS and record sell out of the SECC.

KB: You don't really realise it's been a great year until it's finished. When you go on tour you sort of go in a wee bubble. I've been on tour since the end of May and 8 December is the last night, so after that then you look back and go wow, the amount of people I've played to. It is quite humbling, the amount of people coming out, the queue outside for the DVD, to look at them standing in the rain and that, it's a wee bit... it's just me.

JM: Take us right back to the 17-year-old who thought he might want to be a stand -up comedian. What made you think that?

KB: I had just left school, I was 16 and I had the idea, I think we were in one of my pals' house, he had a house party or something and I left at five in the morning, you know that way where you're just walking home, thinking 'I'm going to be somebody'. I went in, I think half five, six O'Clock in the morning, got my computer up, just e-mailed The Stand, just saying 'I would like to give stand-up comedy a wee go and here's some jokes,' and they got back to me, I'd totally forgot about it, I woke up the next day, never even remembered sending the e-mail, and they said 'we'll book you in for a five minute spot in Glasgow.'... So I

thought I just need to walk on, it's just talking to people. All my pals think I'm quite funny, I just need to try and convey that as naturally as possible, just turning a group of strangers into a group of your pals. I never had an opening line, I had some ideas about being 17. My USP, my unique selling point, is going to be that I'm the youngest guy on the bill. I showed up, and they said, 'There's a 17-year-old on, underager, under no circumstances anybody sell him alcohol, we'll be facing disciplinary action.' All the staff had this wee memo through from the head office in Edinburgh. So I read that, and I walked on stage and said, 'I'm only 17 and I just got sold a pint, so get it up you.' It's not the greatest gag you're ever going to hear, but I think the audience, they erupted. It was my dad that was there, he was quite emotional just going, 'where did that come from?' He just thought I was just a waster at school because he would go to parents' night and the teachers would say 'Kevin's funny, but...' It was always 'but', 'Kevin's funny but...' So I think my dad was almost proud that I had put it to something more creative.

JM: Kevin Bridges, it's been a pleasure.

KB: John, thanks a lot mate. Good man. Cheers.

Like Billy Connolly before him, some have claimed that there are people on every street in Glasgow who are as funny as Kevin Bridges. During our conversation Kevin acknowledged that may be so, but they should do what he did and take it onto stage. I think he does himself a disservice. There are few can do what he does. I saw him have a crowd of 10,000 in the SECC in constant laughter. Few of the bar room funny men could do that. His humour takes me back to my youth. His resurrection of the exclamation 'Yaldy!' is just one of many delights for me.

OSCAR PISTORIUS INTERVIEW
Monday 12 November 2012
Scotland Tonight

Olympian and Paralympian Oscar Pistorius says it will be a dream come true to make his Commonwealth Games debut in Glasgow. The South African sprinter, who is known as the blade runner, spoke of his excitement at 2014 as he received an honorary degree from the city's Strathclyde university. I spoke to him as he visited the university's National Centre for Prosthetics and Orthotics.

JM: Oscar Pistorius, thanks for joining us on *Scotland Tonight*. You're here at Strathclyde University earning an honorary degree for the work that you've done in prosthetics here – what developments are you seeing?

OP: If you look at the way the Paralympic movement has enabled people to see Paralympians and people living with disabilities in a new light, I think that's fantastic, but being here at this centre, and lot of the innovation that's at the forefront of what people are going to be using in the coming years is getting used here, getting trained here, and it's fantastic to see that. The students are very excited and very passionate about what they do, and at the end of the day it rubs off on the users and on the patients here.

JM: Take us into your mindset when you're on the starting blocks about to run against able bodied athletes at the Olympics. What's going through your mind?

OP: I'm pretty sure whatever's going through their mind, it's pretty much the same thing. I grew up participating against kids in my community who didn't have disabilities. When I started running, I participated against guys at the university when I was training. I'd never seen a difference and I probably will never see a difference between somebody that has a disability and somebody that doesn't. I focus on the ability at hand. So when I'm racing in a Paralympic race or an able-body race there's no difference for me, it's the same distance, same track, same preparation, same mindset, same end goal. Ultimately it's more important for me to run a fast time than what it is to win a race. And when I'm lining up at the Olympics it's a matter of getting to the line as quick as possible, focus and make sure that my reaction speed is good, when I come off my blocks the driving phase is good, accelerating out of the corner, being efficient on the back straight, monitoring the race, monitoring the elements, the wind, entering into a final straight and when I have to go, make sure it's as clean and the transition is clean into a top speed and that I maintain it as hard as I can to cross the line. So I don't for any moment think about the other guys and are they able-bodied. That's not an issue for me.

JM: Oscar Pistorius thanks for joining us on *Scotland Tonight*.

OP: Thank you.

DIARY: He lost his legs below the knee almost at birth because his lower legs didn't have a fibula. He runs on blades, giving him the name Blade Runner. He was very pleasant and open and the kids were in awe of him. As usual the flunkies start trying to cut the interview early. Anyway, a good piece for tonight and an inspirational guy.

Two months after this interview Pistorius shot and killed his girlfriend Reeva Steenkamp at his home in South Africa. His trial for murder drew worldwide attention. Pistorius said he had mistaken Reeva for an intruder. He was found guilty of culpable homicide and jailed with a maximum term of five years.

ANDY MURRAY INTERVIEW
Tuesday 13 November 2012

DIARY: My week of interviews continues. Today it was Andy Murray, the tennis champ, whose star has really risen this year following his success in the US Masters and at the Olympics...

Murray is sometimes seen as grumpy, but I found him to be perfectly affable. He was happy to have his photo taken and I was struck by how lean he was – I could feel his ribs. If I hadn't known better I'd think the fellow needed a good feed.

Scotland Tonight
2012 has been the greatest year of Andy Murray's tennis career, with an Olympic Gold on home soil and a Grand Slam triumph at the US Open. Today the World Number Three was in Edinburgh with his mother Judy as part of an initiative designed to get the younger generation to develop the skills required for sport. They took time out to speak to *Scotland Tonight*.

JM: Andy, welcome to *Scotland Tonight*, it has been a fantastic year for you.

ANDY MURRAY: It has been the best year I have had on the tour in my career by a pretty long way.

JM: What do you reflect on most, the Olympics?

AM: Yes, it's very different the Olympics and the US Open. The Wimbledon final as well was probably one of the toughest moments I'd had in my career, but then followed by the Olympics which was the biggest high in my career a few weeks later on the same court. So I had lots of ups and downs this year, but I would say the Olympics as a whole, just because of the magnitude of the event and how well it went, how successful the British athletes were, to be part of that was great.

JM: You've said that sometimes when you had lost a match, it was difficult. It took days for you to manage to get yourself going and for all this training to be worthwhile. And now you realise why pushing yourself was worthwhile, but before you ever got to that stage, what was it that kept you going?

AM: I'm not sure. It used to take me a long time when I had lost big matches and grand slam finals. It took me sometimes months before I felt right again on the court. But after Wimbledon this year, it wasn't like that, it only took me a few days and I felt something change, I don't know if it was in that match in particular, but I got over that loss much quicker than I had in previous big matches and then I practised unbelievably in the build up to the Olympics and then played one of my best tournaments ever there. So I don't know exactly what changed around that time but something did, and I went on to have the best few months of my career.

JM: And Judy, you have always believed that your boys would go to the very top, not just be good, but go to the very top. You have always had that faith, why?

JUDY MURRAY: You don't ever know that they are going to. I think with them really from probably when they were both 14 or 15 they never really wavered from the fact that they wanted to be tennis players and I think as a parent you just try to encourage them as much as you can and try and create the right opportunities for them at the right time, it's up to them to go off and do it and to work hard and to maximise their potential and they have certainly done that.

JM: So we are looking towards next year. How do you push on, Andy?

AM: After the US Open a lot of people had said to me 'do you think it will be difficult to motivate yourself now?' because it is something I was waiting for for so long, it has been the last really five years of my life I have been trying to win a grand slam so to finally do it was great. But actually the few days afterwards, it made me realise that all the hard work and stuff was worth it. So I'm going to go away and train really hard in December, go away to Miami for a three-and-a-half, four week training block and get myself in the best shape possible for the Australian Open.

JM: And Judy, when Andy won the US Masters, we had a discussion on *Scotland Tonight* about how we get more young children involved and there was a lot of concern about tennis perhaps being an elitist sport. We're in Craiglockhart in the capital, it's the only indoor centre and is still quite costly. Is there still a problem getting it open to everyone?

JM: Yes, I think we need more public courts. We lost a lot of public courts over the last 20 years. A tennis court takes up a big space, so we have lost it to housing supermarkets, sometimes even to other sports because there wasn't much of a demand for tennis then, but now you are realising what you don't have because so many kids want to play, so resurrecting local public courts and school courts, I think is absolutely crucial so that more people can play and we certainly need more indoor facilities because our weather is rubbish, but they need to be affordable as well as being accessible and they are quite expensive, sadly.

JM: Andy and Judy Murray, thanks for joining us on *Scotland Tonight*.

AM & JM: Thank you.

Andy Murray went on to win Wimbledon the following season, the first British male to do so in more than 70 years.

Tuesday 11 December 2012

DIARY: Interview with Charles Green. He was distrusted at first because nobody knew him or what he was about, but he's won over most Rangers fans by playing to the gallery to please the Bears – fighting the SFA and SPL and more. The interview covered as much as I could in the time allowed. Celtic fans thought I gave him an easy ride, most others thought I got as much out of it as I could. He stayed on the green room and enjoys holding court. It's entertaining listening to him and he has big plans for Rangers. However, all the stuff he's been saying about the international leagues and owning own broadcasting rights has been said before by David Murray and it didn't happen.

2013

Thursday 10 January 2013

DIARY: First time I've interviewed Alistair Darling – the former Chancellor – now leader of the Better Together campaign in the studio. I found him to be much warmer than his reputation would suggest. The interview was extended, ended up being nearly 12 minutes. I let him make his case, but I also challenged him reasonably at times – uncertainty remaining within the UK and sharing a platform with David Cameron and Nick Clegg. I don't see the point in shouting matches.

Monday 14 January 2013

DIARY: Latest polling showing support for Independence stalled at 28 points – 20 behind those who'd vote No, with almost one in four undecided. It is a big ask, but the Yes campaign remain positive. They have no option.

Tuesday 29 January 2013

DIARY: The day was focused on a sit down with the First Minister Alex Salmond for *Scotland Tonight*. We got a freelancer Stephen Daisley to work on it yesterday so I had a good brief for it. We had a production meeting and structured the interview – social justice/economy/Europe/NATO/polls. I went into the interview well prepared. It was a straightforward interview in the sense that I asked him considered questions and he, in fairness, answered them straight. He didn't waffle. I wonder if I should be a bit more aggressive, but these interviews are increasingly dull and nothing is learned. I'm sure there will be criticism that it's not challenging enough, but there is also praise that I let people answer. Salmond himself was quite relaxed and not full of the bombast that sometimes overtakes him.

Wednesday 30 January 2013

STV News at Six

Should Scotland be an independent country? That's the question you will have to answer in next year's referendum. Today the Scottish Government accepted changes to the question they wanted asked, as all sides united behind the recommendations of the Electoral Commission. But there could be trouble ahead over a commission proposal that the UK and Scottish Governments should agree now what process would be followed in the event of a Yes vote.

DIARY: The Electoral Commission recommended the referendum question be changed from 'Do you agree Scotland should be an independent country?' – which was considered to be leading – to 'Should Scotland be an independent country?' The Scottish Government has accepted that so it'll be a formality going through the Parliament and, therefore, will be the question we will have to answer.

Tuesday 5 February 2013

STV News

The Scottish and UK Governments are at loggerheads tonight over claims from the SNP that Scotland could be independent by March of 2016 following a Yes vote next year. The timetable has been described as ludicrous with the Scottish Secretary insisting the Nationalists are using the issue as a distraction from key

debates surrounding the attempt to break with the Union.

DIARY: The Scottish Government issued a 'road map' outlining their plans for Scotland becoming independent should there be a 'Yes' vote in the referendum. Basically they're saying the process would be all but complete by March 2016. That does seem rather optimistic and they've come under fire for it. However, at least they're setting out what they expect to happen post-referendum. The No campaign haven't, and I don't think they will.

Monday 11 February 2013

DIARY: An interview with John C Reilly – the Hollywood actor. He's been in loads of movies and is one of those guys whose name isn't so well known, but whose face is very familiar. He was clearly very tired and, in fact, the music concert he was promoting with his band had sold out, so he could have pulled out. To his credit he didn't. Very personable and no entourage. I liked him and it would have been good to have had a beer with him.

Monday 25 February 2013

DIARY: The resignation with immediate effect of Scotland's – indeed the UK's – leading Catholic over allegations of inappropriate behaviour made by three priests and a former priest. Coming just ahead of his departure to vote in the conclave for the new Pope, it was dynamite. We did an STV News Special live from St Mary's Cathedral in Edinburgh. Sad day for the Catholic Church and for Cardinal O'Brien, who has the reputation of being a decent man. However, he is outspoken on gay rights issues and the implication is that there was a deep hypocrisy in that.

DIARY CONT: What is the way forward for the Catholic church? One guest on *Scotland Tonight*, Michael McMahon MSP, put it best – the RC Church should focus on the issue in which it excels – charity, support for the poor etc.

Monday 4 March 2013

DIARY: Invited to lunch with some senior execs from the RBS which is one of the biggest bogey banks from the 2008 crisis. It's owned 87 per cent by the tax payer, but they have awful PR – not the guys who do it, but what they have to deal with. Talked about turning the bank around, but what they cannot or will not change is the huge bonus culture (which applies to banking globally) and they will never have public understanding until they do.

DEATH OF MARGARET THATCHER

Monday 8 April 2013

Scotland Tonight

Baroness Thatcher, who died today at the age of 87, was an extraordinary politician whose policies changed the face of Scotland. To her supporters she was a great Prime Minister who saved the country from economic collapse. For others she was a deeply divisive figure who pursued an agenda which decimated industries and destroyed communities.

LORD MICHAEL FORSYTH, Former Scottish Secretary:
I will remember her as a very kindly, caring lady who was a great friend to

me and my family... She was a giant... Not even the hardest line Socialist would argue that it was possible to keep going with mines or steel mills that were no longer competitive and it was important to create new jobs. Now that does not in any way diminish the pain and suffering that was caused by that change. What made Margaret Thatcher unique is that she was a politician who was prepared to do the right thing and take the opprobrium in the interests of the country. Sadly, today I think we have too many politicians in all political parties who are too worried about what next day's press is going to say about them.

LORD GEORGE FOULKES, Labour:
The changes would have come, but they could have come more slowly and more carefully and with more consideration for the people, not as ruthlessly as Thatcher did it... She was actually quite a kind person on a one-to-one basis and this was a dilemma because she was very ruthless and vindictive politically, but kind personally.

JOAN MCALPINE, SNP:
It's all very well saying there needed to be structural reform on the economy, but if we behaved like the Europeans and supported some of our industries, like our shipyards, we'd still have a better manufacturing base than we had after the Thatcher years.

DIARY: She was a huge public figure in my lifetime and remains a divisive figure even now. What is not in doubt is her status as a political giant. A conviction politician who provided strong leadership. Interesting to see the reaction in different areas. The London media were rather uncritical. Hundreds gathered in George Square to celebrate, which I think was distasteful.

Tuesday 9 April 2013

DIARY: Young Pete Smith did well with an interview with Rangers chief executive, Charles Green. Pre-recorded our discussion with a lawyer in the gallery to make sure we didn't cross any line. First time I've done that.

Tuesday 16 April 2013

DIARY: A real error at lunchtime. We reported on a Scot named Chris McKenzie who'd been injured the Boston Marathon Bombing. We even had a photo. Turns out he didn't exist. The photo was indeed of a Chris McKenzie, but just a face that came up in a Google search. STV, the BBC and other organisations all believed an asshole on Twitter who seemed to find it funny. Contemptible. Nonetheless, we fell below our own standards.

Wednesday 8 May 2013

STV News – live from Manchester with Raman Bhardwaj

Good evening, live from Old Trafford – on the day Sir Alex Ferguson announces he is retiring from the beautiful game, ending the most successful managerial career in British football history. In all Sir Alex won 49 trophies, including here at Man United – 13 Premier League titles and major success in Europe. Today's news draws to a close one of Scotland's greatest success stories.

FIRST INDEPENDENCE DEBATE
Thursday 16 May 2013
Scotland Tonight

On 18 September next year the Scottish people will be asked to make the biggest political decision in more than 300 years. The Independence referendum campaign will be fought on various fronts. Tonight, in the first of a series of live debates, we spotlight the key battleground of economics. Joining us are two of Scotland's most senior politicians. From the Scottish Government, we have Deputy First Minister Nicola Sturgeon; from the UK Government, the Secretary State for Scotland Michael Moore. They'll be crossing swords in debate, and will also get the opportunity to cross-examine each other.

The format of the debate was agreed by both sides beforehand. They'd make a statement, I would question them both separately, then they would cross-examine each other for a set period of time each. I could not intervene other than to alert them to how long they had left. It was intriguing seeing them react under a different pressure from what they are used to. Nicola Sturgeon was an obvious winner. Michael Moore allowed her to dominate his cross examination. She would reply to his questions with another question, which he would then try to answer. I think he was too gentlemanly and never really got going against her.

ANDY MURRAY WINS WIMBLEDON
Sunday 7 July 2013

DIARY: **Andy Murray won the Men's Singles title at Wimbledon, finally** ending 77 years of vain hope. He beat Novak Djokovic in three sets and, for the most part, played superbly. He turned round difficult positions he would have lost previously. Up there as possibly the greatest ever Scottish sporting achievement.

Monday 8 July 2013
STV News at Six

This is the STV *news at Six*, live from the hometown of Scotland's sporting hero Andy Murray. Dunblane is where it all began. Where a boy with a racquet, talent and a dream started on the road to becoming a legend. Conquering Centre Court assures the 26-year-old his place amongst the greatest Sportsmen. And what achievements along the way – glory at the Olympics when he won Gold, Grand Slam victory at the US Open and now this very modest young Scot is the first British man to take the Wimbledon men's singles title in 77 years.

DIARY: A scorcher of a day. I was standing on the courts where Murray played as a kid. The Dunblane Tennis Club was very accommodating. Especially during the evening programme Annette (*Annette Wiseman – make-up*) was having to dab my brow between each link. I could feel the heat of the sun through my shoes. The official temperatures was in the high 20s, but our car thermometers were showing it to be 30C plus.

SECOND INDEPENDENCE DEBATE
Thursday 5 September 2013
Scotland Tonight

Tonight, in the second of our series of live referendum debates, we spotlight the key battleground of welfare and pensions. To debate what sort of benefits system we'd have in an independent Scotland, we're joined by two of Scotland's most senior politicians. From the Scottish Government making the case for Independence, is Deputy First Minister Nicola Sturgeon; and from the Scottish Labour Party making the case for staying in the Union, we have Deputy Leader Anas Sarwar.

DIARY: It ended up being quite controversial because of the tactics used by Sarwar. He badgered and nipped at Sturgeon constantly and she rose to it once or twice. I chaired it for the first part and had to take control a few times. However, in the second part they cross examine each other and I step back. That's when it became a shouting match at times. I wanted to step in, but couldn't. 'Politics in the raw' and 'a stairheid rammy' were some of the observations. Sarwar's tactic was clearly to get under Sturgeon's skin. We were trending on Twitter across the UK and there has been a lot of reaction, not all of it favourable. I'm unconvinced that it added much to the debate, but it's maybe a sign of the way it's turning.

Monday 16 September 2013
DIARY: An announcement that Billy Connolly has shown initial signs of Parkinson's Disease and has been treated for prostate cancer. We learned that the Independent MSP Margo MacDonald, who knows Connolly and is also suffering from Parkinson's was at an hotel across the river. So it was a quick dash to get over and set up a

two-camera shoot. My interview was off the cuff, but it wasn't a hard one, just getting her to talk about her own experience. She's a big figure in Scottish politics and has a feisty reputation. I always find her to be good fun and quite flirtatious.

MARGO MACDONALD: When I was diagnosed with Parkinson's (*in 1995*) it was like a bolt out of the blue. I didn't really know what Parkinson's was. I came out of the doctors in a bit of a dwam, went to the hairdressers, had a good drink and had a good bubble with my hairdresser. And after that I decided well I've got Parkinson's, I can't see it, I can't feel it, I'll just get on with it. As you can see I've got a bit of a shake, but that's only because I'm talking to you (*laughs*).

ONE YEAR UNTIL THE
INDEPENDENCE REFERENDUM

Wednesday 18 September 2013

STV News at Six – live from Holyrood
September the 18th 2014. Decision time for Scotland. A year from today we, the voters, will choose the future of our country. Remain within the union or opt for Independence? It's the biggest decision the nation has had to make in hundreds of years. In this special edition of STV News we mark 365 days to the poll.

DIARY: **An STV poll showed Yes 31 per cent No 59 per cent, which is consistent with the trends. The Yes campaign is laying much store on persuading the undecided and soft 'No' vote. It's a big ask.**

Presenting the news from outside Holyrood. We had a camera position marked off with some cones and a very basic set up. We had the First Minister on live. He announced himself as 'Hi, I'm John MacKay!' He's losing weight. He needed to. He actually nicked my water. I told him he was welcome, but I'd already drunk from it. He didn't bother, doing the old childhood thing of wiping it with his sleeve.

Tuesday 24 September 2013

DIARY: **Interviewing film star James McAvoy this afternoon along with controversial author Irvine Welsh about the film 'Filth'. Excellent interview covering the film, the Scottish film scene and Independence. I found McAvoy to be pleasant and grounded and his presence caused quite a stir in the building. Given the darkness of Irvine Welsh's writing, he was surprisingly light and personable. It was a good 'get'.**

IRVINE WELSH, author:
I am obsessed with failure. I think that failure's really interesting because success only comes in one kind of form. If you're successful you think 'this is great', but it doesn't really teach anything, but failure comes in all different types of form so you learn so much from failure. I am fascinated by the way when things are going against us we make our own decisions to compound it or we inevitably make our own decision to compound that. If you're sometimes compelled to keep acting it's just time to stop and let things take their course.

JM: You had Scottish talent, a Scottish director and a Scottish supporting cast, but a lot of this had to be filmed elsewhere. It comes back to this question we hear a lot, the need for a Scottish film studio.

JAMES MCAVOY, actor:
We don't have a proper studio in Scotland and that is a real shame, not just a shame because of job creation, but because culturally we don't have the facility to tell stories about ourselves on a regular, frequent and prolific basis, which we need. It's important for our own cultural confidence and identity and it would be useful. It's not even something you can talk about in business terms, is it economically unfeasible, will we make money back? It's got to be subsidised, it's a service, it's not just an industry. We serve the ego and the collective identity of the culture you represent and we just don't have that. The tangibles of it can't be measured, but they're immense. Huge for your self confidence as a nation.

Monday 7 October 2013

STV News

The Scottish Secretary Michael Moore has been sacked. The Berwickshire MP has been replaced by chief whip Alistair Carmichael. Liberal Democrat leader Nick Clegg said he wanted to 'draw on different experience' in the run up to the Independence referendum.

Many commentators believed that one of the factors which contributed to Michael Moore's dismissal was his performance in the STV debate against Nicola Sturgeon.

DIARY: **Michael Moore was a polite, not un-warm individual whom I always liked. His replacement is the more combative Alistair Carmichael, whom I met during a debate at the last General Election and took to right away. I think we'll see more scrapping. He was clearly uncomfortable about why Michael Moore had been chopped.**

Monday 11 November 2013

STV News

Finally, it has become a Glasgow tradition – the placing of a traffic cone on top of the Duke of Wellington Statue in the city centre. But it could be coming to an end. The city council is considering raising the height of the monument to discourage pranksters from climbing it.

DIARY: **I think the council is misjudging people's views on it – so misjudging that you have to think there is an ulterior motive. Twitter campaigns, Facebook campaigns and by tonight they'd already backed down. We carried it on *Scotland Tonight* and maybe not as light-hearted as I'd have liked, but the guy opposed made some good points – essentially it's a war memorial.**

SCOTTISH GOVERNMENT WHITE PAPER

Tuesday 26 November 2013

STV News

The Scottish Government has unveiled its White Paper on Independence. The 670 page document reveals the priorities the SNP say they will negotiate for Scotland if the nation votes Yes in next year's referendum. Proposals for childcare, economy, defence, currency and pensions are all covered. Critics argue the document is no more than a wish list and cannot be delivered.

DIARY: In recent months we've been told that certain questions will be answered 'in the White Paper'. The launch was a fairly low razzmatazz event at the Glasgow Science Centre, but widespread interest from the UK networks and abroad. First Minister Alex Salmond and Deputy FM made the presentation. The initial impression is of a weighty document, some 670 pages, which doesn't reveal much that is new. I did the lunchtime programme from outside the Science Centre. That was straightforward. This afternoon I went through to Edinburgh, twice dozing off as I read the White Paper. No reflection on the book, which is actually very easy to read. The programme went very well, including live interviews with both Alex Salmond and Alistair Darling on location. They both went off okay – not much you can get in three minutes or so.

Wednesday 27 November 2013
We had another *Scotland Tonight* debate this evening with the Deputy First Minister Nicola Sturgeon up against the Scottish Secretary Alistair Carmichael. Many believe the poor performance of his predecessor Michael Moore in the first debate contributed to his sacking. Carmichael – who has a reputation as bruiser – was no better. Sturgeon verbally floored him. I don't know if he was conscious of holding back because of Anas Sarwar's performance in the last one, but he never got going. Rona hosted.

This debate became famous for the line, 'Help me, Rona'. In fact Alistair Carmichael

didn't say that. He turned to Rona and asked, 'Are we going to stop this?'

Thursday 28 November 2013
DIARY: Tried a new concept on *Scotland Tonight* which seems to have been well received. The regular programme with Rona ran as usual on-air, meanwhile I was hosting a 'Google hangout', which was five guests with me in the Studio and five more joining us from various locations via Skype, including actor Brian Cox – in Switzerland. We ran for half an hour just online, but when the regular transmission ended, we then went on-air on STV for another half hour. We've received much praise for being innovative, but more than that people enjoyed that the Google chat wasn't of political point scoring, rather one of thoughtful discussion. I enjoyed doing it. There is no question the technology could be better quality, but it was good to try it.

CLUTHA TRAGEDY
Friday 29 November 2013
DIARY: I got a text from my son saying 'See a helicopter has crashed into the Clutha Bar in Glasgow?' I actually asked him for the punchline. Tragically, not a joke. A police helicopter came down and crashed through the roof of the pub which was packed with people enjoying a live band. Initially, it looked as if there might be no fatalities, but soon there were reports that people had been killed.

Saturday 30 November 2013
STV News – live from next to Clutha
Good evening. The Clutha vault helicopter crash has been described as

205

a 'Black Day for Scotland' by the First Minister. Three people from inside the helicopter and five from inside the pub are dead. In the city's hospitals 14 others lie seriously injured. The Queen and the Prime Minister have sent their condolences to the bereaved families and tonight emergency services continue their painstaking operation to find those beneath the rubble.

DIARY: **It is so randomly sad. You go out for a beer on a Friday night and you die because a helicopter crashes through the roof. We did a live programme at lunchtime which went well. The wreckage of the pub was behind us beyond the police control. It is still so hard to believe. Back down again this evening and the full scale of the tragedy was now clear. Eight people, including three in the helicopter, had been killed. As I went on-air, there was quite a crowd of people on the other side of the camera. I had no autocue, so was remembering the script. I was aware of a woman waiting with her husband listening intently. When I went on-air saying, 'Eight people have died,' she threw her hand to her face in horror. It's rare to see the impact of the news you are delivering. I hope she didn't know anyone.**

DOUGLAS BARRIE, STV Online Journalist:

I saw it as a retweet and immediately notified the others working in the STV newsroom that night. Colleagues put calls in to the police. It was too early to know for sure but it definitely didn't look like a hoax, so we posted what we could using the tweet for reference.

Barely five minutes later, we had confirmation that it was indeed a helicopter – so instinctively I picked up a digital camera and ran for the door. We had to be at the scene as quickly as possible.

The others began calling other staff members to notify them. Several emergency vehicles passed me on the way and the scene was a sea of blue flashing lights.

I parked at Glasgow Sheriff Court and even from that far away, police officers were asking people to move back. As they did I spoke to as many people as I could –mostly people who had heard the crash rather than seen it, but a few did speak of how they saw the helicopter drop.

As I was sending my recorded quotes back to the office via two mobile phones, I crossed the river and met a contact who knew the band playing the Clutha that night, Esperanza. I sent the extra information to the office and I think we were one of the first to have this angle.

I continued newsgathering through the night as the crowds started to disperse and the recovery operation began.

Twitter and Vine were the main sources for sharing what I was gathering on the street – it was the easiest way to get something back to the office for the team to collate quickly and succinctly. It was also a way to communicate with other colleagues around the scene.

Social media was an integral part of our coverage.

Monday 2 December 2013

DIARY: The helicopter wreckage was finally moved from the Clutha Pub today, revealing one more body. That's the death total now nine. It also allowed for the removal of all the bodies still there. There was a terribly sombre scene when the bodies were taken away and the emergency services lined up and saluted. *Scotland Tonight* was an extended programme. Some very powerful elements – Alleena Coupe, who was in the bar and *Scottish Sun* editor Gordon Smart who saw it come down. The leader of Glasgow City Council Gordon Matheson nearly broke down as he described being part of the official team approaching the barriers where the media and families were for the announcement that there were eight dead. The story will move on now and not be in such focus, but I won't forget it. A Friday night drink and a helicopter crashes into the pub. How random and how awful.

DEATH OF NELSON MANDELA
Friday 6 December 2013
STV News

This is an STV news special, live from Nelson Mandela Place. There can be few places anywhere that the name Nelson Mandela isn't known. And not a single politician who could command the same respect in their homeland or on the world stage. In the end he died peacefully at home with his nearest and dearest. Throughout last night and today politicians, personalities and the public have been paying their respects to the man who inspired a generation.

First Minister Alex Salmond described Mandela as a 'towering statesman.' Former Prime Minister Gordon Brown said he was 'the greatest leader of our generation.'

DIARY: There was a celebration of Mandela's life with maybe about 300 people there. We were right next to the stage and I did fear that we'd have problems with sound. Everything seemed very last minute and I genuinely thought we would have trouble getting on-air. However, it all worked very well. For my part, I'm pleased that we did it, but I'm not so convinced that we should have done it to the exclusion of all other news.

ANCHORMAN CAST
Wednesday 11 December 2013

DIARY: To Claridges for the interviews with the 'Anchorman 2' cast. The journalists are gathered in a room and then called for a designated five minutes. It's just a conveyor belt and not something I would want to do all the time. Anyway, my plan was to ask the actors for advice to take home to the STV News team. First I was with Paul Rudd and Steve Carrell and they played along really well. Will Ferrell – the Anchorman Ron Burgundy – did too. I'd brought props (*ties and false moustaches*) and, although he wouldn't put them on, he was willing to react. Director Adam McKay and I discussed our shared surname. Will Ferrell was asking me about Independence – 'You guys will lose all your money, right?'

Paul Rudd who plays ace reporter Brian Fantana advised our reporters to douse themselves with the strongest cologne they could find, get a chest toupe, grow a moustache and wear polyester pants (*trousers – at least I hope he meant trousers*). Steve Carrell who plays Brick Tamland the weatherman, said roving reporters should go commando 'to capture the essence'.

Scotland Tonight

He's a man who was put on this earth to read the news and have salon quality hair. The legendary Anchorman Ron Burgundy comes from a time when everyone believed what they saw on TV. In short, Ron Burgundy is kind of a big deal. He and his news team have assembled for the latest chapter in the Anchorman saga. I've been privileged to meet the man who knows him best.

JM: I'm a news anchor in Scotland. We all look up to the doyen that is Ron Burgundy. You know him better than anyone. How could he advise me?

WILL FERRELL, Ron Burgundy: From Ron's perspective the first thing I see is that you don't have a moustache. Ron would be appalled. Yeah, you gotta grow some facial hair. Are you wearing cologne?

JM: I'm not. Should I be?

WF: It should be enough cologne that it makes my eyes water from ten feet.

JM: Ron was put on the earth to read the news and have salon quality hair. I can do the first bit, not so much the second. How do I achieve that?

WF: (*laughs*) Your hair is very short, yeah, yeah. You just have to use a lot of conditioner. It's also just DNA and fortunately Ron was given the gift of beautiful hair.

JM: He also wears suits that make Sinatra look like a hobo. These are ties I've worn in the past...

WF: (*laughing*) That's an amazing selection. Are those really from your...?

JM: They're from my illustrious career. Would Ron wear any of these?

WF: Probably that one, the loudest. (*An especially garish tie*)

JM: We've got a lot of big issues in Scotland, Independence and such. Ron very much takes the line of give people what they want, so is that the line we should follow?

WF: It's a big question, right, for Scotland? Whether to go it alone? I think try it for a week. Then if you guys don't like it, come right back.

2014

Monday 6 January 2014

Scotland Tonight

The Year of Decision has arrived, and between now and polling day the two referendum campaigns will be doing everything they can to win the hearts and minds of Scotland's four million voters.

DIARY: This is likely to be the most significant year of my professional life. *Scotland Tonight* kicked off as we are likely to go on – with the Referendum. A pre-recorded interview with Deputy First Minister Nicola Sturgeon and the same with Scottish Secretary Alistair Carmichael. Marking interviews really.

Thursday 16 January 2014

STV News

A major search is ongoing tonight to find a little boy who disappeared from his home after being put to bed. 3-year-old Mikaeel Kular's mother reported her son missing when she woke this morning. She last saw Mikaeel at nine O'Clock last night. Police helicopters are in the sky over Edinburgh. Detectives are on foot and horseback. Locals are helping as gardens, coastlines and homes are searched.

DIARY: Sounds like an abduction to me. I can't see that a 3-year-old would get up, dressed and out of the flat without being seen or heard.

Mikaeel's mother Rosdeep Adekoya was convicted of his murder after his body was found in Fife.

Monday 20 January 2014

DIARY: There was a study by some academic which claimed both BBC and STV are biased against the Yes campaign. Usual lack of insight or understanding of the media they claim to analyse.

Monday 3 February 2014

DIARY: Straight out to the south side home of acclaimed author William McIlvanney for a pre-recorded interview. A very pleasant, warm guy. I enjoyed hearing him talk about the writing process, 'Do you have these doubts?' And, of course, I do.

Back to STV and change for *Scotland Tonight* promo, change again for News promo. Have to check scripts and get into the studio for the *Six O'Clock*. Off air at 6.30pm and straight into preparing for a pre-record on an Edinburgh sex saunas story at 7.30pm. Out to prepare for two significant political interviews. Rehearsals at the back of 9.00pm, pre-record with George Galloway MP at 10.00pm and on-air at 10.30pm. A full day and I prefer it that way.

Tuesday 4 February 2014

DIARY: We had an excellent audience last night – an 11 per cent share peaking at 13 per cent (200,000). For a current affairs programme that is excellent. I do enjoy it. The only downside is the childish and incessant cybernats online who flood our feed. Sifting genuine comment from the clichés can be a challenge.

Wednesday 5 February 2014

DIARY: I hosted an event with Bernard Ponsonby on the art of the political interview. I don't consider myself in Bernard's class so it was interesting to hear. He confirmed what I've always felt, that preparation is the absolute key.

BBC *Scotland* have announced a new political programme at 10.30pm Monday – Thursday fronted by Sarah Smith – the daughter of former Labour leader John Smith. It's about time, but also a flagrant abuse of position. However, we have nothing to be concerned about. We have well established ourselves.

BARRY HUMPHRIES
Tuesday 11 February 2014
Scotland Tonight
He's an entertainment legend who's been making audiences laugh around the world for more than five decades. Barry Humphries is now taking a final bow with a farewell tour. The man behind the iconic Australian suburban housewife Dame Edna Everage is saying 'goodbye possums' with an all-singing, all-dancing spectacular. Tonight he was at the King's Theatre in Glasgow. Before he went on stage, he spoke to *Scotland Tonight*.

DIARY: Interviewing the Australian comic entertainer and satirist Barry Humphries, better known as Dame Edna Everage. I had interviewed one of his other alter egos, Sir Les Patterson, some 15 years ago – perhaps 'was a straight man for' might be more accurate than interviewed. I found him to be charming and a very interesting interviewee. He's 80 next week and it's remarkable how sharp he is. His description of political correctness as

the modern puritanism was, I thought, perfect.

JM: You've been doing Dame Edna since the '50s. That's a long, long time.

BARRY HUMPHRIES: Edna has been in my repertoire, in my life, really.

JM: You're going to miss her, surely?

BH: It's very hard to explain. Edna has a life really of her own. I don't have much to do with it. In the old days, when I first thought I'd invented Edna, it was like having created a puppet. And when I'd done a little show with this puppet Edna, I'd put the puppet in a box, close the lid and forget about it. Next time I came back, however, I'd open the box and the puppet would be wearing funny glasses. The puppet would say things that I would never dare to say to my audience. And I realised that I had invented something rather, to use Edna's favourite word, 'spooky'. Something which did have its own separate life, and so if I have to improvise on the stage I can improvise very easily, because it's as though Edna exists and is a sort of ventriloquist, telling me what to say. It's not a thing I ever analyse. I leave it sometimes to academics, and you know, John, academics do write about me now. That's a sign really of being more or less dead.

JM: You also do satire very well, even now, and a lot of people would think satire comes from a youthful anger, perhaps. How do you sustain that? Where does that anger come from?

BH: I did have a little anger in my youth, which is only proper. I don't approve of a youth who is not angry. But I was brought up in a middle-class background in Melbourne, Australia, and Melbourne was a city in a very remote part of south-east Asia, trying to be English. And it almost succeeded. I felt frustrated living there. It was too cosy, too comfortable, too self-satisfied, for a priggish little know-all like me. And so I began to sort of take the mickey out of Melbourne. I invented characters which somehow to me described the boredom of Melbourne, but people laughed. I couldn't win. They didn't go away hurting, they went away laughing.

JM: Is political correctness damaging do you think?

BH: Political correctness is another form of Puritanism, which I dislike intensely.

JM: You came to the United Kingdom, you were based in London, you worked with a lot of the satirists of the time, Peter Cook and such.

BH: Yes, I did.

JM: How does now, 2014, compare to that era of the 1960s? The world has clearly changed, but has it really?

BH: Well the satire, so-called satire movement of the '60s, the stars of which were people like Peter Cook, Dudley Moore, Spike Milligan, even David Frost, all of those people were wonderfully bright, interesting men. Significantly, mostly men. And I worked with all of them. It was a

very interesting period, the '60s in Britain, because it was just coming alive after the war. So we were still licking our wounds in the '50s. By the '60s we were wearing coloured clothing again, as I'm pleased to see you are. It was a very funny time.

Wednesday 12 February 2014

STV News

The Scottish and UK Governments are at loggerheads tonight over the creation of a sterling currency area in the event of a Yes vote. The Chancellor George Osborne is expected to rule out such a plan when he speaks in Edinburgh tomorrow. A move that has been branded by Ministers here as mere bluff.

DIARY: It throws into jeopardy the SNP's plans for a sterling zone. They say he is bluffing and I'm inclined to think they are right, but I can see it causing doubt. And, of course, the media is being manipulated. Leak it beforehand and then the actual speech and you get two prominent days of coverage. And we can't not cover it.

Thursday 13 February 2014

STV News

In one of the most significant days in the Independence referendum debate, the three main Unionist parties have said they would veto Scottish Government ambitions for a currency Union in the event of a Yes vote. The day started with the Chancellor saying he had received advice from Treasury officials that a currency Union wouldn't work. Labour and the Lib Dems quickly followed with similar statements as the Scottish Government said the parties were trying to bully voters into the No camp.

DIARY: The Chancellor of the Exchequer, George Osborne, made a speech in Edinburgh in which he said an independent Scotland would not be able to share the pound with the UK. The SNP accuse him of bluff and bluster, but it has certainly shaken them. They've been saying all along it would be fine. It's a difficult issue for them. However, Osborne did no sit down interviews, took three questions and he was off. Why they think that coming north, making pronouncements and then running off again without explaining themselves is going to be persuasive to the Scottish electorate is beyond me. It would have been good to have done *Scotland Tonight* this evening. Real meat today.

Saturday 22 February 2014

DIARY: An interview with Oscar winning actor Richard Dreyfuss, who's in Glasgow for the Film festival. We had ten minutes with him at the Malmaison Hotel.

'Okay if we get a quick snapshot?'

'A lot of actors are quite short. Dustin Hoffman isn't that tall, y'know.'

'Er... no a quick snapshot. A photo.'

'Oh.'

Monday 24 February 2014

STV News

The Prime Minister has declared he would not seek to block Scottish membership of the European Union in the event of a Yes vote. Speaking as he and his Westminster cabinet met in Aberdeen, David Cameron also told STV News that he would be delighted to take part in a referendum programme where he would answer questions from undecided voters. But with the Scottish cabinet meeting in the very same city, the two governments went into battle over oil and gas.

DIARY: The UK cabinet was meeting in Aberdeen, only the second time it's come to Scotland in 90 years. Meanwhile, the Scottish cabinet was meeting in Portlethen, some seven miles away. The UK cabinet met in the Shell HQ, the Scottish cabinet in a village hall. It was the usual posturing and game playing. Unlike the Chancellor, the Prime Minister at least did some interviews, as did the First Minister.

Tuesday 25 February 2014

Scotland Tonight

Welcome to the fourth in our series of *Scotland Tonight* referendum debates. Tonight we have with us the two most senior women in Scottish politics. Returning to the fray from the SNP Scottish Government is the architect of the Independence White Paper, Deputy First Minister Nicola Sturgeon; and making the case for staying in the Union, we have the Scottish Labour leader Johann Lamont. They'll be crossing swords in debate, and will also get the opportunity to cross-examine each other.

DIARY: We had expectations that it might give a different tone to the debate, but it didn't. The cross examination was another rabble with the two talking over each other constantly. Nobody will have learned anything from it and many will have been put off. I was doing the analysis with Bernard Ponsonby and Colin Mackay and as we came off-air Bernard said we would be slaughtered for that and we were, on the social networks. Neither of the politicians was happy either. Johann Lamont had left by the time I came out of the studio, but Nicola Sturgeon was saying that both sides know they can't back down in that format.

Tuesday 4 March 2014

DIARY: Alex Salmond was making a speech in London on Independence. He is well regarded in the UK – one of the few Scottish based politicians they'll know. So we went on that in *Scotland Tonight*, plus day two of our poll which shows the SNP are still way ahead in popularity for the Holyrood elections in 2016. Incredible for a mid-term government.

Tuesday 18 March 2014

Scotland Tonight

What happens if there's a 'No' vote in September's Independence referendum? It's a question each of the pro-union parties is under pressure to answer. Today Scottish Labour set out its stall, proposing a package of measures which would give MSPs greater control over income tax and some welfare spending.

DIARY: Scottish Labour announced their increased powers for Devolution in the event of a 'No' vote in the referendum. No sweeping ideas, rather tinkering. It's a compromise imposed,

no doubt, by the Westminster MPs. If there is a 'Yes' vote they'll need to look at themselves.

Monday 24 March 2014

Scotland Tonight

The momentum is now with the Yes campaign. That was the message from the SNP after the latest ICM opinion poll revealed a significant swing in favour of Independence. The survey put support for Independence at 39 percent, just seven points behind support for the Union. How concerned should Better Together be by the findings? Is the No side beginning to look like a campaign in trouble? We're now joined by two senior pro-Union figures who have called for a more positive strategy to connect with voters. At Westminster is the former leader of the Liberal Democrats Charles Kennedy. And in Dundee is the former Labour First Minister Henry McLeish.

DIARY: Interviewing former Lib Dem leader Charles Kennedy on *Scotland Tonight*. It was a down-the-line interview, but I've always been impressed by him. He's always seemed straight and believable.

Thursday 3 April 2014

DIARY: The main story was the quite bizarre decision by Glasgow City Council to feature the live explosive demolition of the Red Road flats as part of the Opening Ceremony of the Commonwealth Games. They says it's 'bold', but most people think it's daft. I'd be surprised if they go ahead with it and it could be fraught with risk if they do.

Friday 4 April 2014

STV News

'The brightest light in the Scottish political firmament has gone out.' With those words Jim Sillars led the tributes as he announced his wife Margo MacDonald died peacefully today at their Edinburgh home. She was 70 years old and had been suffering from Parkinson's Disease for some time. The political world was quick to react, with affectionate recollections of the most popular politician of her generation. The First Minister said she made politics exciting and human.

DIARY: **She was a major political figure in Scotland of the last 40 years, spectacularly winning a by-election in Govan in 1973. From then on she was always a familiar face, very highly regarded for her forthright views and common sense approach. I had the pleasure of interviewing her a few times and always found her fun. A big loss to Scottish politics, especially for Independence, which she campaigned for all her political life. Many, many tributes today, all of them sincere.**

Tuesday 8 April 2014

STV News

The former Secretary General of NATO has claimed Scottish Independence could have a 'cataclysmic' impact on the world. Speaking in Washington, Lord Robertson claimed the loudest cheer in the event of a 'Yes' vote would come from the enemies of the West. However, the Deputy First Minister said she was shocked by the former

Defence Secretary's language and branded his comments insulting and offensive.

DIARY: **It's certainly the most controversial anti-Indy speech there has been and the language does seem excessive. His basic point was that an independent Scotland weakens the UK, which weakens Western security. Did a pre-recorded interview with him. He was complaining about being kept waiting in the green room in Washington for 20 minutes (we were told he was still travelling in his car).**

I do wonder how you can reconcile going from being in CND (Campaign for Nuclear Disarmament) to Secretary General of NATO. People change, of course, but that is quite a journey.

Tuesday 22 April 2014

STV News

Gordon Brown has said an independent Scotland's first annual pension bill would be 'three times the income from oil'. In a speech for the pro-unionist Better Together campaign in Glasgow, the former Prime Minister said pensions would be more secure and cheaper to administer if Scotland remains part of the UK. The SNP accused him of being 'economically illiterate' and said pensions are more affordable here than in the rest of the UK.

Scotland Tonight

Gordon Brown has made his first foray into the cross-party Better Together campaign, outlining his vision of Scotland's future within the UK. Tonight's speech from the former Labour Prime Minister came in the wake of a weekend opinion poll suggesting that Yes Scotland now needs a swing of just over two per cent to secure Independence.

Monday 28 April 2014

STV News

The First Minister has called Scotland a 'lynchpin of the European Union' as he made the case for Independence in the heart of Europe. Speaking in Bruges he said Scotland had a key role to play in the EU citing vast natural resources and human talent. However his speech was somewhat overshadowed by comments he made in an interview about Russian president Vladimir Putin's leadership.

Mr Salmond said that while he didn't approve of Russian actions he admired certain aspects of President Putin, in particular that he had restored Russian pride.

DIARY: First Minister in Bruges talking about Europe and Scotland's place in it. Also some froth about qualified remarks he made about Russian President Vladimir Putin.

Tuesday 29 April 2014

Scotland Tonight

What does it mean to be Scottish? It's a question that has taken on added significance in 2014. A special conference being held tomorrow at Edinburgh University is to explore the different aspects of Scottish identity and how it's been shaped by various forces.

DIARY: Eminent historian Tom Devine was the lead guest, but a good support panel. His basic point was that national

identity is fluid and the 'Scottishness' we have now would be unrecognisable to those from the 18th Century. I would like to have heard more.

Wednesday 30 April 2014

STV News

Parents affected by the Mortonhall baby ashes scandal have been left horrified by a report which revealed their children's remains may have been mixed in with those of adults. That was just one of the grim findings of the official investigation which says families have now been left with a 'lifetime of uncertainty' over what happened to their babies.

DIARY: The baby ashes scandal. Stillborn or premature babies who were cremated without their parents knowledge. It now seems their ashes may have been mixed with those of adults who were cremated first thing in the morning. The pain of the parents is clear. More to do with the standards of the time (started in 1967) than any badness.

Friday 9 May 2014

DIARY: An unfortunate mispronunciation on the news this evening, saying 'webshite' rather than 'website', caused a huge reaction on social networks. My name – @RealMacKaySTV – was trending on Twitter. As I noted on Facebook, 'You read crafted intros and hold chaotic programmes together and nobody notices. You say 'webshite' instead of 'website'? Meltdown!' I apologised and moved on, but knowing all the time that I daren't smile.

Tuesday 13 May 2014

DIARY: *Scotland Tonight*'s subjects – Scottish cultural 'miserablism' and a review of the end of the football season. The cybernats were on their high horse about a poll that wasn't being released at Westminster. They swamped the *Scotland Tonight* feed with their herd mentality. It ruins what social networks can be.

Wednesday 14 May 2014

STV News

The Chancellor George Osborne has told MPs there would be no deal to allow an independent Scotland to share a currency with the rest of the UK. Giving evidence to the Commons Scottish Affairs Select Committee, he said the only way for Scotland to keep the pound was to vote 'no'. But the SNP said he's putting himself on the wrong side of economics and the Scottish people.

DIARY: The SNP says it's bluff and bluster, but it is one of the clearest statements of the entire campaign. I think it's a weakness for the SNP. Even if there is a shared currency, then you are ceding significant control of your economic policy.

Thursday 15 May 2014

STV News

The Prime Minister has told STV that the Unionist parties should work together to agree new powers for Holyrood in the event of a 'No' vote for Independence. David Cameron, in an interview for *Scotland Tonight*, said it would be good 'if the parties could talk to each other about their proposals and put them into place'. It came on the day the First Minister accused the No campaign of being in disarray.

JM: Prime Minister, you're the Prime Minister of the austerity agenda, the bedroom tax, the zero hours contract. You are the embodiment, are you not, of why so many people in Scotland think a 'yes' vote is necessary?

DAVID CAMERON, Prime Minister: Obviously I don't agree with that. We're not voting about the government, we're not voting about policies. This vote, this referendum is about Scotland's future. Does Scotland want to stay in the United Kingdom? Or does Scotland want to separate itself irreversibly from the United Kingdom? That is the question on the ballot paper. Of course I would argue that we're making good economic progress. We've seen another fall in unemployment in Scotland, the economy is growing and strengthening and we're seeing lots of problems being addressed, but that's not the question in the referendum. The referendum is; stay in the United Kingdom with all the advantages that it has, all our family of nations, or go separately irreversibly in another direction.

JM: You have a dilemma, don't you? The fact is that polls here show that the better you perform in the polls moving towards the general election next year the greater the chance of a 'yes' vote in Scotland.

DC: People in Scotland know there are separate questions. This is the most important decision Scotland has had to take for 300 years which is, do we stay as part of the United Kingdom, a successful family of nations or do we forever separate ourselves from it? That is a separate question to who is elected to the UK Parliament.

JM: But however you're saying there are two questions, the fact is that's what people take from it. They are less likely to vote 'no' if there isn't a Conservative Government at Westminster.

DC: I'm just telling you there are two separate questions, I'm making two separate arguments, one alongside Labour, Liberal Democrats and people who have no political affiliation at all that we should keep our family of nations together. Think of the things we've achieved in the past, whether establishing the NHS or defeating Hitler, think of the things we can do in the future as a family of nations, that is a separate question from the outcome of the British General Election in 2015.

JM: Prime Minister, thanks for joining us on *Scotland Tonight*.

DC: Thank you.

DIARY: Interviewed the Prime Minister David Cameron... It focused on the referendum, of course. I pushed him on the unpopularity of his policies in Scotland, on committing to a timetable for more powers for the Scottish Parliament, on a Cabinet Office poll that is not being released and on the dilemma of the fact that the more successful he is in the polls for next year's General Election, the more support moves to the Yes campaign. He answered them all as smoothly as you might expect, but was wobbly on the timetable for new powers – initially suggesting it'd be in the first Queen's Speech of a new Parliament, but then backing away – and on the (*refusal to release details of the*) poll in which there was evidence of steel – 'We just don't.' I found him to be quite personable. When we were setting up I asked him about kids he'd met in Maryhill, he complimented the set, laughed at my usual line about the Bond villain chair, urged us to cover the forthcoming European elections. Then he and his entourage were away, and it was some entourage – MI5, Police Scotland and his advisers and staff. The security staff wanted to know about exits, his staff were all questions – so he's sitting there and he'll be mic'd up? Who does that? All of it being sent back by Blackberry.

When the Prime Minister was in make-up he was briefed by his people about the interview. They described me as a 'straight anchor' and mentioned my Twitter handle @RealMacKaySTV. Evidently they'd checked it, which made my heart sink. Unfortunately, my most recent tweets had been some online nonsense involving photos of my big feet jammed into a pair of stilettos.

Tuesday 27 May 2014

DIARY: The BBC launched their much vaunted new show tonight, *Scotland 2014*, and we wiped the floor with them. They have tried to copy every idea we introduced on *Scotland Tonight* and even come on at the same time. At our *Scotland Tonight* meeting I heard

what they were doing on their first night and knew then that they had got it wrong. They should have had a big splash and didn't.

We had Deputy First Minister Nicola Sturgeon and Scottish Labour leader Johann Lamont. They were head-to-head in one of our debates before and that became a rabble. This one was far more considered – they both knew it had to be better – and there was favourable feedback.

This was utterly shameless by *BBC Scotland*. They saw how successful *Scotland Tonight* was and recognised that their own offering was inadequate. Had they truly wanted to use their public funding to provide a service for the licence fee paying audience, they could have put on a new, original programme at 11.00pm. What they did instead was attempt to challenge *Scotland Tonight* with a cloned version of the same programme at the same time. It has rarely come close to matching *Scotland Tonight*'s audience.

Wednesday 28 May 2014

DIARY: We got one of our best audience shares for *Scotland Tonight*. The BBC took a pasting – half of our audience and poor production decisions. Much satisfaction, but we can't be complacent. They will sharpen up their act. They'll have to.

Friday 30 May 2014

STV News

It's been almost 60 years since a passenger tram last ran through the streets of Edinburgh. It's been more than decade since plans were first mooted to bring them back. Now, after months of testing they are finally ready to roll and early tomorrow morning the first tram will leave the depot at Gogarburn and make the short trip to the nearby Gyle Centre to pick up its first customers.

JM: Edinburgh's trams have become one of the most controversial transport projects in recent years. Years of delays, soaring costs, legal dispute and cuts to the route. One person involved in the project described it as 'hell on wheels'.

Monday 2 June 2014

DIARY: The *STV News* relaunch tonight and it went very well. The new set reflects that a lot of money has been spent on it. It's very blue, big and shiny and I think it's the best set I've worked on.

Tuesday 3 June 2014

STV News

In the clearest signal yet that Labour, the Conservatives and Liberal Democrats could agree a common package of new powers for Holyrood, the former Prime Minister Gordon Brown has told a United with Labour event a deal could be done and legislation passed 'earlier than people think'. It is part of his message to the party's core support who may fear a 'No' vote to Independence will mean an end to any further Devolution of power to Edinburgh. However, the Chair of Yes Scotland, the former Labour MP Dennis Canavan, says Labour values can only be realised through Independence.

Monday 9 June 2014

STV News – live from Holyrood

In 100 days its make your mind up time as we go to the polls to answer the question 'Should Scotland be an independent country?'. Today sees the campaigns for and against the union crank up a gear. Over the next three months both Yes Scotland and Better Together know they must do all they can to win undecided voters to their cause. They recognise getting the message across in the media and on the doorsteps is crucial.

DIARY: Interviewed the leader of Better Together Alistair Darling in a hall in Maryhill where he'd been speaking. Pushed him on the lack of agreement on what extra powers will be delivered in the event of a 'No' vote. That's their weak point. Through to Edinburgh to present the 6.00pm from Holyrood. Two live interviews – Nicola Sturgeon and Ruth Davidson (*Scottish Conservative leade*r). Immediately after I had to do a down-the-line interview with Alex Salmond – he was in Aberdeen. There was a time lag and if you try to interject it all becomes very messy. So it probably appeared I gave him an easier ride. Later accused of being biased by unionists. It's one side or the other.

Wednesday 11 June 2014

DIARY: *STV News* won an RTS Scotland award for our coverage of the Clutha Tragedy last year. I do think we deserved it because it was a cracking programme.

There is a slight discomfort in winning an award for our coverage of a tragedy, but that is the nature of the business we are in and we are at our best during the big stories.

Monday 16 June 2014

DIARY: *Scotland Tonight* went on incursions in Iraq and pledges from the union parties on more powers for Holyrood and the Scottish Government's proposals for a Scottish Constitution. Nobody could really get fired up – the World Cup providing much distraction.

Tuesday 24 June 2014

DIARY: To Glasgow Caley Uni for an interview with Jimmy Wales, the founder of Wikipedia. He was receiving an honorary doctorate. Wasn't sure about him at first – 'Is it okay if I call you Jimmy?', 'That's my name.' Then he was checking his phone as I outlined what we were doing. However, once we got going he was fine. Wikipedia is so very popular because it's free and many wonder if he regrets not making money from it. He says he enjoys it, but it's clear that being free wasn't so much a founding principle, but a necessity of the time – the dotcom bubble bursting etc. A wide-ranging interview. An unremarkable looking man, but he's created a phenomenon.

Tuesday 1 July 2014

DIARY: Interview with Allan Wells, the 100 metre Olympic gold medallist from the Moscow Olympics. He's a genuine childhood hero of mine. I still remember his victory vividly. He was very pleasant and we had a good interview.

COMMONWEALTH GAMES
Wednesday 23 July 2014
STV News

Glasgow has been transformed into a sun-drenched festival city. After years in the planning, the Commonwealth Games of 2014 have arrived. The Queen will formally open the historic event at Celtic Park. It begins at fourteen minutes past eight or 2014 – with the official ceremony at 9.00pm. As the clock counts down, our reporters are live across the city as Glasgow prepares to party.

DIARY: Glasgow is buzzing and I got a sense of that even just at Pacific Quay with the events that are going on. The weather is helping.

Thursday 31 July 2014
DIARY: Every evening of the Commonwealth Games I've stood on the balcony doing the programme. Astonishing the number of people walking along the Clyde and across the Squinty Bridge. The city is throbbing. Just being in the city you get a real sense of something happening. We're picking up medals too.

Monday 4 August 2014
DIARY: *Scotland Tonight* was previewing tomorrow's big debate. The leaders of both campaigns – or chief execs – Blair McDougall and Blair Jenkins seem to get on very well and there is no personal animosity between them, unlike the politicians.

Tuesday 5 August 2014
DIARY: Today was all about the first referendum debate between Alex Salmond and Alistair Darling. No question this was event television. TV crews from various parts and worldwide interest. Just as we were going on-air – in the final ten second countdown – autocue disappeared – apparently all my cameras died – and I was thinking I'd have to busk it – and they reappeared on three secs. Close, very close. In the cross examination section Alex Salmond did not perform well – daft questions on alien invasion and driving on the right side of the road – and Alistair Darling focused effectively on the lack of a Plan B on currency. The Yes camp were very down after it and our reaction and snap polls said Darling won. Maybe not by as much as many were declaring, but a definite win.

Thursday 7 August 2014
STV News

'It's our pound and we are keeping it'. The defiant words of the First Minister Alex Salmond today when he came under sustained attack at Holyrood to reveal a Plan B, if he can't negotiate a post-referendum currency union. Opposition Leaders used Question Time to berate the Scottish Government's lack of contingency on the issue. It's six weeks today until Scotland goes to the polls

DIARY: The First Minister under continued pressure for his perceived failings in the debate. The whole question over Scotland's currency should we not get agreement on the pound is the big issue.

Wednesday 13 August 2014
STV News

The Chief Counting Officer for the

Scottish Independence Referendum has told stv News that the final result should be known at breakfast time on the 19 September. Mary Pitcaithly revealed the ambition as more than four million polling cards were printed ready for distribution in the coming days.

DIARY: **I do sense, especially after last week's debate, a resignation among Yes campaigners. I think they know they'll lose, it's now a case of narrowing the defeat to allow it to be raised again.**

Friday 15 August 2014

STV News – Live from George Square
People make Glasgow. Tonight 5,000 are here in George Square to celebrate the biggest sporting and cultural event the city has ever hosted. In terms of sporting success the 2014 Games were the most successful ever. But the winners, too, were the people of Glasgow and Scotland. Tonight we all join in the victory party.

DIARY: **The programme came live from George Square for the Commonwealth Athlete's Parade. Among our guests was Charlie 'I'm buzzing like a jar of wasps' Flynn – a boxing gold. A great character and one of the personalities of the Games. The crowd adored him. He's just very natural. Good luck to him.**

JM: (*amid loud cheers*) This is one popular man, let me tell you. What did it feel like today coming along in the procession.

CHARLIE FLYNN, Commonealth Gold Medal Winner:
It was like Hydro number 2. (*He'd won his boxing gold at The Hydro*)

Back again. A blast from the past, man. Just like when I won the gold the public are embracing me and I love them for it. (*Huge cheers*)

JM: What have you done since you won your medal? Have you been able to get back to your normal life?

CF: What have I no' been doin', man? I've been everywhere. (*Cheers of Charlie! Charlie!*)

JM: Has the postman been delivering? (*He had been a part time postman before the Games and famously quipped after his medal win, 'The Postman delivers.'*)

CF: I've no' been delivering, I've been chilling. I've been delivering interviews.

JM: And what now, back to training?

CF: Aye, I started back a couple of days ago, trying to get back into a routine, man, let the dust settle and look at the long term boxing plan and get focused again.

JM: And what about this new found fame you've got?

CF: Ah, it's madness, man. I'm like a son of Glasgow, I go in and they're all cheering and everybody loves you. I honestly would love to thank the public for their help and support because I wouldn't be here without them.

Monday 18 August 2014

STV News
The referendum battle has intensified with a month to go before we make one of the most important decisions in our country's history. The First Minister launched a 'declaration of

opportunity' in Arbroath evoking that town's famous place in Scottish constitutional history. Better Together focused on the drive to win over undecided voters with a massive logistical exercise ahead to contact every voter.

DIARY: **A month until the referendum and polls at the weekend showed Yes gaining again. This could be very tight.**

Tuesday 19 August 2014
Scotland Tonight

The Scottish Government has put the future of the NHS at the heart of its referendum campaign, with the Health Secretary Alex Neil claiming today that only a 'Yes' vote can protect our health service in Scotland from cuts and privatisation. The opposition pro-Union MSPs hit back accusing the SNP ministers of peddling lies and scare stories.

DIARY: **The SNP are trying to get the NHS on the agenda because of the hit they've taken on the currency. Health is devolved and any choices on spending are those of the Scottish Parliament. It's a fairly transparent tactic, but could just connect with women voters especially.**

When the Labour spokesperson, Neil Findlay, arrived in the studio before we went on-air he joined in a discussion I was having with the crew about pies and bridies. He ventured that when he was a builder his favourite was a Scotch pie in a Gregg's roll because they were the perfect size for each other. He was thoroughly engaging, just like his counterpart, the SNP's Stewart Maxwell, who has been good chat previously in the hospitality room after programmes. I think it's no coincidence that both men have had experience of life beyond the political bubble. Contrast that with a group of students we had in previously, supporting some guests. They were earnest and eager, but competed with each other in political clichés. It was clear that they were headed for the politics pathway with no diversions. I don't know that it is good for them or for politics.

Wednesday 20 August 2014
STV News

A leading figure in the oil and gas industry has claimed the Scottish Government's North Sea estimates are up to 60 per cent too high. Sir Iain Wood has warned the country will begin to feel the effects of depleting reserves in just 15 years time. The tycoon said an independent Scotland's economy would suffer with significant increases in energy bills. However the Scottish Government insists the future of the industry is brighter than he predicts.

DIARY: **There's no denying that is a blow for the Yes campaign, no matter how they're trying to play it down. It is qualified by him saying that there are further discoveries, but still.**

Monday 25 August 2014
Scotland Tonight

The currency, oil and gas and the NHS were among the key issues as Alistair Darling and Alex Salmond crossed swords for the second time in the referendum campaign. For an hour and a half the First Minister and Better Together leader put forward their cases, cross-examined each other and took questions from the audience in the BBC debate.

DIARY: Second major debate between Alex Salmond and Alistair Darling (*on the BBC*). Salmond had it all to lose after being widely considered to have lost the last time. Much like the last time, the reaction of one being a runaway winner was rather overplayed. Salmond was much better, but Darling wasn't terrible. The Yes campaign will get a big bounce from it.

Tuesday 26 August 2014
STV News

Alex Salmond says his performance in the debate will give the Yes campaign a boost. However, both sides believe the referendum battle will be won or lost on the doorsteps, not on television. A snap poll declared the First Minister the winner last night and the odds of a 'Yes' vote have been shortened by the bookies. Better Together say Yes Scotland still need to answer big questions before the nation decides.

Wednesday 27 August 2014
STV News

The Electoral Commission says there's been an unprecedented surge in people registering to vote in the referendum – but as many as half a million Scots could still be denying themselves the chance to have their say – and they're running out of time. The deadline to register is midnight, next Tuesday.

DIARY: It's all referendum now. A big push on to make sure people are registered to vote. I am getting an ever increasing sense that this is becoming closer and closer.

Friday 29 August 2014
STV News

The Prime Minister has told STV News he'll attempt to forge a cross party consensus on more Devolution should he win the next election. Continuing his visit in Scotland, he gave his clearest signal yet that he'd seek a joint approach with Labour and the Liberal Democrats to give Holyrood more powers in the event of a 'No' vote in the referendum.

DIARY: This is the lull before the storm. The next two weeks might be quiet, but then it'll kick off. Much being made of Jim Murphy MP being 'egged' on his tour of 100 towns in 100 days. Some people saying it is trivial and maybe it is, but I still think it brings the debate into disrepute. This is supposed to be a civilised campaign and that shouting and barracking puts people off. It may be politics in the raw, but it is unpleasant.

Monday 1 September 2014

DIARY: A poll released tonight showing the 'Yes' vote has gained another four points, putting it at No 53 per cent and Yes 47 per cent. That's an eight point shift in a month by an organisation – YouGov – that hasn't typically had Yes high. That result is also within the margin of error. It's all getting very close and no question the momentum is with the Yes campaign. A lot of people are saying 'there is something in the air.' Mind you, after the first debate a month ago the Yes campaign was quite flat, so things can change quickly.

Tuesday 2 September 2014

STV News

A new poll has suggested the Yes campaign need just a three per cent swing to win the referendum. Better Together have said the poll highlights that Scots who want to stay in the union must vote, while the Yes Campaign say the momentum is now with them.

DIARY: The second STV debate – the third televised one overall – was this evening. We went with a different format – three from the Yes and No camps and not the head-to-heads that have been more typical. As a result it was less confrontational and STV received widespread praise because people felt they heard reasoned discussion.

Monday 8 September 2014

STV News

Shares in Scottish companies have fallen sharply after a poll suggested the Yes campaign was in the lead in the referendum. The pound has also dropped to a ten month low against the dollar. Better Together claims the city's jitters have been caused by the uncertainty over the economy –Yes Scotland says the Chancellor George Osborne is to blame. Labour have launched a charm offensive across the country. Some of the party's big hitters were out trying to firm up their vote following the Yes campaign's poll lead. However, Yes drafted in celebrities and claimed they now have the momentum.

DIARY: The weekend polls – and another today – showing how close the camps are has put Better Together into a panic. Now offering more powers, only they aren't more powers, just a timeline for the ones already promised. And they're falling back on Gordon Brown to stem the flow of Labour supporters to Yes. I don't think he's the ace they perceive him to be. I wonder if it's come too early for the Yes campaign and people who are swithering will be panicked by the fact it could be a reality.

Tuesday 9 September 2014

STV News

David Cameron and Ed Miliband have cancelled their weekly clash in the House of Commons tomorrow to campaign in Scotland for a 'No' vote. In a joint statement with Nick Clegg, the leaders of the three main Westminster parties said they wanted to be north of the border, listening and talking to voters. Alex Salmond has predicted their visit will backfire – and provide a massive boost for the Yes campaign.

DIARY: Continuing anxiety in the No camp with the Prime Minister David Cameron, Labour leader Ed Miliband and Lib Dem leader Nick Clegg missing Prime Minister's Questions tomorrow to come to Scotland to campaign. Is that really an advantage to Better Together? I'm not so sure. One vignette that summed up their travails was an attempt to raise the saltire over Downing Street – as they tried to raise it, it fell down!

Wednesday 10 September 2014

STV News

The Conservatives, Labour and the

Liberal Democrats united in Scotland for the United Kingdom. The party leaders made impassioned pleas to voters to stick with the union. But as far as Alex Salmond is concerned, David Cameron, Ed Miliband and Nick Clegg were here just to save their jobs.

DIARY: The Prime Minister David Cameron, the leader of the Opposition Ed Miliband and Lib Dem leader Nick Clegg were all campaigning in Scotland today. The No campaign given a severe jolt by recent opinion polls, although one tonight has No 53 per cent and Yes 47 per cent. The No campaign also had warnings coming from major institutions about financial companies moving HQs, not as much oil etc. Quite the barrage.

Thursday 11 September 2014
STV News

A number of high street businesses say their costs and prices could go up if the nation votes for Independence. Their intervention in the debate comes as historic Scottish banking institutions laid out contingency plans to move their head offices south of the border. The First Minister said none of the moves will have any impact on jobs or the operations of the banks. He said it was about moving 'brass plaques'.

DIARY: The polls swinging back towards No, but still too close to call. However, the supermarket Asda has said prices will rise in an independent Scotland, likewise John Lewis. Now, despite other stores (eg Tesco) saying otherwise, I think that could have an impact. Banks talking about moving is one thing, but Asda is another. No question we are seeing the full might of the British establishment being brought to bear. It could work, too.

Friday 12 September 2014
STV News

Alex Salmond says the Yes campaign are within touching distance of a win, as the polls remain on a knife edge. The First Minister took to the skies today in a tour of cities across the country to galvanise grassroots campaigners for one last push to polling day.

Better Together have again been raising the issue of economic uncertainty on the campaign trail. They've claimed the price of a weekly shop would increase with Independence. It comes as Ed Miliband traverses the country and some famous sporting faces lent their names to the No camp.

Monday 15 September 2014
STV News – live from Holyrood

Good evening from Holyrood at the beginning of this momentous week in Scottish politics. We go into the final days of the campaign with both sides claiming they are heading for victory. The polls are narrower than they have ever been and can't give any side a clear lead. By the week's end we will know our nation's destiny. Both sides have been campaigning relentlessly in these final few days, trying to win over the undecided voters. Today, Alex Salmond repeated his claims that Westminster was behind what he called a 'scaremongering' campaign over what would happen to business in Scotland if there's a 'Yes' vote.

The Scottish Secretary has called on Alex Salmond to 'call off the dogs' and stop intimidation from Yes supporters on the campaign trail. Alistair Carmichael said this behaviour 'came from the top' and was directed only at those who support the Union. The First Minister said both sides 'had a few idiots', but people are energised and empowered by the campaign.

The Prime Minister issued a warning that Thursday's referendum is a 'once and for all' decision as he made a last-ditch trip north to urge voters to save the union. Speaking in Aberdeen, The Prime Minister warned that if Scots vote for Independence it would result in a 'painful divorce'.

DIARY: **Through to Edinburgh for the** *Six O'Clock* **which will be the pattern for this week. Usually I'm just standing on the grass in front of Holyrood, typically without even a pergola for protection. This time a big media village has been built, with gantry positions. There is some clambering up narrow stairs, but we are in an elevated position which will give a good view of the Parliament. Not tonight, though. It was shrouded in mist. A cold, foggy day in Edinburgh.**

Tuesday 16 September 2014

STV News – live from Holyrood
There's now less than 48 hours to go until the polls open and the nation decides its future. But there's been no let up in the fight for every single last vote with more claims, counter-claims and impassioned pleas to the electorate. Today saw Yes campaigners dismiss a Westminster pledge of more powers for Scotland as a 'desperate offer of nothing'. The leaders of the three main parties promised 'extensive new powers' for the Scottish Parliament if the country votes to stay in the union. But the move was described by opponents as a panic measure with no real detail.

DIARY: **In a lovely, sunbathed Edinburgh –– much different from the mist of last night.**

Main line today was a 'Vow' from the three Westminster leaders of more powers for Scotland. Their constant problem with that has been their inability to detail what these powers are. And MPs in England are, understandably, getting aggrieved. Would these powers even get through?

Accusations about the Yes campaign getting overly aggressive. Ed Miliband had to abandon a walkabout in Edinburgh because of the jostling. It has been an aspect of the Yes campaign that has been unpleasant. And it doesn't win votes.

Wednesday 17 September 2014

STV News – live from Holyrood
Good evening from the Scottish Parliament in Edinburgh on the last day of campaigning over the Independence referendum for Scotland.

And on the eve of this historic vote, a new poll for STV tonight reveals the Yes and No camps are neck and neck.

The Ipsos Mori survey puts the pro-Independence camp on 49 per cent and Better Together on 51 per cent.

JM: Our political editor Bernard Ponsonby joins me now. Bernard will they be satisfied with their campaign this evening?

BP: Everybody at this stage of a campaign says that it has been wonderful and will deliver victory. At the end of the day, this was a tactically more difficult campaign to fight because it was always going to have to raise the issues of risk and uncertainty and in doing so was going to stand accused of being negative. But there is no doubt that around the issue of currency in particular, it has been successful in putting the Yes side on the back foot. Whether in the end they perhaps overplayed the currency card is more difficult to tell. It is interesting that yesterday, and again today, Gordon Brown saying to voters, 'if you are unsure, uncertain, you must not gamble with the future, you should vote no'. So even right to the end, the issue of unquantifiable risk is one that the No side are raising in the hope that it carries them to victory tomorrow.

Interview with Alistair Darling (Better Together)

JM: Alistair Darling, we've heard what the polls are saying tonight. It is that close. Have you done enough?

ALISTAIR DARLING: Well I always said it would go down to the line and what it means is that tomorrow when we go to the polls every one of us can tip the balance one way or another. And I do think there is a clear choice now. We can have a stronger Scottish Parliament with more powers so that we can safeguard our health service and education, and at the same time we can have the opportunities that come from being part of something bigger because so many jobs in Scotland depend upon there being no border between Scotland and England. The choice between that and, frankly, taking a leap into the unknown where there are so many unanswered questions, so many doubts about currency, who'll pay pensions? And what I say to people is if you don't know, then you should vote No because otherwise you are taking a real risk, not for yourselves, but for generations to come as well.

JM: Are you glad it's nearly all over?

AD: Well, y'know, I think two-and-a-half years is a long, long time to be discussing our constitution. It's an important matter, passions are running high on both sides, but this is the time we've got to decide. But it's such a big decision, it's bigger than anything that any of us have ever taken before, it's important that we get it right.

JM: If you had one message to give to the many who are still undecided, still not sure how to vote, what would it be tonight to persuade them?

AD: You can get the change you want with a stronger, more secure Scottish Parliament by staying in the UK. You can get the security, the better job opportunities which we desperately

227

need in years to come. The alternative is to take a leap into the unknown. And if you don't know the answers to these questions, if you're taking a big decision of buying a house or deciding to marry someone or to live with somebody, you'd be asking hard questions before you took that leap. We're being asked by Alex Salmond to, y'know, tear down the foundations on which our country is built and he's got nothing to offer in the place. That's not good enough for me and I guess it's not good enough for most people living in Scotland.

JM: Alistair Darling, thanks for joining us on the STV News.

JM: Our political reporter Carole Erskine is in Perth ahead of a Yes campaign rally there this evening... Carole sum up what you have made of their campaign.

CAROLE ERSKINE: This has been a campaign has been a grassroots movement, people of all ages across Scotland becoming engaged in politics and spreading the Yes message. We've seen the traditional door knocking and phone canvassing along with concerts, town hall debates and the creation of many groups for Independence – English Scots for Yes, Carers for Yes and Women for Independence just to name a few. They have been pushing forward what could be seen as a positive message, a message for change. Many people have done this off their own back, some moving back from living abroad to become involved. It has really galvanised the spirit of those who want a 'Yes' vote, the feeling that they didn't want to wake up on 19 September and wish they had done more. No one can fault their enthusiasm but what we don't know is if that will be enough for the majority of the country to go for Independence.

JM: We're now joined by the First Minister Alex Salmond, the leader of the Yes campaign. You've heard tonight's poll, it could not be closer.

ALEX SALMOND: Yeah and it's very encouraging because obviously right through this campaign it's the Yes side who've been gaining ground as we've convinced more and more of our fellow citizens that a 'Yes' vote is best for Scotland's future, to create a more prosperous economy, but also to create a more just society.

JM: The polls open tomorrow. Are you relieved it's nearly all over?

AS: No, I'm enjoying myself wonderfully. I've met so many people and I've learned so much on the campaign. There's been so many points of fun as well as very serious points. But people are really interested, they're taking their responsibilities so seriously. They're taking this great opportunity and they're studying it and they're part of it and it's part of an enlivening process, the like of which I've never seen in Scotland. Perhaps there are few parallels in the whole of Western Europe. That's why it's so much a privilege to be part of this great campaign, this people up campaign, this campaign which is empowering

Scotland and why it's a privilege to present that vision of a Yes vote, that prosperous economy and that just society.

JM: A number of undecided voters tonight going into the poll tomorrow still undecided. What's your final, clear message to them this evening?

AS: Vote for the future. I think we've managed to illustrate to people how so many things are secure in Scotland. We saw today 45,000 new jobs in Scotland. I think that symbolises that political and economic confidence go together. So as we've satisfied immediate concerns, this is about voting for what's to come in Scotland, what the future is going to be. So my advice, and it's advice offered to people who are still making up their mind is, we know this country can be a successful country. We know we want to be a more equal and just society, so vote for that future, vote 'Yes' tomorrow.

JM: First Minister thanks for joining us on the STV News.

JM: There are, then, just hours to go until Scotland goes to the polls. By any measure this has been an unprecedented political campaign fought from city street corners to Highland mountain tops. Our political editor Bernard Ponsonby has been there every step of the way. Bernard, your final thoughts?

BERNARD: John, I would simply say that I have seen nothing like this before. I don't think that anything I've covered before would come anywhere near the kind of excitement that has been generated in Scotland in recent times. There is a sense in which commentators covering events like this get gripped by hyperbole, the word historic is bandied about so often it almost becomes the stuff of cliché. But the decision that this nation will take tomorrow is so profound, so profound in so many different levels that the word historic almost seems inadequate. But be in no doubt about one thing; the politics of this country will never be the same again. The narrative has changed in recent days. The only question tomorrow is what is the end game of that particular narrative? Yes it's been exciting, yes it's been bad tempered at times, but overshadowing all of that, and both campaigns and personalities is one single reality – you, John, me, everybody in Scotland tomorrow is master of their own destiny. A civic duty by Scots tomorrow will make history. And change a country.

JM: That is where we have to leave it tonight. The campaigns are almost run. Tomorrow you will decide. From Holyrood… a very good evening

DIARY: So the campaigning is over and now it's up to the people of Scotland to decide. I spoke to leaders of both campaigns live on-air tonight. I thought Alistair Darling seemed fresher, maybe slightly more upbeat. The First Minister Alex Salmond said he was fine, but I had the slightest sense of flatness and fatigue. No surprise given the pressure he's been under this past while. Alistair Darling has been part of a far wider political team.

They both repeated much the same lines as they have throughout the campaign and I didn't challenge them on that. The idea was that these would be the final summings-up for their campaigns. It was Alex Salmond's final interview of the campaign and, I believe, Alistair Darling's too.

Tonight's polls all favour No marginally, but with narrowing gaps. All you hear is 'too close to call'. I did get a couple of Yes people saying to me that even if it's a 'No' vote things will change. I wonder if they're getting ready for defeat in their own minds. But if you are on the ground it's the Yes campaign that dominates, sometimes boorishly. I wonder if that'll count against them.

A big day tomorrow. The sense of nervous excitement is palpable everywhere.

SCOTTISH INDEPENDENCE REFERENDUM

Thursday 18 September 2014

STV News

Good evening. Live from the Scottish Parliament in Edinburgh. On an historic day for Scotland voting is well under way to determine whether the country should leave or remain part of the United Kingdom. More than three years after the Scottish National Party secured a landslide victory at Holyrood, the long-awaited referendum on Independence is finally taking place. Polling stations the length and breadth of the country opened at 7.00am and people have until ten o'clock tonight to cast their vote, with the result expected to be known by breakfast time tomorrow.

The question facing voters is a simple one: Should Scotland be an independent country?

DIARY: The rules of elections/referendums mean that there is not much that can be reported other than the fact of it and people turning up at the polls. The turnout is expected to be very high.

STV News at Ten – live from Edinburgh

A defining moment in our history. Welcome to a special edition of the *STV News at Ten* live from the capital of Scotland. We have all been asked 'Should Scotland be an independent country?' We the people have given our answer. With the vote on a knife-edge, far too close to call, the eyes of the world are upon us. From every corner of the country, on every street on every village, in towns and cities people have been out en masse to make their vote count. Two political, passionate and at times polarising campaigns fought right down to the wire.

(*The chimes of Big Ben*)

As Big Ben marks ten o'clock on the 18 September 2014, two capitals await. Will the Union remain intact, a shared democracy between Westminster and Holyrood, or will complete sovereignty be restored to Scotland?

(*The bongs of Big Ben*)

The referendum is now over. The polls are now closed. Scotland is ready to count our votes and declare whether or not we are indeed to become an independent country.

I consider this to have been the pinnacle of my career. As Big Ben chimed and I delivered that line to the nation about two capitals waiting, the hairs stood on the back of my neck. It was a moment of history for our nation and no one could know for sure what the next hours would bring and what it would mean for our future.

DIARY: **I was staying in Edinburgh to do a special STV *News at Ten* from the Edinburgh roof. It was very ambitious because the technical capacity of Edinburgh's gallery is not the same as Glasgow's. We had rehearsed the opening link to tie in with the bongs of Big Ben to mark the closing of the polls and it seemed to work very well.**

A train back to Glasgow, where George Square was full of 'Yes' voters. A quick stop at PQ where the results programme was on-air. It already seemed that No had won.

REFERENDUM RESULT

ALEX SALMOND RESIGNS

Friday 19 September 2014

Scotland This Morning – with Andrea Brymer

Hello and welcome to this special breakfast show marking the most momentous political day in our history for 300 years. Last night millions of people answered the question 'Should Scotland be an independent country?' The result? A victory for the No campaign.

MARY PITCAITHLY, Returning Officer: It is clear that the majority of the people voting have voted No to the referendum question.

For First Minister Alex Salmond, a devastating night. A conclusive victory for the No campaign.

ALEX SALMOND, First Minister: There is going to be a majority for the No campaign. And it's important to say that our referendum was an agreed and consented process and Scotland has by majority decided not, at this stage, to become an independent country. I accept that verdict of the people and I call on all of Scotland to follow suit in accepting the democratic verdict of the people of Scotland.

JM: As dawn breaks across the land, celebrations from the victors in the battle for hearts and minds.

ALISTAIR DARLING, Better Together: The people of Scotland have spoken. We have chosen unity over division, positive change rather than needless separation. Today is a momentous result for Scotland and also for the United Kingdom as a whole.

DAVID CAMERON, Prime Minister: Good morning. The people of Scotland have spoken and it is a clear result. They have kept our country of four nations together and like millions of other people I am delighted... The three pro-union parties have made commitments, clear commitments on further powers for the Scottish Parliament. We will ensure that those commitments are honoured in full... Just as the people of Scotland will have more power over their affairs, so it follows that the people of England, Wales and Northern Ireland must have a bigger say over theirs... I have long believed that a crucial part missing from this national discussion is England. We have heard the voice of Scotland – and now the millions of voices of England must also be heard. The question of English votes for English laws – the so-called West Lothian question – requires a decisive answer. So, just as Scotland will vote separately in the Scottish Parliament on their issues of tax, spending and welfare so too England, as well as Wales and Northern Ireland, should be able to vote on these issues and all this must take place in tandem with, and at the same pace as, the settlement for Scotland.

BERNARD PONSONBY: I think that is perhaps the most significant contribution ever made by a British Prime Minister in terms of constitutional change throughout the totality of the nations of the United Kingdom.

DIARY: **Not much time afterwards before I was heading through to Edinburgh again to present lunchtime. A general air of flatness everywhere, I felt.**

Friday 19 September 2014

STV News – Live from Holyrood

It's been a monumental and emotional day for Scotland and for Scottish politics. Tonight Alex Salmond announced his resignation. The shock statement came after the nation voted 'No' to Independence by 55 to 45 per cent. The First Minister said his time may be over, but he said for Scotland 'the dream will never die.' In a dramatic news conference in the capital, he added the country could still remain a real winner, but it's time for someone else to lead that battle.

JM: I'm joined now by our political editor Bernard Ponsonby. Bernard, why has he gone?

BP: For the reason he gave. There are fresh battles ahead and the Government and SNP need a fresh perspective. In his statement he said that if mistakes were made in the campaign he accepted responsibility for them as he led the campaign. Remember there are two priorities; prosecute the case for more powers and ensure the SNP win again in 2016. Realistically I don't think he ever intended to go all the way to 2020 so this makes perfect sense.

JM: The Prime Minister was quick to respond to the 'No' vote this morning. Speaking outside Number Ten David Cameron claimed more powers for Holyrood would be delivered. The unionist parties' last minute plea to give extra powers for the Scottish Parliament was a key feature of the closing stages of the referendum debate with Gordon Brown in particular promising a speedy process. However, that timing could be in doubt tonight and there may be more Devolution for England, Wales and Northern Ireland.

That ends our referendum coverage here in the capital city. It's official. The nation has spoken. The 300 year old Union remains. The break-up of Britain does not begin. Instead, a new settlement is promised, a new chapter in Scotland's story begins. The question now, for tomorrow and the next day is, will Westminster deliver?

DIARY: **Alex Salmond announced his resignation. That threw all the programme plans in the air. We acquitted ourselves well – Bernard's fine bio (delivered to camera without written notes) – live with John Swinney and Johann Lamont and off cleanly. A very good programme and a momentous day. This won't happen again and if it does, not with the same resonance.**

Some trouble caused by Loyalists in George Square, unfortunately.

Monday 22 September 2014
Scotland Tonight

As the debate intensifies over English votes on English issues, the SNP is claiming that the vow made by the main Westminster leaders to strengthen Holyrood is unravelling. They say UK ministers have signalled a threat to Scottish funding through the omission of any reference to the Barnett Formula in the parliamentary motion published today.

DIARY: **Back to work for the post-referendum period and the question, what are we going to talk about now? In actual fact there was plenty, principally on the powers being offered by Westminster – still don't know precisely what they are – and where now for the Yes campaigners?**

Tuesday 23 September 2014
STV News

Alex Salmond has said more powers must be delivered to Scotland as promised. The First Minister said Holyrood would hold the Westminster leaders to their vow. However, Labour leader Johann Lamont gave her personal commitment that increased powers over welfare and tax would be delivered. The exchanges came as Lord Smith who has been tasked with getting the parties to agree on what should be offered to Scotland met with leaders at Holyrood.

Wednesday 24 September 2014
STV News

Nicola Sturgeon has launched her bid to succeed Alex Salmond as the new Leader of the SNP. If elected at the Party's conference in November she is likely to become First Minister. Today, the current Deputy First Minister told STV News that she will not rule out backing another Independence referendum if she judges it necessary.

Thursday 25 September 2014
STV News

One of the world's great sporting events, the Ryder Cup, has opened at Gleneagles. Just one week after the Scottish Independence Referendum, the eyes of the world are once again on Scotland, as Europe and the United States battle it out for the biggest prize in team golf. Forty-five thousand fans will watch the drama unfold each day along with millions more around the world.

Monday 29 September 2014
STV News

The Prime Minister has told STV news he is confident that agreement can be reached with the other Unionist parties to give Scotland the new powers promised in the referendum. But he also said that new powers for the rest of the UK must proceed on a similar time table. He also said he was happy that the issue of Independence has been settled for a generation.

Tuesday 30 September 2014
STV News

Gordon Brown has launched a strong attack on David Cameron over his handling of more powers for the Scottish Parliament. The former Labour Prime Minister has called on Mr Cameron to 'pull back' on his pledge to back English votes for English laws, saying it was never discussed before the referendum. Mr Brown is urging Scots to sign a petition demanding the Prime Minister implement his referendum vow on new powers.

DIARY: This is the same Gordon Brown who brokered 'The Vow' among the Westminster leaders for more powers and who is being given much credit for securing a 'No' vote, now asking people to sign a petition. This 'extra powers' issue is going to drag on.

Monday 20 October 2014
STV News

Shops across Scotland have started charging for carrier bags. Whether you're at the supermarket or just a local takeaway you'll have to pay the five pence levy. It's been brought in by the Scottish Government to try to reduce litter and applies to all bags, whether they're plastic, paper or biodegradable.

Scotland Tonight

Scotland may have voted 'No' in the Independence referendum, but the momentum in Scottish politics appears to lie firmly with the SNP, whose membership has more than trebled since the big vote. For Scottish Labour, it's a very different picture with two of its former First Ministers warning that the party has lost its way and alienated many of its traditional supporters.

Tuesday 21 October 2014
STV News

The first party talks on more powers for Scotland have taken place in Edinburgh. The initial meeting was described as constructive by Lord Smith who has been tasked with brokering an agreement on increased Devolution. However, experts have questioned the commission's tight timetable.

Wednesday 22 October 2014

DIARY: The first meeting of the Smith Commission to decide on new powers for Scotland. This will become a long running political row. On the one hand the nationalists who say we were promised more, on the unionist parties who'll say there was a decisive 'No' vote.

JOHANN LAMONT'S RESIGNATION
Monday 27 October 2014
Scotland Tonight

Scottish Labour has been left reeling by the explosive departure of leader Johann Lamont, who accused the UK party of treating Scotland like 'a branch office' and described some Labour MPs as 'dinosaurs'. As yet no politician has put themselves forward to succeed her, but there is growing speculation that the MP Jim Murphy is poised to stand.

DIARY: Labour's preparation for a new leader and the fallout from Johann Lamont's resignation – Scottish Labour treated as a branch office and too many dinosaurs… Perhaps a new leader could invigorate them, but none of the recent ones have – or (it could) just come to nothing. Fascinating.

Thursday 30 October 2014

DIARY: An STV poll today for the General Election next year shows Labour in meltdown with only four seats, down from 41. The SNP dominate with more than 50 seats. I can't see it playing out like that, but a major shock for Labour.

Friday 14 November 2014

DIARY: Our top story was a guilty verdict in the World's End murder trial – a cold case of two 17-year-olds murdered in 1977. The killer Angus Sinclair is already in jail for other murders, is suspected of more and had spent time in jail as a youth for killing a young girl. Why was he ever released? The usual question we hear so often. He's being called Scotland's 'silent serial killer' because he got away with it for so long. Jury out this afternoon after six weeks of evidence. Much debate over whether they'd be back today or not. I'd no doubt they would be – it's the weekend, there's a big game tonight and his defence wasn't credible. They came back just after 5.00pm.

Tuesday 18 November 2014

DIARY: Alex Salmond stepping down as First Minister. That featured heavily on *Scotland Tonight*. Little doubt he's been a success and leaves on a high, despite actually losing a referendum. We can't forget that when he came to power in 2007 not much was expected. He has transformed his party and while there are domestic issues, his governments have been stable.

Wednesday 19 November 2014

STV News – live from Holyrood
Nicola Sturgeon is the new First Minister of Scotland. She was elected by MSPs this afternoon during a session of Parliament when opposition leaders joined her in marking what is a significant day for women in politics. The SNP leader pledges to be a First Minister for all of Scotland.

JM: The First Minister joins us now from her official residence, Bute House. Congratulations on becoming First Minister.

NICOLA STURGEON, First Minister: Thank you. It is a great honour. I am excited about this but I am under no illusion this is a big responsibility. I will do this job to the best of my ability. I was anxious to stress in Parliament and will do so again now. I am First Minister for all of Scotland, so if you are SNP or not, voted yes or no, my job is to represent and serve you and I will do that to the best of my ability.

JM: And the first female First Minister?

NS: That is, I think, a symbolic

moment. I very much hope my election as First Minister will send a strong message to women and girls all over the country, it doesn't matter your background, gender, if you're good enough or work hard enough you should be able to fulfil your potential and reach your dreams. That is a message that means a lot to me. I have an eight-year-old niece and I want by the time she is a woman for the things that are holding women back now to be in the past. So it is a proud moment and symbolic. I want to extend opportunity to all women that will be more than the simple example of my holding this office.

JM: What will your priorities be?

NS: I have begun setting out those priorities. I have been a member of Alex Salmond's Government for seven years. I am proud of the achievements of this Government and I want to build on them. I am absolutely clear we must do more to tackle the inequalities that afflict Scotland, too many children live in poverty. I have set out clear plans to extend the living wage to more people, not just in the public sector but in the private sector, extend childcare to give our children the best start in life. I understand very well you can't achieve social justice without a vibrant growing economy, so being on the side of business and promoting their interests at home and around the globe will be a key task of mine as First Minister and one that I relish.

JM: Briefly, will we see another referendum while you are First Minister?

NS: That is down to the people. I won't pretend other than that I support Independence and I will seek to continue to persuade people that Scotland should be an independent country, but the decision is not mine to take. I can't impose a referendum on Scotland, no more than I can impose Independence on Scotland. We will only have another referendum when people vote for that in a manifesto. It will be the will of the people, not the will of this or any other First Minister that determines that.

JM: Nicola Sturgeon, First Minister, thank you for joining us.

NS: Thank you.

DIARY: I think she is very capable and will be very effective. Not only is she talented, but, as she says, she has served a seven year apprenticeship as deputy, so she knows what to expect. I anchored a segment from Holyrood. It included a live two-way with her, which was really just a marking interview congratulating her, asking her priorities, will there be another referendum?

Tuesday 25 November 2014

DIARY: *Scotland Tonight* was the three candidates for the Scottish Labour leadership. Jim Murphy is the clear favourite. Neil Findlay has an 'old' Labour position which is the clearest. Sarah Boyack was much improved from the nervous individual I interviewed when she declared her candidacy.

Thursday 27 November 2014
STV News
The Better Together parties say they have delivered on their referendum

vow. Today Lord Smith revealed a deal has been struck which will allow the biggest transfer of powers since the establishment of Holyrood, though the Scottish Parliament budget will stay the same size regardless. The SNP and Greens say the vast majority of tax and welfare powers will remain reserved, branding it not so much home rule, as continued Westminster rule.

DIARY: The headlines are income tax is to be devolved with some welfare. Of course, nothing is clear cut, so it's not really all income tax and it isn't anything like all welfare. It's all way too complex for most people to bother with. The nationalists say it doesn't deliver what was promised, the unionists say it does.

Monday 1 December 2014

DIARY: Gordon Brown – former Chancellor and Prime Minister – announced he's standing down as an MP at May's election. I wanted him to be the political giant people thought he could be (*because of his Scottish background*). He wasn't the genius he's portrayed to be, his sense of entitlement damaged what could have been a transformational Blair/Brown leadership and he's had as many failures, if not more, than successes. History might be kinder to him, but I doubt it.

Monday 15 December 2014

STV News

The new Scottish Labour leader has announced plans to rewrite the party's constitution to say that it will run its own affairs in Scotland. Jim Murphy says he will ask members to agree to a new 'clause four' at the party's conference in March. In his first major speech after being elected on Saturday, he said the move would represent the 'refounding and the rebirth' of the party.

Scotland Tonight

JM: Jim Murphy, thanks for joining us. Congratulations. What do you stand for?

JIM MURPHY, Scottish Labour Leader: I stand for making Scotland the fairest nation on Earth. It's not good enough that there are too many people trapped by poverty, who find it so hard to escape the circumstances of their parents and grandparents, who were born into council estates or council schemes and don't have the chance to get the best school education, to get the chance to go to the greatest universities. I'm not going to use a lot of facts and figures, but there are only 220 pupils in our country to get good enough school results to get a chance to go to our greatest universities. 220 in our entire country each year. That is something I am determined to change. I am really comfortable about people being successful and I think it's something people should celebrate… But saying that we have these problems is not talking the country down, it's the sense of creating Scotland, not just as the fairest nation in the UK, but with hard work and determination, the fairest nation in the world. It can be done.

GEORGE SQUARE TRAGEDY

Monday 22 December 2014

STV News – live from George Square in Glasgow

Good evening. Six people are dead tonight in a tragedy in the heart of Glasgow, amid the Christmas lights and shoppers. A council bin lorry left a trail of devastation after appearing to go out of control and ploughing into people on the street. Several others have been injured.

KAREN GREENSHIELDS, STV Reporter: I was off duty when I happened upon the scene, but within ten minutes I was reporting 'live.' As my shaken husband stood by my side, holding our carrier bags of Christmas shopping, I described to our news anchor in a hastily arranged live 'phone interview exactly what I was seeing around me.

Over the years I have become used to covering breaking news stories, but on that day as I stood in the middle of a city centre street in chaos, I was utterly unprepared. I had neither notepad, nor pen and my mobile 'phone was almost out of charge. (*I was en route to the repair shop to have its smashed screen repaired.*) Nevertheless, I reckoned that I had to be one of the first reporters on the scene and I wanted our viewers to know exactly what was happening.

I encountered two problems almost immediately. Firstly, I couldn't understand why my fingers were trembling so much (*I later put this down to shock*). It took at least six attempts to dial the newsroom number from my key pad. Secondly, I felt suddenly ashamed that whilst hundreds of onlookers stood in shocked silence, I had slipped very quickly into 'reporter mode'. As I approached bystanders to ask what they had seen, I felt unusually self conscious without a camera crew by my side.

I solved the practical problems by borrowing a pen from a passing print reporter. She also gave me an old receipt and I quickly made notes for the imminent interview with studio. Again, I found it difficult to write with a steady hand as I noted the positions of the three bodies I could see just yards from me.

With 45 seconds to go before the live 'phone interview, it dawned on me – no camera no pictures – I quickly imagined myself as a radio reporter, but as I spoke I realised just how much TV reporters rely on the camera to convey the finer details. I struggled to find the best adjectives. As I talked, I walked in a 360 degree circle as I would have done with a camera to capture the totality of the scene. Old habits die hard.

In interviews for the two later bulletins, I felt more composed than usual. In live situations, a watching crowd can sometimes be daunting and that night our location was thronging with TV crews and onlookers. However it was almost a relief, therapeutic even, to give my eye witness account. I was using first person, not third. I instinctively changed my tone. I was recounting an awful event which had affected me and my husband. It didn't feel right to employ my normal detached, dispassionate tone.

Whilst I wish that I had never had to tell the story, I hope that personally and professionally, I struck the right balance.

At about 1.30pm I had finished updating a voiceover for STV's Hogmanay review of the year with details of late developments at Rangers. The producer Brendan O'Hara made comment that he hoped nothing else would happen and the programme would now be complete. I made reference to not being so sure, there was often a tragic news story just before Christmas. It was a throwaway comment. Within an hour, two colleagues phoned the STV newsdesk saying something serious had happened in George Square. At first there was talk of at least one dead and then more. Clearly this was a major breaking story and we mobilised our news team. We then heard that six people were dead, but there was no official confirmation of this despite at least one media outlet tweeting it. The rumours piled on top of each other – the victims included a family of four with two young children, a baby had been killed in its pram, one of the victims was pregnant. By the time we went on-air at 6.00pm the facts had been established. Six dead. It seemed unbearably cruel on the city of Glasgow. Just like a year ago, people looking forward to Christmas dying in a completely random accident.

Tuesday 23 December 2014

DIARY: **There was a strange serenity to the floral tributes at Royal Exchange Square from where we did the programme this evening. Stark contrast to yesterday afternoon when the horror began. The names of the dead were released today – regular folk going about their business. And there is a particular tragedy at Christmas when families are looking to come together. So very sad. And yet in streets nearby people were laughing and joking. What else are they going to do?**

STV News – live from Royal Exchange Square
(*final lines*) This is where yesterday's tragic events began to unfold. The scene now here in the heart of the city is one of serenity. The light canopy provides a soft shroud for the flowers. For the candles. And for the people paying silent tribute.

2015

Friday 22 January 2015

STV News

The battle for hearts and minds on television took another twist today as broadcasters offered to host a General Election debate programme which would include the leaders of all main parties running for Westminster. It means Nicola Sturgeon would go head-to-head with David Cameron, Ed Miliband and Nick Clegg. The leaders of the Greens, Plaid Cymru and UKIP would also be included in the seven-way line up.

Tuesday 27 January 2015

STV News

With a hundred days to the UK General Election David Cameron and Ed Miliband need to battle it out for every single vote. Polls suggest neither Labour nor the Conservatives will win a majority of seats. The SNP hope to hold the balance of power, but they've ruled out any deal with the Tories and Labour. More on the polls, the issues and Westminster coming up. First our Political Correspondent Claire Stewart has been talking to voters in Stirling. A seat once won by the Conservatives, currently held by Labour, but which could be seized by the SNP in May.

DIARY: Everyone saying it's too close to call. From a Scottish perspective what is so fascinating is that the SNP should be the third largest party in terms of seats. They could hold the balance of power. However, they've ruled out a coalition with the Tories and today Labour ruled

out a coalition with them. The SNP's red line on Trident is not acceptable to them. One of our analysts tonight said it wouldn't be in the SNP's best interests either. As the Lib Dems found out, sharing power at Westminster contaminates you. So we might have a coalition of others, or a minority government. Again our analyst – the excellent Steve Richards – said the example of the Labour Government in 1974 was that six months was about as long as you could last. It's going to get very intense. Of course, the polls take one figure and spread it across the country, individuals and local issues in each constituency might disprove them. Nobody seems to expect the SNP will get the 50 seats some polls suggest – 25 seems to be the expectation of most. Still a huge leap forward for them.

Wednesday 4 February 2015

STV News

It's the most detailed General Election survey ever undertaken in Scotland. Sixteen thousand people were asked their views and it's a grim outlook for the Labour leader Jim Murphy. The prediction – rock solid Scottish strongholds stormed, wipeout at Westminster, a landslide victory for the SNP. Potential high profile casualties include the Labour campaign supremo Douglas Alexander and the Shadow Scottish Secretary Margaret Curran. Lord Ashcroft's study looked at more than a quarter of the Scottish constituencies, many of those in Glasgow, and found the SNP to be ahead in 15 of the 16 seats.

DIARY: The recent polls have all pointed towards an SNP dominance of the coming election, but that has been attributing one figure across the country. The Conservative peer Lord Ashcroft has done 16 individual constituencies and they have said the same thing. Labour is facing meltdown and such is the detail of the polling that you can point to individual MPs who look like they're out. In Glasgow they may have only one MP. That is remarkable.

Tuesday 17 February 2015

DIARY: NHS figures – cancelled operations – the main news story. In fairness, it seems the NHS is working well generally, but it's such a huge organisation that it's inevitable there will be issues. There always have been.

Tuesday 24 February 2015

STV News

The oil and gas industry has reported its worst annual performance for 40 years. The industry is warning of heavy job losses and a steep drop in investment in the North Sea unless there are urgent tax breaks to combat the low oil price and rising costs.

Thursday 5 March 2015

STV News

The latest crop of constituency polls from Tory peer Lord Ashcroft have sent fresh waves through Scottish politics today. They suggest Labour will lose Gordon Brown's seat to the SNP as well as that currently held by Alistair Darling. The former Lib Dem Leader Charles Kennedy would also be ousted by the SNP, who are neck and neck with David Mundell in the only Tory held seat in Scotland.

Friday 6 March 2015

STV News

Dave King has taken control at Rangers after a landslide victory at the club's general meeting. John Gilligan and Douglas Park have been appointed to salvage the Ibrox side after the ousting of the current board. Paul Murray will act as chairman while King seeks approval to be appointed as a director.

(*Grant Russell's script*) – It was building up to this day. Rangers fans hopeful of a new dawn for their club after all the uncertainty in recent years. Gone are the old regime who the fans desperately wanted out. In come a group of businessman who the fans hope can turn their club around and put it back on a sound footing – both on and off the pitch.

DIARY: The Rangers board has been cleared out at an EGM today and Dave King and his team are in. I don't know how good they will be, but there seems little doubt they have the club's best interests at heart, unlike the self-serving chancers who have trotted through in recent times. Perhaps this is the beginning there should have been three years ago.

Thursday 19 March 2015

STV News

The Scottish Government is to revise its own figures for oil and gas production. It comes after the UK Office for Budget Responsibility downgraded its projections for oil receipts, wiping billions of pounds off expected revenues in the next five years. Labour said this meant the

SNP's plans for full fiscal autonomy would mean 'devastating' cuts.

Monday 23 March 2015

STV News

Ed Miliband has dismissed claims the SNP could hold power over a minority Labour government. In a speech in Glasgow today the Labour leader said Alex Salmond's claims were nothing more than 'bluff and bluster' and he again ruled out a coalition with the SNP. Though he repeatedly failed to rule out a looser arrangement with the nationalists.

Friday 27 March 2015

STV News

New research on why voters cast their vote the way they did in the Independence referendum suggests The Vow on more powers by the unionist parties made little difference to the final result. Alex Salmond has suggested the move was pivotal, but a survey of 4,000 voters by the Centre for Constitutional Change suggests people voted 'No' because many believed the country would have been worse off.

GENERAL ELECTION 2015

Monday 30 March 2015

Scotland Tonight

The political parties have been out on the streets on the first official day of the General Election campaign. Between now and on 7 May they'll be battling to win your vote in what the polls are predicting will be one of the tightest races in decades.

Tuesday 7 April 2015

STV News

The leaders of Scotland's four main political parties are to go head to head on STV tonight. It's the first time they will have clashed on TV during the General Election. They'll face a grilling from a 200 strong audience in Edinburgh.

DIARY: There were no great revelations. Jim Murphy of Scottish Labour needed a big win – or to land a significant blow at least – and that didn't happen. Nicola Sturgeon had most to lose after her success in last week's UK leaders' debate, but wasn't really pushed on the detail of some SNP policy. Ruth Davidson of the Scottish Conservatives will have come across well – feistier than she's normally seen to be – and with a clearly different argument from the others. The Lib Dems' Willie Rennie is clearly a decent man, but was rather sidelined. No major winners or losers.

Monday 20 April 2015

STV News

The SNP have launched their manifesto with a pledge to make Scotland stronger at Westminster. But in a pitch to voters down south too, Nicola Sturgeon said she'd use any influence the party have after 7 May to bring about positive change for people across the UK. The manifesto commits the party to full fiscal responsibility, but does not lay out the cost of the policy to Scotland.

DIARY: Short notice of a down-the-line interview with the First Minister on the SNP manifesto, which was launched today. They're saying slow the cuts and spend our way out of the deficit and debt. It seems counter-intuitive, but they say it'll work. The opposition say it doesn't add up. The interview was on the manifesto – the only party not talking about cuts, no mention of Independence and full fiscal autonomy now called full financial responsibility and not so imminent. She answered all of these straightforwardly as she always does. Seems to have been an effective manifesto launch with London-based journalists impressed by her 45 minute Q&A session afterwards. They say they don't get that from other leaders. As we sound checked I asked her the best question she'd been asked all day, which rather stumped her. By default that's got to be the winner!

A pre-record with the Proclaimers for next week. Great guys who produce some fine music. I've always liked them. Very down to earth and dismayed by Hibs defeat in the Scottish Cup semi-final and whether they or Rangers will make the play-offs. Wide ranging chat from their music to politics to football.

Tuesday 28 April 2015

Scotland Tonight

All the opinion polls point to an SNP tide sweeping across Scotland at next Thursday's General Election. It's an extraordinary time for the party and its leader Nicola Sturgeon. Tonight she's with us live for the latest in our series of election interviews conducted by STV's political editor Bernard Ponsonby.

DIARY: Bernard pushed her on a couple of areas of vulnerability – one of which is emerging more obviously – the possibility of the SNP being a 'Feeble 50', ie a large tranche of MPs, but no real influence. That's a given if the Conservatives win. But if Ed Miliband wins, the SNP will back him by default. They will have to. So what happens if he proposes something of which the SNP don't approve? Nicola Sturgeon says that her experience of minority government in Scotland is that sometimes, when you couldn't get your policy through you had to go back and change it. But what if Miliband challenges the SNP to vote against him? She contends that a vote against wouldn't necessarily bring a Government down, but it could lead to instability.

Wednesday 29 April 2015

STV News

With just eight days until the country votes, the SNP surge appears to be reaching tsunami proportions. Our exclusive poll shows a seemingly unstoppable tidal wave that could engulf Scottish Labour. The once mighty People's Party faces total wipeout. A landslide victory is forecast, with Nicola Sturgeon's SNP capturing every single seat in the country and returning 59 MPs to Westminster.

DIARY: It's a good headline, but I don't think anyone really believes it. Most will predict the SNP getting 40 plus seats, which is still an almighty achievement. Jim Murphy was interrogated by Bernard in *Scotland Tonight* and is too experienced for it to be the slaughter some expected. However, he didn't put across any message that is going to transform the result over the next week.

Wednesday 6 May 2015

DIARY: The last day of campaigning before the polls open. No one is expecting a majority government, so will it be the same coalition as the last time, a minority government or Labour with the SNP backing? My gut is that the Conservatives will perform better than predicted. I think a lot of English voters about to cast their vote will be fearful of a Labour SNP alliance, however informal.

Friday 8 May 2015

STV News – live from Westminster
A disunited kingdom.

Scotland rewrites political history as the Conservatives return to Downing Street with a majority.

Under the might of the Sturgeon Surge, the people return an army of 56 MPs to Westminster.

It was a disaster for Labour. A wounded Ed Miliband quits as leader.

So the question tonight – where does this leave Scotland in the Union?

JM: Good evening and welcome to Westminster. An incredible result. There has been nothing like it before. Ever. The least predictable General Election in living memory has returned a majority Conservative Government under Prime Minister David Cameron. Alongside an historic, seismic shift in Scottish politics under the leadership of Nicola Sturgeon.

The Conservatives defied the polls and won 331 seats. It was bruising night for the Labour Party, they returned 232 MPs. The SNP won a landslide in Scotland with Nicola Sturgeon's party seizing 56 out of the 59 seats. The Liberal Democrats have been left with just eight MPs. The Greens hold on to one. UKIP also has one MP, leaving 21 MPs from other parties.

DAVID CAMERON, Prime Minister at Downing Street:
In this Parliament I will stay true to my word and implement as fast as I can the Devolution that all parties agreed for Wales, Scotland and Northern Ireland. Governing with respect means recognising that the different nations of our United Kingdom have their own governments as well as the United Kingdom government... In Scotland our plans are to create the strongest devolved government anywhere in the world.

ED MILIBAND, Labour Leader:
Britain needs a Labour Party that can rebuild after this defeat so we can have a government that stands up for working people again. And now it's time for someone else to take forward the leadership of this party. So I'm tendering my resignation.

NICK CLEGG, Lib Dem Leader:
Clearly the results have been immeasurably more crushing and unkind than I could ever have feared. For that, of course, I must take responsibility and therefore I announce that I will be resigning as leader of the Liberal Democrats.

JM: Bernard, this result was a tale of two elections, really, and a tale of two results that have collided spectacularly. What does it mean for the Scottish dimension at Westminster?

BERNARD PONSONBY, STV Political Editor:
In a sense, John, it's also a clash of two mandates. David Cameron has a mandate to pursue deficit reduction, including 13 billion pounds worth of unspecified welfare cuts and he also has a mandate to deliver more powers for Holyrood through the Smith Commission proposals. But Nicola Sturgeon has a mandate to say no to austerity and she has a mandate to pursue further powers for Holyrood. Now, this inevitably is going to lead to a clash. In a sense there can only be one winner – 56 SNP MPs simply cannot trump a Conservative majority at Westminster. But here's where the politics comes in. Does David Cameron look at this and say I have to be slightly more flexible given that there is now a different Scottish dimension? Well today he said, yes there will be more powers for Holyrood, but he said that was more or less it. And if that is more or less it, that will mean conflict. That conflict and how it plays out could determine the political terrain in Scotland in the coming months.

VOX POPS: I voted SNP rather than Conservative, which I'd normally vote, because I want a voice in Westminster. I don't want Independence, I just want a voice in Westminster.

Labour's time in Scotland pretty much is over.

Scotland is a people and we wanted to make that heard at Westminster.

I've came all my life, a working class family, and your heart and your feelings are Labour, that somehow you're maybe betraying what you believe in. But no, I think that I genuinely believe that the SNP is the way forward for the next generations.

It's a wee bit worrying. I think we're probably going to go to a referendum a bit sooner than most people want.

The people are disillusioned with Labour, with them joining the unionists, and they've swung to the SNP for it.

JIM MURPHY, Scottish Labour Leader:
There is a responsibility in good times and in bad times as a leader. And our judgement, and our view and our determination is rebuild from here.

JM: The First Minister Nicola Sturgeon is with me now. Congratulations on a remarkable success in Scotland.

NICOLA STURGEON: Thank you very much indeed. It was a result, I think, of historic proportions. The tectonic plates of Scottish politics shifted yesterday and the Scottish people put their trust in the SNP to stand up for Scotland at Westminster and make Scotland's voice heard and that's exactly what we intend to do.

JM: How are you going to be able to do that, though, given that 56 MPs at Westminster, but you're up against a Conservative majority.

NS: The fact that we're up against a Conservative majority is something I didn't want and unfortunately that's because Labour weren't strong enough to beat the Conservatives in England. But the fact that is, the scenario we face makes it all the more important there is that big team of SNP MPs to stand up for Scotland and to protect Scotland's interests and make our voice heard. The second point I'd make is this; the Government cannot ignore what happened in Scotland yesterday and it can't be business as usual. There has to be a recognition that people in Scotland in significant numbers voted for an end to austerity, voted for stronger investment in our public services and voted for a more empowered Scottish Parliament. So these issues that we put at the heart of the Election campaign, our MPs will now seek to put at the heart of the House of Commons.

JM: But, nonetheless, it is a majority Conservative Government, which nobody expected, on an austerity agenda. They can ignore you, it could be the Feeble 56.

NS: But they can't ignore Scotland and if they do it would be completely unacceptable. Scotland didn't just vote in small numbers for a different part yesterday. Some of the swings we saw across Scotland yesterday were unprecedented in Westminster political history. Scotland decisively voted against austerity and for an alternative approach. I briefly spoke to the Prime Minister this afternoon and made it clear that it cannot be business as usual, the democratic will of the Scottish people as expressed in that election yesterday has to be recognised. So our MPs and me as First Minister will be working hard to make sure that those issues that were so dominant during the election campaign are just as dominant down here in Westminster.

JM: What did the Prime Minister say to you in that conversation?

NS: It was a brief call, it was an opportunity for me to congratulate him. I didn't want him to be Prime Minister again, but he has won the Election and I congratulated him. He was gracious to congratulate the SNP on our success. We'll meet as soon as possible and discuss these issues in more detail, but I made it clear it can't be business as usual.

JM: You said throughout the campaign this was not about the referendum, but you now have a position that you have a Conservative majority, a very large tranche of SNP MPs. Does it make a second Independence referendum more likely?

NS: No, I don't think it does one way or the other. I said during the Election that this election wasn't about Independence and it wasn't a vote for a second referendum. I said very explicitly, very directly to voters across Scotland if you vote for the SNP I will not take your vote as an endorsement of Independence. I'm not going to turn my back on that, I'm going to stick to my word. If there's ever another referendum in Scotland on Independence, that will only come about if people vote for that in a Scottish Parliament election.

Yesterday's election was a vote to make Scotland's voice heard and the 56 SNP MPs that will be shortly coming to this place behind us here are here to make Scotland's voice heard and that's exactly what they intend to do.

JM: First Minister, thank you for joining us.

JM: Thank you.

JM: The General Election of 2015 might be considered as two elections. In Scotland the predicted SNP landslide. Across the UK the unexpected Conservative majority. Tonight the SNP have a powerful grip of Scotland. Here at Westminster David Cameron and the Conservatives hold power in the UK. The next big question – what happens now?

DIARY: The Conservatives have won a majority with 331 seats, which almost no one saw coming. The SNP won 56 – all but three of the seats in Scotland. That had been predicted, but the SNP leadership, like the rest of us, were unconvinced it'd be on that scale and played it down. Labour have been destroyed in Scotland – only 1 MP – and they have only themselves to blame. I don't think this is a protest vote, I think the SNP have replaced Labour as the party of the Left. It can be seen as two elections and I used that in my scripts – the UK elections and the election in Scotland. The Lib Dems have been reduced to a rump – punishment for being part of the Coalition and not getting anything of their key principles passed in return. Labour failed in England, too, quite aside from their Scottish collapse. I don't think people

ever saw Ed Miliband as being Prime Minister right from the moment he was chosen leader.

It made for straightforward programmes with a clear narrative. I interviewed Nicola Sturgeon on the 6.00pm news. The important point was on whether it brings a second referendum closer. She said this election was not about Independence, and she wouldn't make it so. I'm sure she's sincere on that, but I wonder what pressure some of the new MPs will bring to bear.

She'd been up all night and was saying she wasn't sure she could remember her own name, but impressive as always. Also, a chat with John Swinney on Abingdon Green. He said that on the day after the Referendum he'd wondered what would become of his party. He has no such doubts now.

Monday 11 May 2015

STV News – live from Westminster
Good evening from Westminster. After a landslide victory in Scotland, 56 SNP MPs are here promising Scotland's voice will be heard like never before. As the majority Conservatives had their photocall with the Prime Minister next to Big Ben, the SNP stood together with the First Minister at Westminster – a large saltire flying nearby. The party says being the third largest in the Commons will open up unparalleled opportunities to make their case and be a principled opposition.

DIARY: There was the usual media crush as Nicola Sturgeon stood in front of them all. This is an image that will be shown again and again in years to come. It was a remarkable sight. Earlier, David Cameron had posed with the new Tory MPs, Big Ben in the background. That was very grand compared to the rather squeezed area for the SNP photocall at St Stephen's Entrance. I wonder if it'll be a metaphor for this Parliament.

During the photocall there was a vivid demonstration of the tensions between established and new media. The BBC cameraman transmitting live pictures of the event had his picture spoiled by another guy holding up his iPhone. When the cameraman asked him to drop his phone lower the response was,

'Periscoping mate. I'm periscoping', ie he was broadcasting pictures using an app from his phone.

'How many followers you got?' queried the increasingly irate cameraman.

'Couple of hundred,' the periscoper claimed.

'Well these pictures will be seen by millions and you're ruining them.'

The periscoper carried on regardless.

At first I thought it was similar to the experience I used to have as a sports correspondent when the newspapers resented the presence of electronic media. It's not. The issue at root there was that we would transmit stories before the papers, but we didn't impede the newspapers from covering the story. That continues today in a different form. Twitter breaks news instantly and other media have to deal with it. The question is should the image seen by potentially millions of people be spoiled by the intrusion of somebody broadcasting to a few? That's not to say that the periscoper

should be denied the chance to broadcast, but they should abide by the same protocols as the rest.

Friday 15 May 2015

STV News

David Cameron has said he will consider any proposals for further devolved powers for Scotland, following talks with the First Minister. The two met today for the first time following last week's General Election. Nicola Sturgeon told STV News she will now put forward priority powers to be handed to Holyrood as soon as possible along with arguing for full fiscal autonomy.

Tuesday 2 June 2015

STV News

Politicians from all parties have united in paying tribute to the former Liberal Democrat leader Charles Kennedy, who died suddenly in his home in the Highlands yesterday. Just 23 when he was first elected, he was an MP for 32 years. To his friends he embodied decency. Among his opponents he commanded respect. And to his constituents, he was Charlie – one of them. Reaction from Westminster, Fort William and our Political Editor to come, but first our Chief Reporter David Cowan on the shock death of one of Scotland's most talented politicians.

DIARY: He was respected across politics because as many have said, he could disagree respectfully and without rancour. That's rare. I never met the man, I don't think, although I interviewed him up the line from

Westminster. I was always struck by how reasonable and human he was. It says much that so many people, like me, who didn't know him were deeply saddened by the news.

Wednesday 10 June 2015

STV News

Scotland is facing a housing crisis unless substantial numbers of new homes are built. That's the warning from an expert commission which says one hundred and fifty thousand families are on social housing waiting lists. The Scottish Government says it has invested heavily, but there are concerns that aren't anywhere near enough to tackle the problem.

DIARY: Given that I'd made the observation about it being a running problem for decades I suggested digging out previous reports with the same message. It worked rather well.

Thursday 11 June 2015

STV News

The SNP is demanding that the UK Government gives full tax-and-spend powers to the Scottish Parliament. The Party is tabling an amendment to a bill now going through Westminster which seeks to give Holyrood the right to Full Fiscal Autonomy. The UK Government will oppose the move, but some Conservative backbenchers are backing an amendment of their own saying Scotland should have all the powers it wants, and as quickly as possible.

Monday 15 June 2015

STV News

The outgoing Scottish Labour leader Jim Murphy says there will be a second independence referendum and the Conservatives will give the SNP the excuse they need to bring it about. In a farewell speech given to the London based think tank – The Policy Exchange – he said David Cameron was putting party above country by appealing to English Nationalists in his drive to make sure that only English MPs can vote on English laws. He also urged the Labour Party not to forget the lessons of Tony Blair's three election victories.

Tuesday 14 July 2015

Scotland Tonight

The UK government has pushed back a vote on fox hunting in England and Wales after the SNP announced they would vote against the reforms. The nationalists said their decision to vote on the measure was in protest at the handling of English votes for English laws. The Prime Minister has described the SNP's position as entirely opportunistic.

DIARY: Significant because the SNP had used that as an example of when they wouldn't interfere with English votes. Nicola Sturgeon could not have been clearer. Then they changed their minds to send a message to the PM over the English Votes for English Laws debate and lack of movement on new powers for Scotland. Certainly they won a victory without even having to vote, but I think it is short-sighted. There could not be a clearer example of the SNP going back on their word. Their supporters will be happy and political buffs will admire the politics. However,

it will give many people more reason to distrust party politics.

Monday 17 August 2015

STV News

She has one of the toughest jobs in Scottish politics. Following her landslide victory as Scottish Labour leader Kezia Dugdale is now set on tackling a series of problems confronting her demoralised party. She began her first full week of campaigning with a visit to a nursery in Paisley.

DIARY: She comes across well and people respond to her warmth, but some criticise her for not saying anything of substance in her answers. That may be a lack of assurance from inexperience. If she can bring more of herself through, she may do well. It's a thankless task, but they have to start rebuilding somewhere. It might not be made any easier depending on the outcome of the UK leadership contest.

Monday 24 August 2015

Scotland Tonight

The leadership of Scottish Labour is seen by some as the poisoned chalice of British politics. But Kezia Dugdale has boldly taken up the challenge of reviving the once-dominant force left devastated by the all-conquering SNP. She joins us now from Edinburgh.

KEZIA DUGDALE: I'm going to focus on Labour values first and foremost, tell people why I'm Labour, what I believe in, what that means in 2015 and then explain to people how I'm going to go about making that real for them with the detailed policies they want to see. So first and foremost, I'm going to talk about education, about closing the gap between the richest and poorest kids in society. Making sure that every Scot can realise their potential and use the power of government to do that.

DIARY: She has warmth, but during our interview there was a straight question about whether she agreed with her new deputy Alex Rowley that there should be a referendum on Trident. A straight question which didn't bring a straight answer. That doesn't serve her well. She did talk about political cooperation and it'll be interesting to see if that is something she can develop. She has a long haul ahead, but she has got time on her side because nobody is expecting much from Labour in next year's Scottish Elections.

Tuesday 25 August 2015

Scotland Tonight

There were 613 drug-related deaths in Scotland last year, the highest figure ever recorded and an increase of 72 per cent over the past decade. The minister responsible for the country's drugs policy has admitted that some users have been failed by the system.

A recurrent issue throughout this book.

EndNote

Scotland has been transformed since this reporter first pulled on his trench coat. This book has charted that change.

We know where we've been. The question now is where are we going?

The past can help inform us about the future. The wheel always turns, patterns are often repeated.

I go back to what I said right at the beginning. Twenty years ago few would have imagined that Scotland would come quite so close to Independence so soon. In that time I have interviewed many informed people, heard from experts and academics, and had the views of bar room bores and social media know-alls foisted upon me. No one has called it right every time.

We all may have our ideas about where we are headed as a nation and a society, but none of us knows.

That makes what lies ahead so fascinating. Just like what's gone before.

Some other books published by **LUATH** PRESS

The Road Dance
John MacKay
ISBN 978-1-910021-93-4 PBK £7.99

Life in the Scottish Hebrides can be harsh – the edge of the world some call it. For the beautiful Kirsty Macleod, the love of Murdo and their dreams of America promise an escape from the scrape of the land, the repression of the Church and the inevitablility of the path their lives would take. But as the Great War looms Murdo is conscripted. The villagers hold a grand Road Dance to send their young men off to battle. As the dancers swirl and sup, the wheels of tragedy are set in motion.

Powerful, shocking, heartbreaking.
THE DAILY MAIL

John MacKay gives an enlightened portrayal of the Hebridean culture of the time, with its strict religious observances, prejudices and oral traditions... an absorbing, powerful first novel.
SCOTS MAGAZINE

It conjures up the atmosphere of fear that stalks a community where the church casts 'sinners' into the wilderness.
SCOTLAND ON SUNDAY

Heartland
John MacKay
ISBN: 978-1-910021-90-3 PBK £7.99

A man tries to forge a new future for himself by reconnecting with his past. Iain Martin hopes that by returning to his Hebridean heartland and embarking on a quest to reconstruct an ancient family home, he might find a new purpose. But as he begins work on the old blackhouse, he uncovers a secret from the past which forces him to question everything.

Praise for *Heartland*

...broody, atmospheric little gem set in the Hebrides.
THE HERALD

Where indeed do you seek sanctuary when your past has changed irrevocably, your memories are false and your future is uncertain? A gripping plot full of credible characters... set in a convincing background.
SCOTS MAGAZINE

A combination of Changing Rooms and Agatha Christie, MacKay's Heartland demonstrates the Scotland Today presenter has a readable easy-going prose style.
SCOTTISH REVIEW OF BOOKS

Last of the Line

John MacKay

ISBN: 978-1-910021-91-0 PBK £7.99

When Cal MacCarl gets a phone call to his bachelor flat in Glasgow asking him to come to the bedside of his Aunt Mary, dying miles away on the Isle of Lewis, he embarks on a journey of discovery. With both his parents dead, his Aunt Mary is his only remaining blood link. When she goes he will be the last of the family line.

In a place where everyone knows everything about everybody, Cal finds that secrets are buried deep. He begins to understand that Mary was not the woman he knew and he might not be the person he thought he was.

A heartfelt account of personal, and family, discovery.
THE HERALD

There is a vigour in the telling of this story that breaks through the risk of mere nostalgia. Its characters are alive now, in the twenty-first century... The whole is bound together by the colours of the Hebridean landscape.
NORTHWORDS NOW

A tightly plotted story... with some lovely details of remote island life.
THE INDEPENDENT

The Girl on the Ferryboat

Angus Peter Campbell

ISBN 978-1-910021-18-7 PBK £7.99

Maybe it had just been a matter of time: had we had more time, what we would or could have achieved, together. Had we actually met that first time round, how different things might have been. The world we would have painted. Had we really loved each other, we would never have separated.

It was a long hot summer... A chance encounter on a ferry leads to a lifetime of regret for misplaced opportunities.

Beautifully written and vividly evoked, *The Girl on the Ferryboat* is a mirage of recollections looking back to the haze of one final prelapsarian summer on the Isle of Mull.

An exceptionally good novel. This is among the best pieces of narrative literary fiction to have emerged from Scotland in the 21st century, in any language.
WEST HIGHLAND FREE PRESS

Despite its gentle tone, the questions it raises about fate, chance, and love persist after the book is closed.
THE HERALD

Transcendently beautiful... a delight in any language.
SCOTLAND ON SUNDAY

A memorable love story.
THE DAILY MAIL

Trancendentally beautiful.
THE SCOTSMAN

Reportage Scotland: History in the Making

Louise Yeoman
Foreword by Professor David Stevenson
ISBN 978-1-842820-51-3 PBK £7.99

This eclectic mix covers nearly 2,000 years of Scottish history. Historian Louise Yeoman's rummage through the manuscript, book and newspapers archives of the National Library of Scotland has yielded an astonishing amount of material. Ranging from a letter to the King of the Picts to Mary Queen of Scots' own account of the murder of David Riccio; from the execution of William Wallace to accounts of anti-poll tax actions and the opening of the new Scottish Parliament.

Louise Yeoman, a thoroughly professional historian, has produced a marvellously illuminating and wonderfully readable book telling 'the story of Scotland' through the eyes, prose and Gaelic verse, of a succession of biased, axe grinding and sometimes barely articulate witnesses.
SCOTLAND ON SUNDAY

Louise Yeoman makes a much-needed contribution to the canons of Scottish historiography, providing eyewitness, or as near as possible, to events which have shaped the country over two millennia.
THE HERALD

A Word for Scotland

Jack Campbell
ISBN 978-0946487-48-6 PBK £12.99

The inside story of a newspaper and a nation. Five tumultuous decades as they happened.

A Word for Scotland was Lord Beaverbrook's hope when he founded the Scottish *Daily Express*. That word for Scotland quickly became, and was for many years, the national paper of Scotland.

Jack joined the infant newspaper at the age of 15 as a copy boy and went on to become the managing editor. He remembers the early days of news gathering on a shoestring, the circulation wars, all the scoops and dramas and tragedies through nearly half a century of the most exciting, innovative and competitive years of the press in Scotland.

This book is a fascinating reminder of Scottish journalism in its heyday. It will be read avidly by those journalists who take pride in their profession – and should be compulsory reading for those that don't.
JACK WEBSTER

Scotland: A Graphic History

Jeff Fallow

ISBN 978-1-908373-12-0 PBK £9.99

How did Scotland get to be what it is today?

A land of kilts, coos and whisky. A picturesque country of jagged peaks, mysterious glens and bottomless lochs.

There is much more to Scotland than the tartan-wrapped clichés which blur its proud and turbulent history.

Jeff Fallow begins with Scotland's prehistoric origins south of the equator and covers everything from dinosaurs to David Cameron in this persuasive presentation of Scotland's rich culture and history. This book dispels outworn romantic myths and takes you on a striking visual journey through Scotland's history.

Whatever your view on Scotland's future within or outwith the Union, *Scotland: A Graphic History* is essential reading for teachers, pupils, visitors and anyone with an interest in Scotland's past, present and future.

This is Scotland: A Country in Words and Pictures

Daniel Gray and Alan McCredie

ISBN: 978-1-910021-59-0 PBK £9.99

A Scotsman and an Englishman, a camera and a notebook...

McCredie's lens and Gray's words search out everyday Scotland – a Scotland of flaking pub signs and sneaky fags outside the bingo, Italian cafés and proper fitba grounds. A nation of beautiful, haggard normality.

Gray has been one of the finest wordsmiths around for some time.
SCOTTISH REVIEW OF BOOKS

... an honest account of real places and people, often captured in poetic prose. This book has uncovered a country that is lived and living. It's a refreshing journey which makes you wonder, what is Scotland to you?
THE SKINNY

... lively commentary... much more than the 'fond glimpse and flirty glance' they claim is their aim.
SUNDAY HERALD

Luath Press Limited
committed to publishing well written books worth reading

LUATH PRESS takes its name from Robert Burns, whose little collie Luath (*Gael.*, swift or nimble) tripped up Jean Armour at a wedding and gave him the chance to speak to the woman who was to be his wife and the abiding love of his life. Burns called one of 'The Twa Dogs' Luath after Cuchullin's hunting dog in Ossian's *Fingal*. Luath Press was established in 1981 in the heart of Burns country, and now resides a few steps up the road from Burns' first lodgings on Edinburgh's Royal Mile. Luath offers you distinctive writing with a hint of unexpected pleasures.

Most bookshops in the UK, the US, Canada, Australia, New Zealand and parts of Europe either carry our books in stock or can order them for you. To order direct from us, please send a £sterling cheque, postal order, international money order or your credit card details (number, address of cardholder and expiry date) to us at the address below. Please add post and packing as follows: UK – £1.00 per delivery address; overseas surface mail – £2.50 per delivery address; overseas airmail – £3.50 for the first book to each delivery address, plus £1.00 for each additional book by airmail to the same address. If your order is a gift, we will happily enclose your card or message at no extra charge.

ILLUSTRATION: IAN KELLAS

Luath Press Limited
543/2 Castlehill
The Royal Mile
Edinburgh EH1 2ND